AN INTRODUCTION TO THE DRAMATIC WORKS OF GIACOMO MEYERBEER

I must number Meyerbeer with the chief moulding forces in the musical development of the nineteenth century...in some of his best operas there are scenes which in beauty, truth, power and originality have not been surpassed by any composer whatsoever.

Friedrich Niecks

An Introduction to the Dramatic Works of Giacomo Meyerbeer

Operas, Ballets, Cantatas, Plays

ROBERT IGNATIUS LETELLIER
University of Cambridge, UK and Maryvale Institute, UK

ASHGATE

Published by
Ashgate Publishing Limited
Gower House
Croft Road
Aldershot
Hampshire GU11 3HR
England

Ashgate Publishing Company
Suite 420
101 Cherry Street
Burlington, VT 05401-4405
USA

Ashgate website: http://www.ashgate.com

British Library Cataloguing in Publication Data
Letellier, Robert Ignatius
    An introduction to the dramatic works of Giacomo Meyerbeer: operas, ballets, cantatas, plays
    1. Meyerbeer, Giacomo, 1791–1864 – Criticism and interpretation
    I. Title
    782.1'092

Library of Congress Cataloging-in-Publication Data
Letellier, Robert Ignatius.
    An introduction to the dramatic works of Giacomo Meyerbeer: operas, ballets, cantatas, plays / Robert Ignatius Letellier.
        p. cm.
    Includes bibliographical references (p.   ).
    ISBN 978-0-7546-6039-2 (alk. paper)
    1. Meyerbeer, Giacomo, 1791–1864. Dramatic music. 2. Dramatic music–19th century–History and criticism. I. Title.

    ML410.M61L38 2007
    782.1092–dc22

                                                                                2007012916

ISBN 978 0 7546 6039 2

Printed and bound in Great Britain by TJ International Ltd, Padstow, Cornwall.

MEYER~BEER

Frontispiece: Giacomo Meyerbeer as a young man. Print from the Schlesinger
                  vocal score of *Il crociato in Egitto* (Paris, 1825)

Contents

List of Illustrations

The age of some of the images has limited the quality of reproduction in a few instances.

List of Music Examples

Introduction

The figure of Giacomo Meyerbeer is one of the most enigmatic in musical history. During his life, and until the First World War, he was counted among the pantheon of great composers, and his operas dominated the stages of the world with a hegemony that seemed unassailable. The growth of nationalism, an emergent, vociferous school of critical prejudice inspired by Robert Schumann and Richard Wagner, changes in musical taste, a move away from the heroic (except for Wagner) and the decline in the traditions of bel canto singing, are a few of the factors influencing this cultural phenomenon. A slow process of revival and re-examination began in the 1950s, but the size of the operas, their insistence on team cooperation (which mitigates against their being chosen as a vehicle for a single great star), the dearth of published scores and absence of definitive performing editions, the enduring negative public perception of his musical worth, ignorance of his life and the overall range of his *oeuvre*, have all contributed to holding back the reviving impetus. The production of *Gli Ugonotti* at La Scala Milan in 1962 nonetheless was a landmark in a process of rediscovery that is currently finding an unexplored world of freshness and originality in the Italian operas of the composer's early career. In 2004–05, in addition to revivals of *L'Africaine* in Strasbourg, *Le Prophète* in Münster, and *Les Huguenots* in Metz and Liège, *Margherita d'Anjou* was produced in Leipzig and *Semiramide* given for the first time since 1820 at the Rossini Festival in Bad Wildbad. In 2006 *Semiramide* was also given at Martina Franca. Opera Rara further released a recording of the forgotten *L'esule di Granata*.

The aim of the present study is to carry the process of rediscovery forward in a small way by presenting an introduction to Meyerbeer's work, not just to his famous French operas, but to all 17 of them in the context of the whole of his whole dramatic *oeuvre*. From his nineteenth year he began writing for the theatre (his ballet *Der Fischer und das Milchmädchen*, 1810), while his religious cantata *Gott und die Natur* (1811) served as a vital testing ground for the dramatic and vocal skills, and large-scale construction he would need for his first operas. *Jephthas Gelübde* (1812), *Wirt und Gast* (1813) and *Das Brandenburger Tor* (1814) showed the young composer reacting to the heritage of his times—assimilating the examples of Handel, Gluck, Mozart and his teacher the Abbé Vogler in his own very personal way. The high drama of the *tragédie lyrique*, the Oriental pleasures of the Turkish opera, the more homespun charms of the *Singspiel* are all essayed with skill, imagination, thematic fluency and a developing sense of orchestral colour. The last of these three operas was an important moment for Meyerbeer in working out his somewhat ambiguous relationship with patriotism, nationalism and his Prussian homeland.

The first major move of the composer's artistic life was his extended sojourn in Italy, where he confronted and reacted to the overwhelming operatic genius of the age, Rossini. Meyerbeer's response was not simply to imitate him, but to digest his example in the context of the late eighteenth century, to absorb the traditions of bel canto into his own rapidly developing dramatic instincts. All these ideas were confronted symbolically in the secular cantata *Gli amori di Teolinda* (1817) which constitutes a kind of overture to the Italian years. Using a text by Gaetano Rossi, his friend and principal collaborator at this time, and cognizant of a musical inheritance that included the generation before Rossini, he succeeded in this monodrama (for soprano and concertante clarinet) in summing up important musical features of the age—the concern for vocal production, ornamentation and the obbligato traditions of the preceding century.

The six Italian operas which followed between 1817 and 1824 established Meyerbeer as a significant composer in Italy, with an international reputation growing more or less incrementally with each new work. The operas divide themselves into three pairs of two: *Romilda e Costanza* (1817) and *Semiramide [riconosciuta]* (1819) are characterized by a pure, serene, naive quality, as the composer, working within the formulae of the contemporary *melodramma*, produced his own response that took account also of pre-Rossinian models, and showed an instant mastery of the language of Italian lyricism. The next pair, *Emma di Resburgo* (1819) and *Margherita d'Anjou* (1820), the composer's first international successes, were alert to wider Romantic impulses of romance and history, and in a growing personal adventurousness of form and sound, vigorously reinterpreted the operatic language of the day. The impulse was carried even further in *L'esule di Granata* (1822) and *Il crociato in Egitto* (1824) where the development of the Introduzione, a fluent handling and modification of structure, an imaginative expansion of forces, showed an awareness of both the French traditions of grandeur and Rossini's experiments in the *opera seria* in Naples. All these operas are concerned with situations of exile and imposture, search and restitution, confusion and fulfilment, and certainly reflect a subliminal thematic treatment of issues at work in the composer's life: his view of himself as a searching artist, an alien Jew, an outsider living away from his Prussian home and seeking his true métier.

The success of the *Crociato* allowed Meyerbeer to effect a move to Paris, the operatic capital of the world, where, working with Augustin-Eugène Scribe, the principal collaborator of his career, he was able, over the next 40 years, to make his outstanding contribution to the history of opera and music in general with the creation of his four *grands opéras*, all of which became worldwide successes, and established a type and style of opera that had its effect on all who came after him. Using the legends and history of France, the first two, *Robert le Diable* (1831) and *Les Huguenots* (1836), established Meyerbeer as the most important opera composer of his day. The radical treatment of form, the development of scenic complexes and greater plasticity of structure and melody, the dynamic use of the orchestra, and close attention to all aspects of presentation and production, set new standards in Romantic music drama and dramaturgy. The last two, *Le Prophète* (1849) and *L'Africaine* (op. post., 1865), coming considerably later, continued the process, each contributing a unique and powerful response to the carefully chosen plot and recurrent themes of faith, power, politics, and love. Taken as a whole, they constitute a type of thematic tetralogy in which the chosen ideas are developed. *Robert le Diable* used the mythologies of medieval and Romantic Gothic legend, while *Les Huguenots* and *Le Prophète*, considering tumultuous events from the sixteenth-century wars of religion, constitute a type of Reformation diptych in which issues of religion and history are considered in their dark implications for human freedom. *L'Africaine* sees the theatre of spectacle and reflection expanded to issues of global exploration and imperialism, with a return to mystical and legendary elements.

The other operas from the period of Meyerbeer's maturity show a continuing concern with genre and its concomitant formal and stylistic demands. His appointment as Generalmusikdirektor to the king of Prussia in 1842 resulted in works commissioned for special court occasions, like the masque *Das Hoffest von Ferrara* (1843) and the German *Singspiel Ein Feldlager in Schlesien* (1844), where elements of the composer's dramatic vocabulary were developed and expanded in almost ceremonial contexts. The incidental music to *Struensee* (1846), a play about the flawed but idealistic Danish politician by Meyerbeer's tragically short-lived brother Michael Beer, provided a different kind of theatrical response, an overture and suite of powerful and affectingly dramatic music with impressive elaboration of the composer's enduring interest in leitmotif—in all an unique and unjustly neglected achievement.

The 1850s saw the fulfilment of Meyerbeer's dreams to write for the Opéra Comique. *L'Étoile du Nord* (1854) and *Le Pardon de Ploërmel* (1859) work on military and pastoral themes, topoi favoured in the operatic language of the day, that had reappeared often in the composer's chosen scenarios, and which treat at various levels the themes of destiny, exclusion (wandering, exile, disguise, delusion, madness), sacrifice, integration and fulfilment of various kinds. Both works can seem predictable, light, almost frothy, but careful listening reveals an intricate beauty that is really captivating—a beauty that shows Meyerbeer's musical and dramaturgical skills refined and carried to new extremes of technical achievement. Both these highly textured scores have much to offer.

In light of the great range of historical subjects and figures tackled by Meyerbeer in his operatic works, it is unsurprising that significant religious and social issues should be touched upon. However, these themes seem far from coincidental in their appearance within the corpus of his *oeuvre*. Indeed, it would seem that numerous themes not only recur in many operas but were, in fact, developed and refined during his career. Key religious themes within the operas include the core Judaeo-Christian notions of creation, sin, salvation and the eschatological destiny of humanity. Contained within this framework are numerous important subjects which pre-empt much secular and ecclesial thought of the twentieth century. Of particular importance in this regard is Meyerbeer's consideration of the role of women, oppressed groups, cultural imperialism and the need for reform in the Church. A recurring theme is the importance of mediation in both existential and metaphysical contexts. Whilst diary entries indicate that he was neither atheistic nor agnostic in his beliefs, it does appear that Meyerbeer's views on religion were somewhat ambiguous but most deeply felt.

In tandem with the stage revivals has been a growing body of literary work on Meyerbeer. After the groundbreaking book by William Crosten (1948), Heinz Becker began his collation and editing of Meyerbeer's papers, the *Briefwechsel und Tagebücher* (= *BT*) (1960–2006), a seven-volume work carried on in cooperation with Gudrun Becker, and more latterly by Sabine Henze-Döhring. My translated edition of Meyerbeer's diaries (1999–2004) has given the biographical dimension to the composer's life some reality in the English-speaking world.

The libretti and dramaturgy of Meyerbeer's and Scribe's work have received attention in the studies by Christhard Frese (1970) and Karin Pendle (1979), while the complete texts and English translations of the libretti have appeared in the work of Richard Arsenty with introductions by Robert Letellier (2004).

Meyerbeer's life and art have been considered in detail by some modern German scholars, especially in biographies by Heinz Becker (1980) and Reiner Zimmermann (1991, rev. 1998). Sieghart Döhring has produced the most thought-provoking views of the composer's art, especially the concept of Meyerbeer's four *grands opéras* as *Ideendramen* (dramas of ideas) (1983). His interpretation of this historical notion, and detailed information of the production histories of the Meyerbeer operas, especially in the German-speaking lands (1986–97), are of central importance to any study of this *oeuvre* and essential supplements to Alfred Loewenberg (1943, rev. 1970) and Stéphanie Wolff (1962). Marco Pellegrini, with Robert Letellier, has researched modern productions of Meyerbeer's work, 1950–2006, and has provided a complete bibliographical guide to research on the composer (see Letellier and Pellegrini, 2007).

Growing interest in the Italian operas has resulted in significant contemporary research, such as that of Armin Schuster (2003). Many of my own ideas about Meyerbeer's work have appeared in anthology as *Meyerbeer Studies* (2005).

I acknowledge a debt of gratitude to all these scholars.

Research on Meyerbeer has burgeoned in recent years; productions of his operas are increasing. But there is still a general ignorance about his achievements and the nature of his work: there is no general study of his whole dramatic *oeuvre* in any language. The present exercise seeks to rectify this omission and provide a way into what is unknown terrain to most music-lovers. From Meyerbeer's first stage work in 1810 to his great posthumous accolade in 1865, some 24 works mark the unfolding of this life lived for music and the stage. While the reputation of the famous six French operas lives in the public consciousness, the other works have perhaps never been heard of by most. This book seeks to provide a path into this unknown, trackless but exciting achievement—old but still full of freshness and novelty.

For the sake of convenience, the works have been divided into their generic types for quick reference and helpful association, with indication of the place of each chronologically in the composer's life and artistic development. Each section provides a brief history of its origins, an account of its plot, a critical survey of some of its musical characteristics, and a record of its performance history. The bibliography has been selected to draw attention to the most helpful and influential studies on the composer in general, and on each work in particular.

The musical examples were prepared with great care and professionalism by Veronica Henderson, in many cases from original, poorly legible manuscripts. I am very grateful to her.

The iconography is drawn from my own collection. It encompasses playbills, manuscripts, early printed editions, portraits (especially of singers), stage and costume designs, arrangements, and some of the famous commercial cards that were so indicative of the ubiquitous popularity enjoyed by Meyerbeer's operas in the late nineteenth and early twentieth centuries.

This book is dedicated to the memory of Terry Letellier—cousin, beloved friend, my rock of strength—who died on 7 February 2007.

PART 1
Ballet and Cantata

Chapter One

Ballet

Meyerbeer, the child of rich Jewish burghers from Berlin, received his first musical education as a seven-year-old from the music teacher to the Prussian Court, the pianist and composer Franz Lauska. Rapid progress on the piano directed the child prodigy along the path of a performing virtuoso. Lauska was no more able to bring out the child's compositional gifts than the leader of the Berlin Music Academy, Carl Friedrich Zelter, and the director of the Berlin Court Opera, Bernhard Anselm Weber, who served as Meyerbeer's teachers in the following years. Weber, nevertheless, as a devotee of the theatre, provided the young Meyer Beer (as his name originally was) with his first experiences in the area of dramatic composition. Under his direction the 19-year-old composed a one-act ballet pantomime *Le Passage de la rivière, ou La Femme jalouse*, planned and choreographed by the veteran ballet master Etienne Lauchery.

1.1 ***Der Fischer und das Milchmädchen oder Viel Lärm um einen Kuss [The Fisherman and the Milkmaid, or Much Ado about a Kiss]***

Ländliche Divertissement [pastoral divertissement in one act]
Scenario: Etienne Lauchery
First performance: Hofoper, Berlin, 26 March 1810

In spite of his infantile precocity, the protection of his parents and extraordinary conditions of study, Meyerbeer was already 19 years old when his first stage work was performed. The name of the composer of this *ländliche Divertissement* was not mentioned. The French ballet master at the Court Opera, Etienne Lauchery, devised the scenario entitled *Le Passage de la rivière ou La Femme jalouse* (the crossing of the river, or the jealous woman) and choreographed the piece himself. The autograph score is headed *Der Schiffer und das Milchmädchen / oder / Viel Lärm um einen Kuss / Ein pantomimishes Ballet in einem Aufzuge / Musik von Meier Beer*. The hour-long work had four performances, and if the scenario has disappeared, it is still an attestation of Meyerbeer's first encounter with the stage, and with French artists. The Fisherman was danced by Monsieur Telle, the Fisherman's wife (the Hostess) by Madame Telle, the Milkmaid by Madame Lauchery, and the Sister of the Hostess by Mademoiselle Joyeuse, with Fräulein Holzbecker as the Niece and Herr Moser as the Forester.

It is a harmless tale of some countrywomen who should be doing their washing in a river, but are invited to dance by some young foresters. The Hostess and then the Chief Forester chide them all, but eventually end up dancing with them. The

Fisherman comes with a catch that the Hostess wants to take to the village magistrate, because her husband is tired after work and wants to hang his nets to dry. A young peasant with milk jugs asks to be ferried across the river by boat. As reward, the Fisherman steals a kiss off her, which she resists. The Hostess comes back at this moment, berates the young girl, and throws her jugs in the river. The Milkmaid in her turn breaks the spinning wheel of the Hostess, annoying the jealous wife exceedingly. The Forester who happens to be passing by, listens to it all, laughs at the women, and calms the quarrelling.

This friendly little story emerges from the time of the *ancien régime*, when Marie Antoinette had a neat little stylized village with artificial landscape built at the Petit Trianon. It is a harmless diversion provided with a prudish Prussian conclusion, for which Meyerbeer wrote music for 22 numbers. From a pastoral overture through an Allegro galante, an Air de Chasse, to the final Contredanse générale, the score contains everything that could be expected of a ballet-divertissement. Both small and large numbers show themselves heirs to the eighteenth century just passed, and are not distinguished melodically and harmonically from the minuets and contredanses of Mozart and Beethoven. The scoring for pairs of flutes, oboes, clarinets, horns, and the usual strings corresponds to contemporary standards. They are by no means all employed throughout, but rather differentiated woodwind writing brings an element of variety to the movements. Each number is self-contained, but there are recognizable relationships and similarities between individual parts, a turn of semiquavers that recurs in the melodic structure of several of the numbers, and works in its unconscious effect to create a sense of harmony and integration.

This is no youthful masterpiece, but a conscientiously constructed artefact, capable of sustaining a pleasing general impression.

Example 1.1 *Der Fischer und das Milchmädchen*: thematic patterns

Chapter Two

Cantata (Oratorio/Dramatic Monologue/Duodrama)

In the same year that he composed his ballet *Der Fischer und das Milchmädchen* (1810), new and exciting artistic prospects were opened for the young composer when the famous music theorist and composer Georg Joseph Vogler invited him to Darmstadt as his pupil. Here his fellow students were Carl Maria von Weber and Johann Gänsbacher. Meyerbeer's compositional and aesthetic development was to be authoritatively and enduringly influenced by the learned and cosmopolitan Abbé. The artistic consequences of two years of intensive study were to find expression in the oratorio *Gott und die Natur* (1811) and the opera *Jephthas Gelübde* (1812).

2.1   *Gott und die Natur [God and Nature]*

Lyrische Rhapsodie [lyrical rhapsody—sacred cantata]
Text: Aloys Wilhelm Schreiber
First performed: Singakademie, Berlin, 8 May 1811

In February 1811 Meyerbeer received the text of an oratorio *Gott und die Natur* from the poet and professor of aesthetics Aloys Wilhelm Schreiber, an acquaintance of the Abbé Vogler from Heidelberg. The young composer applied himself so fervently to the task, that as he wrote to Gänsbacher on 27 February 'he could not unfortunately even think about letter-writing'. This work, overwhelmingly lyrical in character, contains much of significance in the composer's later dramatic development, and represents a milestone in his career. It was composed at Darmstadt at Vogler's home, and consists of a loosely connected series of solos and choruses setting forth the creation of the world, its end in the Last Judgement, and culminating in praise of God. The orchestra comprised the usual strings, double woodwinds (with piccolo, a third bassoon and double-bassoon), four horns, three trumpets, three trombones, three timpani and harp. Schreiber had observed in his *Lehrbuch der Asthetik* (# 356): 'Opera music has its great difficulties because music already by its very nature cannot be dramatic, whereas the play, when it does not want to unite with music, of necessity must take on a lyrical character.' Whether Meyerbeer knew of this opinion, hardly encouraging for his future career, remains doubtful. In his oratorio he did not in the first place need 'dramatic music', but rather united all the effects of counterpoint and tone colour then at his disposal, and wrote a work in which one notes the models of Handel, Hasse and Haydn without hearing them.

Mittwoch, den 8. May 1811.

CONCERT SPIRITUEL,

in dem

Saale des Königlichen National-Theaters.

Ouvertüre zu Regulus; von Weber. Hierauf folgt unmittelbar:

1) Gott und die Natur; lyrische Rhapsodie, vom Herrn Professor Schreiber in Heidelberg; in Musik gesetzt von Mayer Beer.

2) Psalm: de profundis; von Gluck.

3) Arie: Singt dem göttlichen Propheten, von Graun; gesungen von Demoiselle Schmalz.

4) Dreistimmiger Trauergesang auf Haydn's Tod, von Cherubini.

5) Der Gang nach dem Eisenhammer, declamirt von Herrn Beschort, mit musikalischer Begleitung von Weber.

Der Text, von der lyrischen Rhapsodie, vom Psalm und Trauergesang ist a 2 Gr. Courant; und der Text vom: Gang nach dem Eisenhammer, ebenfalls für 2 Gr. Courant, an der Casse zu haben.

Die Soloparthien in der lyrischen Rhapsodie, und im Trauergesang, haben gefälligst übernommen: Demoiselle Schmalz, Herr Eunike, Herr Grell; Herr Gern.

Billets im Saale à 16 Gr., und zu den Logen à 1 Rthlr. klingend Courant, sind beim Herrn Kastellan Leist im National-Theater, und am Abend des Concerts am Eingange zu haben.

Anfang 7 Uhr; Ende nach 9 Uhr.
Der Eingang des Saals wird um 5 Uhr geöffnet.

Illustration 2.1   *Gott und die Natur*: the playbill of 8 May 1811 (from the collection of the late Heinz Becker)

Example 2.1a   *Gott und die Natur*: the opening chorus and fugue (creation)

Unlike Haydn's late masterpiece *Die Schöpfung* (1798), with its classical dramaturgy moving from nothing to light, *Gott und die Natur* is a song of praise for God's creation and saving power. The opening chorus and fugue, in their downward rushing impetuosity, exalt the primordial and cosmic divine intervention (No. 1) (ex. 2.1a).

The existence of living things (No. 6, the Chorus of Flowers) or the birth of the elements are celebrated (No. 8): Air (soprano), Fire (alto), Earth (tenor) and Water (bass) each have a particular theme linked by a short four-part bonding motif, so that in all eight themata are unfolded, set over against each other, intensified, and then contrapuntally fused, a feat Weber greatly admired. The solo contributions show an operatic sensibility. The Song of Air is notable for the tracery of the flute part that plays around the vocal line. The Song of Fire, with the colour of the alto voice, is dominated by a chorale-like theme 'Meine Kraft ist still und rein' (my power is silent and pure), sustained by solemn chords of the trumpets, horns and bassoons, with the trumpets penetrating the leading horns, and the wide intervals of the supporting bassoons lending the chords a hollow sound. After a credal confirmation of the divine metaphysics by the chorus (No. 10) that 'Er war, er ist, and er wird seyn' (God was and is and will be), there is debate in duet form (No.11) between a doubter (*Zweifler*) and an atheist (*Gottesleugner*). The young composer attains an extraordinary intensity of expression in the last numbers. The Day of Judgement (No. 12) is powerfully portrayed. Strings enter mysteriously with 'Hörst du die Posaune klingen?' (Do you hear the trombone sound?), and over grave clarinets, horns and trumpets the voices of the chorus float whisperingly. A tremendous crescendo roll on the timpani sees the fortissimo entry of the whole orchestra, with the chorus proclaiming 'Sieh des Grabes Riegel springen' (See, the grave's bolt sprung). Demisemiquaver strings rush above the words 'dunkel heulenden Meer' (dark howling sea), and at the words 'Jehova spricht' against contrasting chords, followed by a fading sound effect depicting the horror of impending chaos, the chorus intones the words 'Dumpfe Donner hallen, alle Sterne fallen' (Dull thunder rolls, all stars fall) while the orchestra, in downrushing, chromatically diminished seventh chords, sinks into soundless darkness. A hollow roll on the timpani punctuates the silence, whereupon from on high the soprano announces the general resurrection: 'Es lebt, was je geboren war' (All lives that was ever born). The other soloists join in with a chorus hushed in awe, underpinned by subsiding strings like rays of hope. Edgar Istel (1926, 83) goes so far as to see this as a 'tone-picture reminding one of Michelangelo's famous frescos'. The closing male-voice chorus announces a confident and faithful expectation of redemption, a broadly conceived fugue on the ascending theme 'Im Tod ist der Sieg, im Grab ist Licht, das Wort des Herrn, es trüget nicht' (In death is victory, in the grave is light, the Word of the Lord does not deceive). This is elaborated into a double fugue with technical mastery, and reveals a talent for formal artistic development (ex. 2.1b).

Example 2.1b   *Gott und die Natur*: the closing fugue (redemption)

In the tersely elegant themes, stately tempi and choral fugues in lengthened notes, Meyerbeer carries over into his dramatic music the magnified style of his earlier Klopstock songs. The treatment of the chorus and the attraction of musical pictorialism show the influence of Handel where there is a similar intermingling of theatrical and oratorio styles. It was very important for the young composer to learn how to dispose big movements formally, a task he would be called to confront constantly in the challenges that lay ahead.

There have been two performances of this work in recent times: a live broadcast from the Teatro Communale in Bologna on 21 February 1996 (with Anja Kampe, Monica Minarelli, James McLean, and Andrea Serra Giaretta, with the Chorus and Orchestra of the Teatro Communale di Bologna, conducted by Rüdiger Bohn), and a concert in the Basilica of Kevelaer on 21 November 1999 (with Christine Alexander, Monica Mascus, Thomas Ströckens, Marcus Lemke, with Wolfgang Seifen on the organ, and the Basilikachor Kevelaer and orchestra conducted by Boris Böhmann).

The first work completed by Meyerbeer after his move to Italy in 1816 was a small scenic cantata for soprano, male chorus, ballet and orchestra, with instrumental obbligato, composed for the benefit of some friends.

2.2   *Gli amori di Teolinda [The Loves of Theolinda]*

Cantata di scena per soprano, clarinetto, coro e orchestra [stage (secular) cantata for soprano, clarinet, chorus and orchestra]
Text: Gaetano Rossi
First performance: Verona, 18 March 1816

Meyerbeer's stay in Munich, and the production there of his first opera *Jephthas Gelübde,* are intimately bound up with the careers of two great artists: the clarinettist Heinrich Baermann who played the first clarinet in the Munich Hofkapelle and was considered one of Europe's finest instrumentalists, and his lifelong companion, the soprano Helene Harlas Baermann,. Carl Maria von Weber composed his First Clarinet Concerto for Baermann, who used a method of soft-blowing and was able to produce such sensuous tones that he was known as 'the Rubini of the clarinet'. The young Meyerbeer was particularly impressed by his legato and breathtaking staccato, and wrote him a clarinet quintet to show off his skills. Harlas was a gifted singer, a star of the Munich Hoftheater, and it was her performance as the heroine Sulima in Meyerbeer's first opera that secured its successful premiere. Meyerbeer, enchanted by her range of expression and agility, studied her capabilities and wrote two scenes in *Jephthas Gelübde* especially adapted to her personality. The friends were to meet up again in Vienna in 1813 during the heady year of Meyerbeer's life in the Habsburg capital. Harlas accepted an engagement in 1815 in Venice, a factor which must have precipitated the composer's decision to spend time in Italy. He hurried from Paris to Italy at the beginning of 1816, and was soon in Verona where his friends were living. Harlas's tour had been arranged by Baron Brioli from the entourage of Prince Eugène. As a gift Meyerbeer presented the couple with a scenic cantata *Gli amori di Teolinda*, dated 'Verona, 18 Marzo 1816', with a text by Gaetano Rossi, a native of that city and a famous librettist, who would soon provide his first full Italian opera *scrittura*.

The cantata, effectively an occasional work, was probably intended for a benefit performance, the usual practice to conclude a prima donna's engagement. It was an old tradition for composers to write arias or instrumental pieces especially tailored to the abilities of the artist in question, and dedicated to them. Alternatively, the cantata could have been intended for evening festivities held by Baron Brioli. The cantata is remarkably and rather extraordinarily written for soprano and solo clarinet. Here Meyerbeer was simply utilizing an old Venetian tradition where, since the seventeenth century, the public had applauded vocal competition with a solo instrument (like the trumpet). Vocalist and instrumentalist would try to outdo each other in daring displays of coloratura, or in witty interchange, questions and answers, or in echoing effects. In this cantata, or pastoral monodrama, the shepherdess Teolinda is consumed by love for the handsome but unfaithful shepherd Amidoro, whose imagined closeness is personified for her by the sound of the 'panpipes'—the clarinet. It was devised by Meyerbeer as a piece of refined vocal and instrumental virtuosity influenced by older melodic models of Italian origin. The alternating concertante passages of the soprano follow a slight story line, and there are indications in the score for scenic presentation.

The brief prelude (Andante, A minor/A major) presents a tonal summary of the work. A dusky, mysterious atmosphere of muted strings, questioning and answering motifs, a timid but blossoming cantilena for the cello and bassoon, leads by way of crescendo and stringendo to the major and the opening aria, like an emotional flooding with light. The sun is rising as Teolinda apostrophizes nature. Her thoughts, however, constantly stray to her would-be lover, whose proximity is soon announced by the off-stage sound of the clarinet (ex. 2.2a [a]). At first incredibly soft, the sound grows to fortissimo, a display of virtuosity certainly designed to show off Baermann's talents. Voice and instrument alternate in echo-effects, finally flowing and blending together in a brilliant finale. The full spectrum of the clarinet's range and effects is exploited while Teolinda sighs and aspires over her amorous illusions. The chorus provides an interlude in the guise of a group of happy peasants going about their rural chores. The score indicates that the chorus should dance while singing, a revival of the seventeenth-century French tradition of the *choeur dansé* so familiar from the *opéra-ballets* of Lully and Rameau (ex. 2.2a [b]).

Example 2.2a   *Gli amori di Teolinda*: a) Teolinda's Longing, b) the Chorus of Shepherds

Teolinda gazes sadly after the country-folk as they disappear in the distance. She then launches into a romance (Andante con variazioni) in which she longs for some word of love from the ungrateful Armidoro (ex. 2.2b). The chorus of shepherds intrudes upon her reverie. At first angered, Teolinda is soon calmed by the renewed melisma of the clarinet, a sound impossible to resist. She grows ever more ecstatic, trembling with fantasies, beside herself with devotion, until both she and the chorus are overcome by the enchantment of this pastoral dream.

Example 2.2b   *Gli amori di Teolinda*: the Andante con variazion*i* finale

The piece is in fact a pastorale, a genre popular since the seventeenth century. The picturesque scene is also pure eighteenth-century, a small pastoral intermezzo, conjuring up an idealized past and frame of mind. The voice of the girl and the tones of the clarinet are interwoven, complement each other, and culminate in jubilant harmony in thirds. There is a succession of eight aria forms, recitatives, variations and long instrumental passages, with the highpoint reached in the final Aria con coro (Allegro molto moderato) that belongs to the formal achievements of the preceding years in Italian opera. Use of monodramatic *accompagnati* and the commenting chorus take up the French tradition of the *choeur dansé*, and show Meyerbeer experimenting and expanding on the traditional dramatic cantata. He would have been introduced to this form by the Abbé Vogler. The addition of the solo instrument, the amalgam of concertante with cantata features and dramatic stylistic elements were, however, the composer's innovation. The clarinet part reveals the rich spectrum of opportunities and virtuosity open to the performer of that era. Meyerbeer's music provides some notion of Baermann's tone quality and technical abilities, his extreme agility in arpeggios, his alternation between legato and staccato. The vocal part similarly reflects the timbre and individuality of Harlas. Not only was it a musical portrait of the two friends, it alsooffered them both the opportunity to display their virtuosity.

Solo cantatas with obbligato instruments had been popular throughout the eighteenth century. Meyerbeer took up this tradition and carried it forward, ever intent on developing the connection and relationship of voice and instrument according to contextual and dramaturgical exigency. The work therefore looks both backwards and forwards. The Italianate nature of the work has a spicy admixture that make it the first example of Meyerbeer's adaptation and reformulation of the whole ethos of bel canto and the new Rossinian codification of received tradition. The melodic concept reveals Meyerbeer's own nature at work: the phrases are short, thematic and motival possibilities are not developed in a necessarily expected or extended way. A certain astringent quality in the melodic design counteracts any sentimentality or luxurious lingering. The whole instrumental cast of the work, the intense technicality of soprano and clarinet, contain many presentiments of the orchestral and vocal virtuosity that Meyerbeer was to display in his later operas.

Perhaps most significantly, the cantata presents a distillation of the pastoral genre and several related generic forms, and becomes a point of reference in what would be a recurrent and vital aspect of Meyerbeer's symbolic and dramaturgical preoccupations, with important statements in *Margherita d'Anjou*, *Robert le Diable*, *Les Huguenots*, *Ein Feldlager in Schlesien*, *Struensee*, *Le Prophète*, *L'Étoile du Nord*, and most especially *Le Pardon de Ploërmel*. (The latter takes up and reflects on the pastoral tradition in itself, making it central to the concerns of the opera and Meyerbeer's whole artistic life.)

The cantata has been revived in recent times: in recordings by Julia Varady (soprano) and Jörg Fadle (clarinet) with the RIAS Kammerchor and Radio-Symphonie-Orchester Berlin, conducted by Gerd Albrecht (Berlin, September 1981, released in 1983); Mariana Nicolesco (soprano) and Dieter Klöcker (clarinet) with the Ludwigsburg Festival Chorus and Orchestra conducted by Wolfgang Gönnerwein (Stuttgart, February 1983, released in 1984); and in concerts by Nelly Miricioiu (soprano) and Emma Johnson (clarinet) with the Chorus and Radio Symphony Orchestra of the Netherlands conducted by Julian Reynolds (Utrecht, May 1988); Opéra Berlioz, Montpellier, 1989; and by Michal Shamir (soprano) and Eli Heifetz (clarinet), with the Philharmonia Singers and the Israel Chamber Orchestra conducted by Mats Liljefors (Tel Aviv Museum of Art, 1–2 June 2003).

The recent revivals have revealed the genuine theatrical qualities of this small work which dramatically renews an old concertante genre.

2.3 *Der Bayerische Schützen-Marsch [The Bavarian Sharpshooters' March]*

Cantata for four soloists and brass orchestra
Text: King Ludwig I of Bavaria
First performed: Munich, 18 March 1831

This cantata was written by Meyerbeer in 1829 in honour of its poet, the King of Bavaria. Ludwig I (1786–1868, reg. 1825–48), a liberal and German nationalist before his accession to the throne, when he had defended the Bavarian constitution of 1818 against Metternich, became conservative upon accession. He was an enthusiastic patron of the arts and turned Munich into the artistic centre of Germany. His poem reflects upon his youth under his father, Maximilian I (1756–1825, reg. 1806–25) who as the elector of Bavaria (1799–1806) had been forced into war against France (1799), then sided with France (1805), gaining territory for Bavaria, becoming king, and remaining loyal to Napoleon until just before the Battle of Leipzig (1813), after which he renegotiated a treaty with Austria. The poem ('Töne die ihr mächtig mich bewegt') (Sounds that powerfully move me), written in January 1814, is an imaginative reflection on this dramatic change in the king's political allegiances and Ludwig's own helplessness as prince. Its eight stanzas present a kind of monodrama, a dramatic monologue for two tenors, two basses and male chorus accompanied by a brass orchestra (of seven trumpets, seven horns, four bassoons, one alto, one tenor and two bass trombones, serpent and contrabassoon, with timpani, *tamburro rollante*, and *gran cassa e piatti*).

The work can be regarded as a type of military sequel to *Das Brandenburger Tor*, a belated musing on the tumult and upheavals of the Napoleonic Wars, some twenty years after. The period, with its calls on patriotism and nationalist fervour, had provided a personal and moral dilemma for the young Meyerbeer who had remained in self-imposed exile in Vienna while his first brother Wilhelm had signed up for the final stage of the War of Liberation.

The poem captures the mood of the heroic times recalled ('The greatest delight is enjoying this blessing of victory, / To live in Germany's finest hour. / But destiny always demands resolution, / Dying in return for attaining the goal'). Immediately, however, there is an undercutting of the militarism—the ferocity of the conflict is for a noble cause: 'For only through struggle comes lasting peace. / The blood that is shed leads to wise governance.' Heroism is countered in a verse of dark disappointment as the prince muses bitterly on his personal situation which prevents him from partaking in the forthcoming conflict: 'The blood in my veins stopped flowing, / And I was forced to accept my lot / —That I could not take part in the battle; I must stay here, / Out of action, I alone, away from the troops... / Uncomforted, I alone, only I.' The mobilization is a type of personal reproof, but also the call to a noble mission of freedom: 'Yes, trumpet calls, you admonish me, / To advance, to France, to the people's battle, / Until we complete the great undertaking, /Until we bring peace to the world.'

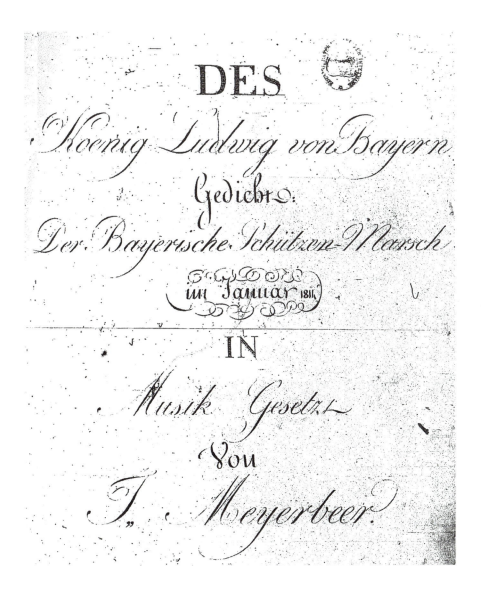

Illustration 2.2 *Der Bayerische Schützen-Marsch*: the manuscript title-page (courtesy of the Bayerische Staatsbibliothek, 1831)

This extraordinary perspective on recent history, politics, nationalism and soldiering adds another dimension to the tacit pull between militarism and pastoralism addressed in *Das Brandenburger Tor*. It would be revisited in *Ein Feldlager in Schlesien*, the opera honouring Prussia's national hero, Frederick the Great.

The cantata is also of interest in the celebration of harmony, the eight-part choral writing, and the extraordinary richness and versatility of the brass orchestra. Like the earlier *Singspiel* it uses an actual folksong, the Bavarian Sharpshooters' March (ex. 2.3 [a]), and a variety of choral and instrumental variation in the setting of the eight verses, strong male voice writing, with a cappella (sometimes for the soloists, sometimes with the chorus) alternating with a parte setting, sinking away in depicting the prince's despair ('Tatlos, ich allein, nur ich') (Deedless, only I alone, only I) (ex. 2.3 [b]), all underpinned by the extensive four-part bassoon writing that looks forward to the sound world of *Le Prophète* (ex. 2.3 [c]). Then all gradually builds up: a fugal finale begins, with four-part interlocking vocal roulades and engagement of the whole orchestral force, leading to an eight-bar moment of solo lento repose before the final apotheosis, with the instruments instructed to play 'upwards into the air', for maximum acoustic effect for the rapturous aspiration ('Bis die Welt den Frieden wir gegeben, / Bis das grosse Werk durch uns vollbracht') (Until we have given freedom to the world, Until we have accomplished the great work) (ex. 2.3 [d]).

Example 2.3 *Der Bayerische Schützen-Marsch*: a) the introduction, b) destiny demands resolution, c) the despair of inaction, d) the fugal finale

Meyerbeer's diary gives us a few hints about the performance of the cantata. He records on 27 January 1831 a visit from Fräulein Vespermann, the Royal favourite: 'She told me many good things, on the King's behalf, about my *Schützenmarsch*...[he] has ordered it to be performed this Lent.' On 25 February he wrote to his brother to whom he had entrusted the Munich arrangements: 'Sketched a letter to Michael: he has unsuspectingly accepted a conductor for the performance of the *Schützenmarsch,* who, while apparently obliging, is more likely to ruin the work. I am also anxious about the choice of the four singers, that the wind instrumentalists should practise on their own first, and that there should be choristers for the performance in the amphitheatre.' Engaged in the composition of *Robert le Diable,* the composer was not able to attend, and on 1 April his fears about both conductor and balance of forces were realized. He confided that 'the performance of my *Schützenmarsch* (18 March)...according to Michael's report, made little impression (apparently, he says, because the accompanying brass drowned out the chorus)'.

2.4 *Maria und ihr Genius [Maria and her Good Spirit]*

Kantate zur Feier der silberen Hochzeit Ihrer Königliche Hoheheiten, des Prinzen und der Prinzessin Karl von Preussen, für Sopran und Tenor Soli mit Chor und Orchester [Cantata in celebration of the silver wedding of Their Royal Highnesses, the Prince and the Princess of Prussia, for soprano and tenor solos with chorus and orchestra]
Text: Goldtammer
First performed: Schloss Wannsee, Berlin, 26 May 1852

After the premiere of *Le Prophète*, Meyerbeer entered the apogee of his fame. Apart from his restless artistic travels to oversee productions of this latest sensation of the musical theatre, he lived quietly in Berlin, enjoying the rich artistic life of the city, and the favour of the ruling family.

Meyerbeer's friendship with members of the Royal House of Prussia was close and enduring. Apart from King Friedrich Wilhelm IV, he was an intimate of the monarch's younger brother Prince Karl and his wife. So their silver wedding on 26 May 1852 provided Meyerbeer with the opportunity of expressing a long-held esteem. Composed between 27 April and 8 May 1852, his cantata for the occasion is also interesting on account of the symbolic place it occupies in his work, coming as it did halfway between *Le Prophète* and *L'Étoile du Nord*. This small work is different from the series of odes and festal songs he wrote for other public or state occasions (like those honouring Gutenberg, the Duke of Saxe-Coburg-Gotha, Queen Victoria, Rauch, Schiller and King Wilhelm I). It is constituted rather as a little duodrama for soprano (Maria) and tenor (the Genius) with a three-part chorus, in four pieces—opening and closing choruses encapsulating an exchange, a song and an answering arioso. It is a celebration of all the pastoral virtues of love, loyalty, marriage, dance and song—a dream of ideal happiness proposed, lost and sometimes found in various guises throughout Meyerbeer's *oeuvre*. It picks up on ideas unfolded in the works of his adolescence, in the balletic games of love (*Der Fischer und das Milchmädchen*), in the celebration of creation (*Gott und die Natur*), of love sought with ardour in the pastoral world (*Gli amori di Teolinda*). This world becomes a major vector of his thematic concerns in the *grands opéras*: found in *Robert le Diable*, slipping away in *Les Huguenots*, tragically glimpsed and lost in *Le Prophète*, and regained in the *opéras comiques* and *L'Africaine*—but only through suffering. This is a countersign to the harsh reality of human mutability and destructive passion, of deforming ideology and uncontrolled character.

Illustration 2.3   *Maria und ihr Genius*: the printed title-page of the Schlesinger
score (Berlin, 1852)

The opening chorus of the cantata sets the scene: 'The sovereign couple stands
reminiscing, / Their memory recalls both joy and sorrow, / The dream of life has
passed so quickly.' Maria's aria establishes the pastoral dream and initiates a series
of images intensively developed in this brief work; the couple are seen in terms
of a pathetic fallacy: 'the myrtle with the rose entwined'; the joy of marriage is
idealized, life is filled with riches: 'You clothed it in your magic spell / With your
love, your heavenly joy, / You gave me what my soul desired.' The pastoral topos of
mutability ('et in Arcadia ego') is referred to in reminiscence of the passing years
('Soon perhaps the sun will set forever, / O treasured time, O golden dream'), in

yearning for the lost days of youth . The Genius provides a pious reassurance, a pledge of immortality ('The divine blossom of eternal love / Never fades, never wilts'). The final chorus led by the Genius solo re-emphasizes the insights of the preceding dialogue, with the red of the rose, the green of the myrtle, the white of the trousseau thrown into a new exciting perspective by 'the lustre of silver' in the crown (of royalty) that has been a part of this nuptial gift. Finally there is the climax: 'And then some day in the evening glow / The promise will turn to gold', with the tenor rising to an impassioned climax of delicate embellishment in *diminuendo*: 'it represents virtue and fidelity' (ex. 2.4). The configuration of double crowning at the end of *L'Étoile du Nord*—in Catherine's marriage to Tsar Peter and her coronation as empress—is already being prepared.

Example 2.4 *Maria und ihr Genius*: the final peroration

PART 2
Opera

Chapter Three

German Operas: *Singspiel*

3.1. *Jephthas Gelübde [Jephtha's Vow]*

Oper in drei Aufzügen mit Ballet [opera in three acts with ballet]
Text: Professor Alois Schreiber
First performance: Hofoper, Munich, 23 December 1812

After the success of *Gott und die Natur*, the time had come for Vogler to entrust his pupil with his own dramatic work. Both devised a plan based on the story of Jephtha and his vow from the Old Testament (the Book of Judges, 11:30–40) which Alois Wilhelm Schreiber shaped into a libretto.

Plot
Biblical times in Ancient Israel, during the period of the Judges (11th–12th centuries BC).

Act 1. Scene 1. Introduction, chorus and dance of the vintage harvesters, with a romance for Tirza, Sulima's confidante, who sings of a peaceful idyll. But it is war, and the Amorites are threatening the Israelites. Sulima, the daughter of Jephtha, a noble-hearted, brave but illegitimate warrior, says that she will accept the suit of her beloved Asmaweth when he has distinguished himself through bravery in the war. If he should fall, her life will be turned into a grave. Asmaweth, in a big aria, confirms his love and willingness to face battle. The scene is overheard by Abdon, one of the tribal leaders, who is also in love with Sulima and who lies in wait for her. Her promise of love provokes Abdon's jealousy, and he swears to be avenged on Asmaweth.
Scene 2. At the city gates. Sulima and her friends are bidding farewell to the departing warriors. Jephtha promises Asmaweth Sulima's hand if he is victorious. He refuses to lead the Israelites, even when the first refugees reach the city: 'Ich hatte ein Vaterland: ihr habt mirs genommen' (I once had a fatherland which you took away from me), he says to the tribal leaders who have always disregarded him on account of his origins. But the people plead with him, and when the devastating news of the battle arrives, he takes up his sword. Jephtha vows that if he is victorious, he will offer up to God the first creature he meets on his return. A thunderclap indicates that God has accepted the vow. He confidently leads the warriors out to battle.
Act 2. Sulima prays at the tomb of her dead mother. Abdon announces the victory of the Israelites, but pretends that Asmaweth has been killed. At the same time he berates the mourners. But Asmaweth appears, much to Sulima's joy, and they celebrate their love in a duet. Rejoicing is heard, and the victorious Jephtha enters. Overjoyed, Sulima rushes to meet him, and Jephtha is horrified to see his daughter the victim of his vow. Abdon insists that the vow be fulfilled, while Asmaweth wishes to save her.

Act 3. Scene 1. Jephtha agonizes over the situation, and resolves to offer himself. Sulima, however, is prepared to confront death. She takes her leave of her father, and her beloved. Asmaweth stands ready with his companions to fight for Sulima's life against Abdon's followers who press forward. Jephtha intervenes: he would rather sink the steel into his own breast.

Scene 2. In the temple, all is prepared for the sacrifice. Suddenly the high priest proclaims that God does not demand blood: he is pleased to accept Jephtha's obedience. The people praise God for his mercy.

Illustration 3.1.   *Jephthas Gelübde*: manuscript of Sulima's Act 3 aria (courtesy of the Bayerische Staatsbibliothek, 1812)

The colour of the opera was meant to be Oriental, which, after the Turkish wars in South Germany and Austria, had become so popular. Most of the pieces are not Oriental, however, in spite of occasional echoes of Janissary music, but more about German citizens in Turkish costume. The musical language, the thematic invention, the harmonic style show the influence of his teacher. The music dramatist Meyerbeer is, however, unmistakably in evidence at those moments where he discovers possibilities for characterization. This is particularly evident in the verbal instructions he inserts in the score. So when the rival lover Abdon broods over his rejection and plans his vengeance, his aria has the indication '*er verliert sich in wollüstiger Rückerrinerung*' (he loses himself in lustful recollection) in order to direct the singer to visualize dramatically what the music is suggesting psychologically in its deep, obsessive ostinato, unctuous sixth chords in second inversion, and the fraught vocal plunge of an octave (ex. 3.1a).

Example 3.1a   *Jephthas Gelübde*: Abdon's aria (Act 1)

The Act 2 finale begins with the chorus of warriors behind the scenes. To clarify the envisaged spatial experience, the composer directed: '*Anfänglich in weiterer Entfernung kömmt aber nach und nach immer näher*' (Beginning in the further distance, [it] comes ever closer). Such dramaturgical concern for spatial detail would remain a constant feature of Meyerbeer's future work. Indeed dynamic finesse also serves the sharpening of the dramatic, as, at the fatal moment when Sulima meets her returning father, four horns sound in triple forte with the special instruction '*Schallstücke aufwärts*' (Instruments upwards). The Death March that opens the third act of this serious opera begins with measured crescendo for horns, trumpets and drums from pianissimo to forte. Here Meyerbeer builds on the traditions of the dynamic and versatile Mannheim school. Passages of a musico-dramatic character are also discernible in vocal gestures. In the trio (no. 12) Sulima announces her preparedness to die. At the words 'Die Erde hat nur Leiden' (the earth contains only sorrow) she sings an extended coloratura melisma of four bars, which, despite a certain awkwardness, proclaims another enduring feature of Meyerbeer's vocal writing in his constant concern to realize psychic states musically. Here he has already embarked on the route he would faithfully follow. Jephtha's internal agony at the outcome of his vow is illustrated by convulsed leaps of sevenths and ninths in the vocal part ('Ich will dich an meinem Busen erwärmen. / Wach auf! Du sollst nicht sterben') (I want to cherish you on my breast. / Awake! You should not die).

This trait, traceable to Mozart (cf. 'Come scoglio' in *Così fan tutte*, 1790), appears a few years later in the Romantic operas of E.T.A. Hoffmann (*Undine*) and Spohr (*Faust*) (both 1816). Sulima's other aria ('Ich will mein junges Leben') (I would like my young life), on the other hand, shows an obvious Italian influence, with *imitando la voce* passages for the voice in rivalry with an obbligato violin, a style which made its appearance well before the Italian period, and which was not therefore copied from Rossini, but rather derives from Handel and the eighteenth-century traditions of *opera seria*.

There is also a fondness already discernible for characterization by means of instrument groups. When Jephtha broods over the fatal vow, his recitative is accompanied by three solo bassoons, reflecting the darkness of his despair; his song, sinking into the depths, is joined by a double bass and a bassoon in canonic intertwining which captures the inescapable compulsion of fate. Destiny is symbolized by sforzandi of the strings in the lower register, and repeated rising threatening basses. Meyerbeer's depiction of the doomed Sulima's desperation is consistently masterful, with the same fateful double basses rising from the depths, the violins silent, as low-pitched woodwinds play above the sombre violas and basses, the clarinets below the bassoons. The flutes when they enter play prophetically from the burial song in Act 3, and Sulima, in an ecstasy of dread, hears the voices at her own graveside, and faints, as her maiden companions soothingly sing a song of supplication. Sulima's scene bears a striking melodic resemblance to the passage 'Darf Furcht im Herz des Waidmann hausen?' (Can fear lurk in the heart of a forester?) from the Act 2 trio in *Der Freischütz* (1821). Weber would certainly have known Meyerbeer's opera well: both composers may have been influenced by the spectral scenes in their teacher Vogler's operas *Castor und Pollux* (1791) and *Hermann von Unna* (1799).

The Act 2 finale provided the young Meyerbeer with the opportunity for dramatic writing. His arrangement of the score is surprising, with tripartite chorus, soloists, and orchestra strongly reinforced, especially in the brass. Encouraged by Vogler, his score develops on Gluck's style, and embodies numerous features later thought to originate with Spontini. The vigorous and dramatic treatment of the chorus already looks to the Paris period. The Act 3 finale contains other prophetic features. When Jephtha, in anguish, decides to perform the sacrificial act, a sinister motif, descending in minor thirds and carried by the strings and bassoons, enters at the words 'Lasst ihr mir grausam keine andre Wahl!' (Terribly you leave me with no other choice) (ex. 3.1b).

This idea will appear again at various times and guises in the later operas as a marker of gruesome situations—from the Conspirators' Chorus in *Il crociato in Egitto*, as a characteristic sound for Bertram in *Robert le Diable*, to the destruction of the castle at the end of *Le Prophète*. There are also grandiose features in the true Meyerbeer manner, as in the transition from the burial chorus (the minor third dying away until only the tonic E remains), passing into the E major of the full orchestra entering brilliantly on the words 'Nein, du sollst leben!' (No, you should live). Here the motifs of Jephtha and Sulima resound for the first time in the major. For Edgar Istel (1926: 100) the use of leitmotif remains an extraordinary achievement, where the psychological development of a struggling soul is musically depicted in truly dramatic fashion by dismemberment and distortion of motifs and veiled allusion to them.

Example 3.1b   *Jephthas Gelübde*: from the Act 3 finale

Many of the religious themes developed by Meyerbeer in his French operas are already present in *Jephthas Gelübde*. It is possible that it formed an enduring psychological stimulus for ideas that he would work out later in life. Sulima and Sélika, in his last opera *L'Africaine*, both in their own ways represent themes of sacrifice and unfulfilled love in a selfless woman. The biblical story is traumatic, and one can see how it could provide the basis for a lifelong struggle with the nature of what is required of us by faith or religion, and the purpose of sacrifice. It is also powerful in communicating other social and political thoughts recurrent in the composer's work.

With his first opera Meyerbeer, because of the his of spoken dialogue, appeared formally to adhere to the generic limits of the *Singspiel*. The musical language, however, in its variety of expression in which the influences of Gluck, Mozart and Vogler appeared in a most original adaptation, far exceeded any narrow generic characteristics. Its two performances at the Court Theatre in Munich, while earning Meyerbeer the approbation of the professionals, was only a *succès d'estime*, in spite of the brilliant casting of Helene Harlas, Georg Weixelbaum and Georg Mittermayr.

3.2. *Wirt und Gast, oder Aus Scherz Ernst [Host and Guest, or A Joke Turns Serious]*

Lustspiel mit Gesang in 2 Aufzügen [comedy with songs in two acts]
Text: Hofschauspieler Johann Gottfried Wohlbrück
First performance: Hoftheater, Stuttgart, 6 January 1813

Even during the rehearsals of *Jephtha* Meyerbeer had begun composing a new opera, on a comic theme this time, with a text drawn from the *Thousand and One Nights*.

Plot
From the Arabian Nights. In medieval Baghdad, *c.*800.

Act 1. Scene 1. In front of the house of the rich young merchant Alimelek receivers and spongers have congregated, and with comically melodic sighing and syncopated accents, they hope to wheedle alms from Alimelek. The grotesque situation is underlined by the exaggerated emphases of individual musical elements.
   Scene 2. In the house hides Irene, the niece of the Caliph Harun Al Raschid, who has been missing for weeks. Only occasionally does she dare go out in daylight. In a romance she sings of her happiness at being with her beloved Alimelek.
   Scene 3. The Caliph, who is travelling around the city incognito, visits the merchant and is received with warm hospitality. Refreshments are offered, and in a drinking song about the fleeting nature of happiness, they begin a conversation. Alimelek says how much he would love to be Caliph for just one day. The guest promises fulfilment of his wish through magic. In his high spirits Alimelek becomes careless and calls for his beloved. She immediately recognizes her uncle, although he hides his astonishment and maintains his disguise. He infuses a sleeping draught into Alimelek's wine, and has him carried to the palace.
   Act 2. Scene 1. Alimelek awakes as Caliph and plays the ruler for a day with great enthusiasm. At night he again receives a sleeping potion, and wakes up in a dungeon. Because he has abducted the Caliph's niece, he is condemned to death. The transformation music that accompanies Alimelek's awakening quotes motifs from the preceding scenes in depicting Alimelek's dream of becoming ruler for a day.
   Scene 2. The Caliph puts Alimelek's constancy to the test. He promises him pardon from all punishment if he will marry another woman. Alimelek remains steadfast, but when he hears that Irene is threatened with the same fate, he gives in.
   Scene 3. The Caliph subjects Irene to the same test, and she also remains constant and spurns the proposed suitor prince. The faithfulness of the lovers leads the Caliph to bless their union. The opera closes with a happy ballet and chorus celebrating the Caliph's magnanimity.

Illustration 3.2   *Wirt und Gast*: manuscript of Alimelek's Drinking Song (courtesy of the Württembergische Staatsbibliothek, 1813)

The overture, unlocking a mythical domain, introduces a note of real comedy, born of the exuberance of youth, and not heard again in again in Meyerbeer's work until *Dinorah*, a work of his late maturity. The young composer's mastery of his craft is evident in the construction, and in the development of climaxes and contrasts. Contrapuntal skills are evident in the opening fugato episode, an original artistry in the treatment of the woodwind, and striking use of the pizzicato. The middle parts are characterized by a chromatic leaning which would recur extensively in his later Paris period (especially in *Robert le Diable*). This early occurrence suggests a derivation from Cherubini rather than Spohr, as was often thought later. Cherubini's works were performed in Berlin under Bernhard Anselm Weber from 1791 onwards, and would certainly have been known to the youthful Meyerbeer. The overture is dominated by Alimelek's Drinking Song, the medium of elation, intoxication, fantasy and change, both as alcohol and sleeping draught, the recurring thematic key to the opera that returns in the Transformation Music and the finale, lending a unity to the musical whole (ex. 3.2a [a]).

Example 3.2a   *Wirt und Gast*: themes of intoxication

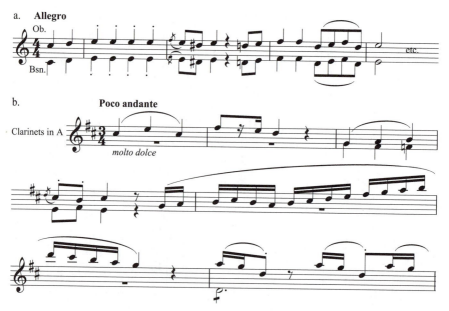

The Turkish veneer, as exemplified in the introductory chorus, establishes a certain similarity with Weber's *Abu Hassan* (1811). But Meyerbeer's work differs from Weber's in the more ample dimensions of the aria and ensembles (like the extended Act 1 finale, with its interpolated romance and canon). There is a deeper characterization of the principal characters, especially Irene, whose music throughout builds a definite personality: the simple melody of her opening aria soon takes off into enraptured virtuosity expressive of her resolution and determination. The opening of the Introduction in its handling of the rising treble figure, with its echoing, rhythmically punctuating sixths in the bass, reveals an Italianate element at work. The first act indeed is characterized by an interplay between German and

Italian styles. The second act, on the other hand, is steeped in a glamour of fabulous Romanticism that provided a stimulus to the young composer, and is especially evident in the handling of the choruses. The entr'acte music, with chorus and dance (No. 6), depicts Alimelek, transferred to the Caliph's palace, lying in the stupor induced by the sleeping draught. He is enveloped in mysterious static chords, his confusion of mind suggested by clarinets wandering vaguely, hovering over horn and bassoon tones (ex. 3.2a [b]). As he awakes, a chorus in strongly marked beat and full orchestra begins: Meyerbeer himself wrote in the direction that it should be played 'with rhythmic precision, as it is sung with the intention of bewildering Alimelek'. The chorus No. 9 develops the local colour, dramatically depicting the whirling dervishes, who are conjured up in sudden anticipated woodwind figures, edgy trills in the strings, and percussive crashes on the big drum and cymbals.

The unusual situation of the duet of testing for Alimelek and Irene (No. 7) indicates something of the young composer's special orchestral flair: the atmosphere of bewilderment induced by the 'böse Zauber' (bad magic) that seems to surround them and rule their lives is conjured up by a double-bass ostinato figure (rising from a quaver through an upward semiquaver run to a crochet) beneath a tonal haze of strings (ex. 3.2b).

Example 3.2b   *Wirt und Gast:* from the duet for Alimelek and Irene (Act 2)

The harmonic effect would be borrowed by Weber, again in the Act 2 trio of *Der Freischütz* ('Ich bin vertraut mit jenem Grausen') (I am used to every terror). But perhaps the most striking piece in the whole opera is the Transformation Music (No. 10) that accompanies Alimelek's sudden downfall from the throne to the depths of the dungeon. The history of the action is given in orchestral compression, with the various themes of the characters, love and ambition, presented in various tonal and thematic guises, with leading motifs combined in growing polyphonic interplay, as Alimelek struggles to regain consciousness.

A comparison with Weber's *Abu Hassan* shows that Meyerbeer's contribution to the genre of the 'Turkish opera' is marked by a strong characterization of the bizarre and the semi-tragic. The work, revised and expanded by Meyerbeer, made its appearances on several stages. The first performance in Stuttgart in 1813 (with Johann Baptist Krebs as Alimelek and Karoline Wilhelmine Mayer as Irene, conductor Conradin Kreutzer) was followed by productions in Vienna (1814, as *Die beiden Kalifen*, with Catinka Buchwieser as Irene), Prague 1815, and Dresden 1820 (this time as *Alimelek*), the last two both conducted by Weber.

3.3 *Das Brandenburger Tor [The Brandenburg Gate]*

Singspiel in einem Aufzug [opera with spoken dialogue in one act]
Text: Dr [Johann Emanuel] Veith
First performance: Schauspielhaus, Kammermusiksaal, Berlin, 5 September 1991

Carl Maria von Weber had become Kapellmeister at the Ständische National Theatre in 1813, and in August 1814 travelled to Berlin for a concert, where his collection *Leyer und Schwerdt* to a text by Theodor Körner was performed to great enthusiasm. His songs captured the contemporary patriotic tone perfectly. Meyerbeer's family were anxious that he should be seen to be involved in the national effort for liberation, like his brother Wilhelm who had volunteered for the free corps. In spite of the efforts of Carl Friedrich Zelter and the dramatist August Wilhelm Iffland (1759–1814), Goethe could not be persuaded to write any words, but eventually the text was provided by E. Veith. Meyerbeer took two weeks to set it to music ('as one only can in 14 days, i.e. very hurriedly', he wrote on 3 August to his tutor Aron Wolfsson [1754–1835]) (*BT*, 1:238).

Plot
The little *Singspiel* is set in Berlin. People are awaiting the return of the king from the defeated France. A veteran of the Seven Years War, Sergeant Schroll, fetches a drum, and Christoph, a young soldier, plays it, gathering the people together to greet the monarch: 'O Tag der Freude, Tag der Wonne, Tag der Lust. / Unser König kehrt zurück' (Oh day of joy, day of rapture, day of pleasure. / Our king is returning). The home guard remember the war and praise Prussia. During the ritornello, several detachments are sent to man observation posts of the streets. Schroll recalls camp life during the war, and how he lost his leg in battle. Wilhelm, his son, who is in love with Luise Staudt, extols the political alliance that has changed the tide of war, with the people praising the leadership of the three monarchs: 'Held Alexander zog heran, und Friedrich Wilhelm schloss sich an, / Und Ost'reichs weiser Herrscher. / Hoch lebe Blücher; hoch Gneisenau; hoch lebe York...' (The hero Alexander steps forward, joined by Frederick William / And Austria's wise ruler. / Long live Blücher, Gneisenau, York). The guard marches off in quickstep. Wilhelm goes on to explain that a young, attractive man can have success with the ladies only if he wears a uniform, and therefore decides to enlist. Staudt, a fashionable man about town, opposes any union with his daughter Luise until there is complete peace, a situation

which causes pain to the young lovers. Luise speaks of their longing to see the king, the father of the nation. All dissension is resolved by the patriotic fervour stirred by the sighting of the royal party. The Quadriga, the Winged Victory surmounting the Brandenburg Gate, is unveiled: 'Viktoria, er kommt...Den König begrüssen wir wieder' (Victory, he is coming. We will salute the king again). The opera ends with Schroll's marching song extolling patriotic pride, based on an actual folksong: 'Wohl mir, dass ich ein Preusse bin' (Lucky me, to be a Prussian).

Illustration 3.3   *Das Brandenburger Tor*: a modern copy of the introduction (courtesy of Reiner Zimmermann, 1991)

The text united all the traumatic feelings elicited for Meyerbeer by the nature of the state of Prussia. Nothing seemed to go right with the composition, and the chance of having it produced was missed because the score was sent to Berlin too late. Meyerbeer had lost interest in it: in fact he read in the papers that the king of Prussia had already left for Vienna in July, and so would not have been able to hear the little opera in any case.

Both Meyerbeer's first two operas had been *Singspiele*: the first, despite its modest format, had tuned into a heritage deriving from Handel, Gluck, Mozart and Cherubini. It had also looked forward to developments by Beethoven and Weber. The second likewise acknowledges Mozart and Weber in its realization of Turkish ideas. Both operas handle large forms effectively, with grand dramatic gestures. Now with this miniature scenario and limited scope, Meyerbeer associated himself more with the more modest traditions of Hiller, Himmel, Weigl and Wenzel Müller. The nine numbers of the score punctuate a scenario about ordinary folk observing and reflecting on the great forces of history. In the midst of a tumultuous military world of battles and political manoeuvring, there is a yearning for peace and the re-establishment of the happy values born of reconciliation and social integration—the traditional métier of the pastoral. Six of the nine numbers extol the military life in the appropriate forms of signals, marches, military couplets, strophic ballads about military exploits and patriotic resolves. The middle three numbers are more reflective and domestic, and pertain to the pastoral aspiration. This covers Wilhelm's humorous song about the mystique of uniforms (an instance of real *bürgerliche Gemütlichkeit*) (ex. 3.3a), with its reassuring shift from A minor in the verses [a] to A major in the refrain [b]: the quintet of disappointment about the postponed marriage, and Luise's buoyant and touching rondo ('Soll uns nicht die Lust beleben') (Should hope not inspire us). The latter is a key to the proper understanding of the scenario: here the king is transformed from absolute military overlord to loving father of his people, and

Example 3.3a   *Das Brandenburger Tor*: Wilhelm's Lied

a symbol of hope, the one who will bring peace and change society. Luise's ability to combine personal optimism with a perception of the almost mystical potential of monarchy, the integrating and transforming capacity for true kingly leadership, results in an overlapping and fusion of the public and private spheres in what can only be understood as a 'military pastoralism'. This concept would be worked out in greater detail in the patriotic opera about King Frederick the Great, *Ein Feldlager in Schlesien* (1844), some 30 years later. *L'Étoile du Nord* (1854) would do the same in a less overt way with its romanticized, popular image of Peter the Great.

Meyerbeer had hoped to recommend himself to his country and home city with this small work. Appreciating its specific purpose and patriotic purpose, he used the Prussian folksong 'Wohl mir, dass ich ein Preusse bin' as the logical emotional, if sentimental, highpoint of this celebration (ex. 3.3b).

Example 3.3b   *Das Brandenburger Tor*: Schlussgesang (Prussian Folksong)

Perhaps something of his innate awkwardness about nationalism is bound up with his reticence in completing and sending the score. By the time it did reach Berlin, the Quadriga had already been positioned on the Brandenburg Gate, and the ostensible purpose of the score had passed. During a stay in Berlin in 1823, and possibly to placate his friend Weber, Meyerbeer tried in vain to secure a performance at the suburban theatre in the Königstadt. It was destined to languish untouched until the occasion of Meyerbeer's bicentenary when, on 5 September 1991, the premiere took place at the Schauspielhaus in Berlin, a particularly appropriate gesture of honour from the city of Berlin to one of its most famous sons, and just a year after the reunification of the divided Germany on 3 October 1990. The cast was: Luise (Stephanie Möller, soprano); Wilhelm (Julian Metzger, tenor); Christoph (Friedemann Körner, tenor); Offizier/Trommler (Dietrich Wagner, tenor); Schroll (Edmund Mangelsdorf, bass); Staudt (Joachim Heyer, bass); Habakuk Traber (pianist); Werner Kotsch (conductor).

3.4 *Ein Feldlager in Schlesien/Vielka [A Camp in Silesia]*

Singspiel in drei Akten, in Lebensbildern aus der Zeit Friedrichs den Grossen [opera with spoken dialogue in three acts, in tableaux from the times of Frederick the Great]
Text: Heinrich Friedrich Ludwig Rellstab, after a scenario by Augustin-Eugène Scribe
First performed: Königliches Schauspielhaus, Berlin, 7 December 1844

The Berlin Opera House was destroyed in a fire on 18–19 August 1843, and it was decided by King Friedrich Wilhelm IV to mark the reopening of the restored theatre with a *Festspiel* especially written for the occasion, on a theme drawn from the history of Prussia. Meyerbeer, who had been in his official post for a year, was entrusted with the composition from the very first: in fact the idea may well have originated with him. His regard for the 'bright, genuinely humane king' (Meyerbeer to Heine on 28 September 1841, *BT* 3:368), whose accession in 1840 heralded a liberal era in the cultural life of the realm, may well have played a role, as also the intention to disarm anti-Semitic resentment against himself by writing a 'patriotic' work. Furthermore, at the time, Meyerbeer's Parisian projects were stagnating: *Le Prophète* (1849) and *L'Africaine* (1865) were comprehensively on hold, their productions beset with casting problems. In the choice of a librettist Meyerbeer further felt himself bound to take cognizance of national sensitivities. The author of the text was also on this occasion his esteemed French librettist Scribe, whose authorship was, by mutual agreement, to be kept secret. The official librettist, the Berlin poet and critic Ludwig Rellstab, actually only translated and versified Scribe's prose version. That it was Meyerbeer who also gave the decisive impulse to the opera is clear from the composer's entries in his appointment calendar for 28 October 1843: 'To Scribe...the plan must be scene by scene. At least 2 acts. 2 full hours duration. —Féerie. Spectacle. Ballet. Opera. Dessauer march. Müller Arnold—Seven Years War, patriotic. Flute—no Friedrich in person' (*BT*, 3:455). Meyerbeer's decision to work on a theme concerned with the person of Frederick the Great (on a suggestion he received from his friend Alexander von Humboldt) occurred at a time of increased scholarly discussion about the Prussian king. Quite special were the illustrations by Adolph von Menzel for Franz Kugler's *Geschichte Friedrich des Grossen* (1840) which from 1849 reinforced a new, artistically determined perception of the king's reign that Meyerbeer obviously tuned into. Already in October 1843 it had been decided that the person of the king would not be represented on stage, but suggested by the flute. These thoughts were made clear on 13 November: 'The king must not come on stage, only his flute' (*BT*, 3:464). A further important development took place in autumn 1843 when Meyerbeer heard Jenny Lind, and spontaneously decided to write the principal role in the opera for her. Intrigues in Berlin necessitated a compromise in this matter: Leopoldine Tuczek was chosen for the premiere, and Lind's debut was postponed to a later performance.

Plot
In Silesia and in Potsdam towards the end of the Seven Years War (1756–63).

Act 1. Conservatory on an estate in Silesia. Saldorf the owner, together with his niece Therese and his foster daughter the Gypsy Vielka, is about to bid farewell to his foster son Conrad, a flautist. Vielka, who has inherited psychic powers from her dead mother, prophesies the future, and pledges her love for Conrad. Conrad sets out on his journey, but soon returns with a stranger. He is in fact the king. During an excursion from his camp, Frederick II has been surprised by a troop of Croatian cavalry, and forced to flee. Saldorf hides him in the house. When the pursuing cavalry arrive, led by Tronk, Vielka appears as a fortune-teller, inflames their superstitions, encourages them to drink and ride on. The king is disguised as Conrad, and about to set out in his stead. Before he can leave, they are interrupted by a suspicious scouting party. They require that 'Conrad' show his skill on the flute before he sets out. The king is able to fulfil this requirement, and is allowed to leave.

Act 2. A Prussian camp in Silesia. In the background are the Riesengebirge, capped with snow. The various regiments proclaim their valour. An old peasant sings of the blessings of peace. The rumour that the king has been taken prisoner circulates, and causes much unrest among the troops. Saldorf arrives at the camp to tell of the king's successful escape, but is arrested as a spy. News comes of the king's safety, Saldorf is released, and is able to inspire the troops out of their despondency and into new resolution.

Act 3. A reception hall in the palace of Sanssouci. After the Prussian victory in the recent battle, Conrad is invited by the king with Saldorf and his family to Potsdam. Here the old soldier hopes for news about his son Leopold, the betrothed of Therese, who has been sentenced to death for a breach of discipline. As they await the audience, they hear the king playing his flute from an adjoining apartment; Conrad joins in with his flute. Vielka tells Conrad to ask for the pardon of Leopold as his reward when he meets the king. He returns with the news that the king has granted the pardon, promoted Leopold to captain, and he, Conrad, to a member of the court orchestra. Saldorf and his family rejoice in their happiness. Vielka, taken up in a trance, can see what the king is dreaming, and prophesies a future full of happiness and glory for the royal dynasty and Prussia.

Epilogue. Six *tableaux vivants*, depicting the dreams of the sleeping king, show scenes from the history of Prussia: 1) an allegory of the war; 2) an allegory of peace; 3) Frederick the Great with his Kapellmeister Friedrich Graun in the Opera House; 4) the volunteers of the 1813 War of Liberation at the Rathaus of Breslau; 5) the unveiling of the Brandenburg Gate in Berlin as the Quadriga, the Winged Victory surmounting the monument; 6) Apollo and the Muses in glory above the new Opera House.

The authentic episodes from the life of Frederick the Great unite idyllic and picturesque elements and anecdotes in the manner of a Prussian fairytale (Heinz Becker, *Meyerbeer*, 1980: 76). The figure of the monarch, although the constant reference point, remains a mythical, entranced incarnation of Prussia, physically present only through the medium of music when twice in the action his presence behind the scenes is indicated by his flute-playing (the Act 1 finale, and at the beginning of Act 3 in Vielka's aria). Important themes are conveyed exclusively in hidden action, like the events surrounding Saldorff's son Leopold. His story involving the themes of law and emotion, society and the individual, and the reconciling Royal mercy, is handled in the manner of Heinrich von Kleist's *Der Prinz von Homburg* (1810). This indirect, oblique mode of presentation establishes a free space which allows the composer to pay homage to the historical ruler as a prince of peace and the arts in archetypal and ideal terms. So Sanssouci appears not so much as a national shrine, but rather a Prussian Arcadia and utopian idyll in which love and the arts hold sway rather than weapons.

The simple Biedermeier tone of much of the music (like Saldorf's 'So geh getrost mit Gottes Segen' [Go confidently, then, with God's blessing] in the introduction, and his 'Gott! Dir danken meine Zähren' [O God, my tears thank you] in Act 2) elicited admiration from Adolf Bernhard Marx (1865: 235) and Eduard Hanslick (1875: 151), who were surprised by this aspect of the composer's art. There is no general tendency on Meyerbeer's part to adjust his style, make some calculated turn to German music, because such passages are not typical of the work as a whole: the German tone serves to identify a certain milieu. Completely different means are used to characterize the Gypsy sphere. So in Vielka's Act 1 romance narration of her mother's death the vocal line is doubled by high muted string solos; and when it recurs in the Act 3 finale, the sound texture is subtly opened up further (solo strings con sordino and in harmonics, with two harps and cor anglais as well as a female chorus behind the scene). In Vielka's virtuoso aria in Act 3, with two obbligato flutes positioned in different places, the vocal line, imitating the double echo of the flutes in elaborated coloratura filigree, is transformed into pure sound. The whole of Act 2 constitutes the spectacular showpiece of the opera. Meyerbeer has grasped the complex problem of presentation and *couleur locale* as a compositional and technical challenge. He does not use the huge forces (full regular orchestra, soloists, chorus and three stage bands) for the achievement of crude advertising effects to force emotional identification from the audience, but instead employs them in various plays with forms, colours and audio-spatial perspectives in almost abstract combination. The principle of a thorough spatial organization of the acoustic whole is stamped by Meyerbeer's characteristic technique of vertical montage, here carried to the extreme: four contrasting themes, among them a quotation from the Dessauer March, are first heard singly, then in combination and finally all simultaneously in counterpoint.

It is interesting that for all its military characteristics, the Camp Scene does not aspire to a glorification of war. This is made clear by the dramaturgically contradictory placement at the heart of the tableau of a bitter-sweet song for an old peasant, Steffen ('Den Waffen Ruhm, dem Frieden gröss're Ehre!') (The glory of arms—the greater glory of peace): the refrain of the first strophe exposes an unmistakable pacifistic counter-gesture: 'Seid ihr bereit, fürs Vaterland zu sterben, dafür zu leben, das ist unser Teil' (Even if you are prepared to die for the fatherland, our task is to live for it). It was thought better to protect the public from the potentially explosive power of this appeal which encoded Meyerbeer's personal credo. By the time of the premiere this strophe had already been cut, and later the whole episode followed suit (Döhring 1991, 4: 142).

Illustration 3.4   *Ein Feldlager in Schlesien*: Jenny Lind as Vielka, Leopoldine Tuczek the creator of the role (contemporary lithographs, 1845)

The *tableaux vivants* that unfolded after the third finale required rapid transformations from the stagehands. In the second of them, *Der Frieden* (Peace), the personified Borussia declaimed verses over Vielka's special theme, this time scored for cor anglais, bass clarinet and harp, while an invisible chorus sang: 'Hold ist des Friedens lächelnden Anlitz' (How radiant is the smiling face of peace) (ex. 3.4). A silhouette of Frederick the Great on his dappled steed appeared, an allegory of peace, and then the interior of the old opera house, with Frederick sitting behind his Kapellmeister Graun, as the aria 'Mi paventi' from the latter's *Das Tod Jesu* is heard.

Example 3.4 *Ein Feldlager in Schlesien*: the Theme of Peace from the *tableaux vivants*

The leading forces of the Opera House performed under Meyerbeer's musical direction (with Leopoldine Tuczek as Vielka, Pauline Marx as Therese, Eduard Mantius as Conrad, Louis Bötticher as Saldorf). The stage designs were created by Karl Jakob Gerst (Acts 1 and 2) and Carl Wilhelm Gropius (Act 3), the choreography by Michel-François Hoguet and Paolo Taglioni, and the stage direction by Karl Stawinsky. Jenny Lind's appearances in the following performances created a sensation. The critics were well-disposed towards the work, although they regretted the muted heroic presentation of Frederick the Great. In spite of its success, Meyerbeer was always conscious that the *Feldlager* could hardly hope for effective presentation outside its intended patriotic milieu. He tried to find a solution to the problem by means of two revisions. The first, *Vielka* (Vienna, 1847), focused entirely on Lind (with Vielka no longer a Gypsy, and recast as a full-blown mediatrix), was not radical enough, while the second (*L'Étoile du Nord*, Paris, 1854) was in fact a new work using only elements of Act 2. The score was never published, only an anthology of melodies arranged by Anton Diabelli.

In Berlin, *Ein Feldlager in Schlesien* was retained in the repertoire for decades as a type of Prussian national opera, and attained 67 performances by 1891. Act 2 was frequently given alone at special Court occasions. The whole opera was revived in concert in Berlin in 1984 (Norma Sharp as Vielka, Ruthild Engert as Therese, Volker Horn as Conrad, Jörn Wilsing as Saldorf, with Fritz Weisse conducting).

Chapter Four

Italian Operas: *Opera Seria*

At the end of 1814 Meyerbeer went to Paris, a sojourn he regarded as 'the first and most significant place for my dramatic and musical education', as he wrote to his father Herz (*BT*, 1:248). The overwhelming impressions of the cultural metropolis of Europe provoked a creative crisis in Meyerbeer, the resolution of which was paradoxically ended only by his move to Italy. The experience of Paris strengthened him in his cosmopolitan cultural convictions, making him aware of the need for some vital experience of Italy. And indeed, contact with the works of Rossini (whose operas were still unknown in Paris) initiated an aesthetical process that fascinated the young composer, so open to all new things.

After observing the scene in Italy for a year after *Gli amori di Teolinda*, Meyerbeer undertook his first new operatic venture in Padua: on 14 May 1817 Rossi agreed to provide a libretto *Romilda e Costanza*, and on 1 June Meyerbeer signed the contract.

4.1 *Romilda e Costanza [Romilda and Constance]*

Melodramma semiserio in due atti [semi-serious melodrama in two acts]
Text: Gaetano Rossi
First performed: Teatro Nuovo, Padua, 19 July 1817

Plot
In Aix-en-Provence at the Castle of Senanges.

Act 1. A big hall in the palace of the Prince of Provence. The announcement of the victorious return of Teobaldo from the wars angers his twin brother Retello, since it now appears decreed that Teobaldo will succeed their late father. Teobaldo had once sworn his troth to Costanza, but, far from the country, has fallen in love with Romilda. She, disguised as a page, has followed him secretly. Costanza now observes the page and Teobaldo's behaviour with suspicion, especially since a confidential letter speaking of a broken engagement has played into her hands. At the opening of the paternal testament, Teobaldo's wishes are more than fulfilled, since he is not only named as successor, but is also instructed to marry Romilda rather than Costanza. The uproar that ensues among those present when Costanza is taken ill is used by Retello for his own purposes. He instigates a revolt and a duel in which he defeats Teobaldo, and then has his brother incarcerated.

Act 2. While Retello and his cronies plan Teobaldo's murder, Romilda, still disguised as a page, is seeking to free him. She persuades Costanza to intercede for Teobaldo, and together they succeed, with the help of a local peasant, Pierotto, in reaching his tower prison, but are themselves caught. When the situation seems hopeless, rescue arrives in the person of Teobaldo's squire Ugo and his loyal troops who succeed in defeating Retello and his followers. Teobaldo eschews vengeance, however, and pardons his brother and co-conspirators.

The libretto moves both dramaturgically and thematically within the trusted confines of the mixed genres of Italian opera, which around 1815 was beginning to settle down into the descriptive category of *melodramma semiserio*. However, *Romilda* does not develop the tradition of the *comédie-larmoyante*, which only a few weeks before had experienced a timely renewal in Rossini's *La gazza ladra* (31 May 1817), but instead follows another French type, the *pièce de sauvetage* as it was embodied in the relevant works of Giovanni Simone Mayr and Ferdinando Paer. The characteristic features of this type dominate the action of *Romilda*: a picturesque setting (Gothic castle with mountainous panorama); disguise as a precaution against persecution (Romilda); liberation from captivity (Teobaldo); and a contrasting comic figure from the peasant class (Pierotto). Unusually, but not uniquely (and one has only to think of the various Leonore operas), the typical roles are reversed: the persecuted innocent is not the heroine, the rescuer not the hero.

Judgements about the music singled out one particular aspect: that on his first attempt Meyerbeer had apparently achieved a nigh perfect mastery of a musical-dramatic idiom hitherto foreign to him. Already he begins to impress his own mark on this newly acquired style, but one has to look for what is typically Meyerbeerian less in the musical structures and more on the level of style. His turn to Italian opera is not so much a natural development in a tradition nor an exercise in alien adaptation, but more a conscious choice and personal decision, stamping it with the individual aesthetics of his manner. In fact Meyerbeer had taken over the opera model of the Rossinian period more as a frame than a copy. In his melodic ideas he uses older Italianate models, particularly Mozartian ones, which he sometimes rather startlingly alienates through use of harmony or instrumentation (Döhring 1991, 4:112). This is evident in what became the most famous number in the opera, the slow first movement of Romilda's Act 2 aria 'Se il fato barbaro'. Here the melody with its rocking arpeggiated accompaniment, which could easily derive from Paisiello, is invested with a novel dramatic quality: the technical parameters of movement and sound are reinterpreted, as in the diminished secondary seventh chord in the third bar of the ritornello (ex. 4.1 [a]). The large-scale structural disposition also corresponds favourably with contemporary standards: long scenic episodes are integrated into closed forms (as with the entry of Ugo and his followers in Romilda's aria). The audio-spatial unfolding of a scene provides the musical structure of the number, as in the Act 2 quartet which is built around Teobaldo's stage romance: this provides the vital link with the incarcerated prisoner, whose voice is heard *di dentro* from the tower. There is a sustaining of atmosphere, and the opera is invested with a dreamy lyricism, characterized particularly by the recurrence of the dulcet harmonized writing for the two leading female roles, a feature of the bel canto tradition which would recur throughout Meyerbeer's *oeuvre* (*Semiramide*, *L'esule di Granata*, *Il crociato in Egitto*, *Le Prophète*, *L'Africaine*) (ex. 4.1 [b]).

Illustration 4.1   *Romilda e Costanza*: the printed title-page of Costanza's cavatina (Milan: Ricordi, 1818)

Example 4.1 *Romilda e Costanza*: a) the introduction to Costanza's cavatina (Act 2), b) from the Act 1 finale

An excellent ensemble was assembled for the premiere: Luigi Campitelli and Eliodoro Bianchi as Teobaldo and Retello, Adolfo Bassi as Pierotto, Catterina Lipparini as Costanza, and most especially the contralto Rosmunda Pisaroni as Romilda. Their performance was received with such resounding enthusiasm that it attracted press reports even beyond Italy. The opera was given on several different stages: with moderate success in Venice in 1817, as a near fiasco in Milan at the Teatro Carcano in 1820. This was because of poor preparation, from which Meyerbeer distanced himself in advance. Far more positive was the production at the Teatro della Pergola in Florence, also in 1820 (with Domenico Bertozzi, Antonio Parlamagni, Niccola Tacci, Maria Marchesini and Rosa Mariani). Outside Italy there were productions in Munich and Copenhagen (both in 1822). The opera was revived in Lucca on the occasion of the opening of the Teatro Nota detto del Castiglioncelli during the Carnevale of 1829 (the libretto was published by Benedini e Rocchi). (See Loewenberg 1970: 655–6; Döhring 1991, 4:113; Schuster 2003, 2:49–57.)

Meyerbeer's successful Italian debut with *Romilda e Costanza* (1817) attracted the attention of many impresarios. Out of several offers, he accepted one for the Teatro Regio in Turin, and chose for his next *scrittura* a classical text of eighteenth-century Italian *opera seria* by the legendary Pietro Metastasio which was transformed for him into a contemporary *melodramma serio*.

4.2 *Semiramide [riconosciuta] [Semiramis (recognized)]*

Dramma per Musica in due Atti [music drama in two acts]
Text: Pietro Metastasio (1729), adapted by Conte Lodovico Piossasco Feys, with later additions by Gaetano Rossi (1820)
First performance: Turin, Teatro Regio, 3 February 1819

Plot
In Ancient Babylon, *c.*850 BC

Act 1. At the Assyrian court of King Nino several foreign princes have gathered in the hope of winning the favour of the young Princess Tamiri of Bactria. Among the first suitors are the Scythian Prince Ircano as well as the hesitant Egyptian Prince Mirteo, who grew up at the Bactrian court and already knows Tamiri. The third aspirant is the Indian Prince Scitalce. Tamiri is enthusiastic about this ardent and apparently warm-hearted prince.

The young King Nino is actually Semiramide, the widow of the late monarch, in disguise, who has assumed the throne in the place of her weak son. The moment she hears the voice of Scitalce, she is frightened. The voice is that of her earlier lover Idreno, whom she knew under this false name, and with whom she, an Egyptian princess, fled her homeland, only in the same night to be inexplicably struck down by him. Scitalce also recognizes Semiramide. Thunder and lightning suddenly herald ill fortune. Nino/Semiramide announces that Tamiri's decision will be postponed until the evening.

Sibari, who has likewise come to Babylon on the occasion of the marriage celebrations, was also earlier at the Egyptian court. He knows the history of Semiramide and Scitalce, and has slandered Scitalce to Semiramide. An old letter could betray him. Sibari, who has secretly adored Semiramide, has also recognized her through the disguise, and comes to speak with her. Scitalce appears. He believed himself betrayed by Semiramide, and thought that he had killed her. This unexpected encounter has confused him. Without giving themselves away, Semiramide and Scitalce sound each other out, and try to understand their feelings. Sibari also tries to find out how Tamiri feels, but he must first remove Scitalce because the latter knows of his earlier crime. Nino/Semiramide also makes the other princes jealous in order to prevent an attachment between Tamiri and her beloved Scitalce. Ircano rages with helpless anger and jealousy. Sibari explains to him that he intends to poison the drink which, after ancient custom, the one chosen by Tamiri will receive at the wedding. Nino/Semiramide sings a wedding song, an epithalamium, in preparation for the feast (canzonetta, 'Il piacer, la gioja scenda' [May pleasure and joy fill your hearts]).

Tamiri choses Scitalce as her groom. But he hesitates to accept the proffered wedding chalice when his glance falls on Semiramide. Ircano angrily demands that he should drink. Tamiri is deeply hurt and now offers Ircano her hand, but he also refuses the poisoned cup. All turn on Scitalce and demand his death. Nino/Semiramide intervenes decisively, and takes him as her personal prisoner.

Act 2. Tamiri feels sorry for the loving Mirteo, but her feelings are really for Scitalce alone. Ircano demands that Sibari should reveal the intrigue about the poisoned chalice. Sibari proposes instead that Ircano should abduct Tamiri. He should call the soldiers waiting on his ship to his aid. Nino/Semiramide explains to Tamiri that Scitalce should die, but Tamiri, no longer seeking recompense, does not think this necessary. Scitalce demands his sword back from Semiramide, hurting her unnecessarily. They part in extreme discord.

Ircano's attempted abduction is beaten back by Mirteo and his followers, and Ircano is taken prisoner. Mirteo thanks Sibari who had warned him in time. Sibari now incites Mirteo against Scitalce, apparently the murderer of his sister Semiramide. Mirteo is enraged and wants vengeance. Ircano, as a free if unarmed prince, rebels against Nino/Semiramide's order to depart. He challenges Scitalce to combat, and admits that Nino shows an inexplicable fondness for Scitalce. Scitalce nonetheless wants to fight, and Nino/Semiramide sadly allows that the two people she most loves want to kill each other. Scitalce is ready for combat.

Just before the duel is about to begin. Scitalce explains why he struck down Mirteo's sister. When Sibari's letter is read, it becomes clear who contrived all the intrigues. Sibari not only reveals his love for Semiramide, but also exposes Nino/Semiramide as a disguised woman.

Semiramide explains herself and reminds the people that she was always a good ruler even though she belongs to the weaker sex. She is reconciled with Scitalce and her brother Mirteo, sends the vengeful Ircano away, and forgives Sibari. Inspired by the manifestation of such nobility of spirit, the people acclaim their queen.

Metastasio's libretto *Semiramide* (1729, written for the church musician Leonardo Vinci) was set in the course of the eighteenth century at least 40 times, most notably by Vivaldi (1732), Hasse (1744), Gluck (1748), Graun (1754), Sacchini (1762) and Salieri (1784). Only at the end of the century did composers begin to favour a later version: Voltaire's drama *Sémiramis* (1748). Unlike Metastasio, in his version of this tragedy Voltaire did not depict the triumph of the Assyrian queen, but the last moments of her life. Rossini's composition (1823) was based on this version.

In 1819, the young Meyerbeer launched this, his second experiment with Italian opera, two years after the successful production of *Romilda e Costanza*, in the midst of his relentless travelling between the opera houses of Italy during 1818, he received a contract from the Royal Opera House in Turin to produce there an opera on the myth of Phaedra, a theme later changed for unknown reasons to that of Semiramide.

In the long letter diary Meyerbeer wrote to his brother Michael Beer in September 1818, the name of Rossini recurs constantly, especially in the light of the performances he attended. The third act of *Otello* particularly struck him: 'The third act of *Otello* so firmly established Rossini's reputation in Venice that even a thousand follies could not rob him of it. But this act is divinely beautiful, and what is so strange is that all the beauties are blatantly un-Rossinian: outstanding, declaimed, even passionate recitative, mysterious accompaniments, lots of local *couleur*, and the antique style of the romance in its highest perfection' (1 September 1818). Meyerbeer wished to approach this ideal without imitating Rossini, something he regretted and censured in Vaccai. All Meyerbeer's knowledge and discoveries were now bound up with a specific concern that would soon dominate all his Italian operas: the fate of the emigrant wanderer, returning from exile, often living disguised under a false identity. Themes of this kind were already an established and popular motif in the operas of the day, but in Meyerbeer's work the recurrence is remarkable:

- In *Romilda e Costanza* (1817) Romilda disguises herself as a man in order to follow her beloved Teobaldo and work secretly in his interests;
- In *Semiramide* (1819) the exiled queen has to pretend to be a man in order to seek justice and find her true love.
- In *Emma di Resburgo* (1819) Count Edemondo is falsely accused of parricide, and must live as an outlaw. On his return, he and his wife, both in assumed personas, are involved in life-threatening situations in their search for justice.
- In *Margherita d'Anjou* (1820) King Henry VI's widow is forced into exile by Richard, Duke of Gloucester and has to fight to win back her position of power; Isaura, disguised as a youth, seeks to regain the love of her estranged husband.
- In *L'esule di Granata* (1822) Almanzor, the ruler of Granada, calls back the banned former rulers of the Abercerages because he wishes to marry Azema of their tribe. Suleman returns in disguise to explore the scene and bring vengeance on his enemy.
- In *Il crociato in Egitto* (1824) the Crusader Armando lives under a false name and assumed religion in the midst of his former foes in Damietta where he has a secret love-child hidden in the harem. His fiancée Felicia comes to find him disguised as a man.

Meyerbeer did not promote anything novel here, but his repeated choice of this subject certainly related to something profoundly personal in his experience, in both racial and personal terms, and distilled a sense of loneliness and fruitful enterprise in his years of self-imposed exile from Prussia.

In Turin, as throughout Europe, the spirit of Restoration was in the air. The Congress of Vienna which finally sealed Napoleon's defeat, and led to the return of the old rulers to their thrones, had ended. Bringing one of Metastasio's works to the stage must be seen against this background. The old poet, who had worked at the Imperial Court in Vienna for many years, was almost a symbol of a bygone age, and any revival of his work would have been seen as a gesture suggesting that the French Revolution had never happened. Without doubt such a decision would have had a political dimension and a reactionary impact. In Turin the return to Metastasio went on unhindered, as it did in the following years. In 1824, for example, *Demetrio*, with music by Giovanni Simone Mayr, was produced. Metastasio's old libretto was adapted for this occasion by Count Lodovico Piossasco Feys who had done a similar service for Saverio Mercadante, with *Didone* (1823) and would again later with *Ezio* (1827). So although there is nothing to verify this, it is more than likely that the same Count Feys, and not Rossi as has always been presumed prepared *Semiramide* for Meyerbeer.

Feys arranged the libretto in the same way that Caterino Mazzolà had rewritten Metastasio's book *La clemenza di Tito* for Mozart (1791). During the time of Leonardo Vinci and Nicola Porpora, who set *Semiramide* in both 1724 and 1729, the opera contained some 30 arias with their inserted recitatives. But, by the time of

Meyerbeer and Rossini, duets had gained in importance as the appropriate medium for the musical confrontation of the principal characters, with the most important moments in the action marked by ensembles with chorus (particularly the introduction and first finale, the longest and most complex numbers of an opera). Metastasio's extremely long recitatives (*recitativi secchi*) had to be shortened and replaced with *recitativi accompagnati*, the old arias had to be thinned out and replaced with new ones more appropriate to the new style, and the right places found for the insertion of ensembles and choruses.

The distribution of the voice types is typical of the *opera seria* of the early nineteenth century, with a soprano/mezzo-soprano as prima donna (Semiramide), a mezzo-soprano or contralto as the primo uomo/musico (Prince Scitalce, her earlier lover), and a *tenore* or high tenor, sometimes a *barytenore* in the tertiary role (Prince Ircano, the suitor of Tamiri). The older tradition groups a set of three secondary characters around the central trinity: a basso (the Egyptian Prince Mirteo, the secret brother of Semiramide), the *seconda donna* (Princess Tamiri who returns the love of Scitalce), and the *secondo tenore* (Sibari, the confidant and lover of Semiramide). As in Metastasio's libretto, the action centres less around the interplay of the couples, and more around the central triangular relationship. The other figures (Tamiri, Mirteo) are more in the background, do not participate in any duets, and are provided with smaller arias that both contextually and musically are of less importance.

The title role was devised by Meyerbeer for the phenomenal singing abilities of the contralto Carolina Bassi Manna, a celebrated interpreter of Rossini. Indeed, the fine casting of other roles (like Claudio and Lodovico Bonoldi) allowed him greater stylistic freedom in the vocal writing. Bassi, who created one Rossini role (in *Bianca e Falliero* at La Scala later in 1819), was one of the most important singers in the wider dissemination of Rossini roles, specializing as she did in the trouser-roles (Tancredi, Sigismondo, Arsace). The nature of the surviving eighteenth-century conventions, which led to the institutionalization of the mezzo male lead in the early nineteenth century, gave rise to an unusual relationship between the leading (female) voices at the time.

On paper the voices could hardly be distinguished, but aspects of colour, timbre and range made all the difference. It is a matter of debate whether or not the Semiramide Carolina Bassi had a darker voice than that of the *musico*, Adelaide Dalmani Naldi. Like Bassi, she sang both soprano (Desdemona, Elena) and mezzo roles (Cenerentola, Isabella) in her repertoire. Meyerbeer, however, distributed the ranges of these two voices in their two duets, with Semiramide having the higher tessitura in the first, and Scitalce taking this on in the second.

The role of the tenor is also unusual in its avoidance of the high register. It was written for Claudio Bonoldi who created several roles for Rossini (*La pietra del paragone*, *Sigismondo*, *Armida*, *Bianca e Falliero*). Meyerbeer's part for him is vocally similar to that of the women, with many passages of dynamic coloratura and a sparing use of high notes. Contemporary reviews thought of him as a baritone.

The opera is characterized by a type of gigantism (critics spoke of a giant opera and its extreme length in performance, almost as if it had been a forerunner of the *grands opéras*). This had something to do with the material, treating, as it does, a grandiose antiquity full of queens and princes, vast palaces and statuesque postures.

Illustration 4.2a *Semiramide [riconosciuta]*: Alessandro Sanquirico's design for Act 1 (watercolour from Antonio Basoli, *Collezione di varie scene teatrali*, Bologna 1821)

The sets by Alessandro Sanquirico were sensational in design and overwhelmingly architectural in impression, projecting a striving for extremes of greatness, splendour and pomp which has further extension in the music. This is manifested in the sublime and overweening singing roles, in which the extensive vocal decoration serves as means of statuesque characterization, as well as in the largeness of the musical forms. The Act 1 finale is indeed of ambitious proportions, and reaches an excited stretta climax in a melodic sequence of cascading double semiquaver iterations in thirds and a rising staccato figure in octaves (dominant to mediant) derived from the development section of the D major overture (ex. 4.2 [a]). The duets and the arias also take on unusually extended form, reduced to only 12 in number in order to control the length of performance. In the duet for Semiramide and Ircano, and in Semiramide's grand five-part final scena, the focus is on form and lyricism more than on action; a pared simplicity and beautiful singing take precedence over dramatic exigency. The unison writings for the female voices achieves an idyllic character that becomes rhapsodic in the cabalettas.

There is also a carefully controlled play of voice and orchestra. In the first finale, the ensemble of surprise is characterized by a section of a cappella singing in which the voices of Semiramide, Scitalce and Ircano are joined in hurried descending melodic spirals, or in the second finale that begins with some 40 bars of Semiramide singing without accompaniment. On the other hand, there is a typical search for orchestral vividness, with a penchant for solo obbligato instruments (the horn, the clarinet, the harp), massive sonority (like the march at the opening of the opera, with piccolos, flutes, oboes, clarinets, bassoons, four horns, two trumpets, trombone, percussion, triangle, Turkish band and strings), or a controlled, exquisite orchestral palate, like the idyllic opening chorus and radiant *finaletto*, all of which helps to sustain the dominating mood of serene detachment (ex. 4.2 [b] and [c]).

Example 4.2 *Semiramide [riconosciuta]:* from a) the overture, b) the Act 1
        introduction and c) the Act 2 finale

Similarities with Rossini's later work are particularly evident in the introduction.
Gaetano Rossi consciously devised his opening (with the help of Isabella Colbran) on
the lines of the model established by Meyerbeer as early as this second of his Italian
operas. Both operas open with a grand court scene of pomp and circumstance, in which
the aspirant princes from various countries sing of their hopes. The proceedings are
then dramatically interrupted by a supernatural event, a thunderclap, portentously
fateful, that throws the scene into confusion. An innovative development is now the
entrée of the prima donna at the beginning of the opera without her usual entrance
aria. In both instances this will effectively be postponed until later in the act, when the
heroine in each case has her decisive and characteristic moment: in Meyerbeer it is
Semiramide's Canzonetta con variazioni, in Rossini it is 'Bel raggio lusinghier'—both
the most famous pieces in the respective operas. If there are echoes of Beethoven (in

the solemn introduction to the overture), Mozart (in the quartet of suitors) and Gluck (in the chorus of dismay after the thunder), then Meyerbeer paid homage to Rossini in this variation genre, already famously represented in *Armida* and *La Cenerentola*. Meyerbeer gives the form his own stamp in the melodic contour and colouring, the striking use of the supporting chorus, entering in varied syncopations during the verses as well as separating them, and the diverse and virtuoso treatment of the obbligato harp which leads an almost independent life of its own and characterizes an orchestral brilliance and flair.

At its Turin premiere on 3 February 1819 the opera found much favour and underlined Meyerbeer's unusual position in the contemporary Italian operatic scene, accepted critically as mediating between the Italian and German schools. *Semiramide* achieved a rather good degree ofsuccess. News of it even spread over the Alps and it was reported in the *Osterreichische Allgemeine Musikzeitung*. The Italian critics were full of praise for the music, with features of the Italian school paired with that of the Germans, and with the whole reflecting and infused with a philosophical peacefulness. The effects elicited by the arias of Semiramide and her duet with Ircano were so great that the audience was moved to enthusiasm. Meyerbeer himself seemed so pleased with the achievements of Carolina Bassi that he presented her with the manuscript, inscribed with a personal dedication.

Illustration 4.2b *Semiramide [riconosciuta]*: Carolina Bassi as Semiramide (contemporary print, 1818)

A year later the opera was staged in Bologna on the opening of the opera house after a two-year restructuring, This time, however, there was criticism this time about the choice of a work by a foreign composer. Meyerbeer used the opportunity to make some changes, adding an overture (that of *Romilda e Costanza* with a new introduction) and replacimg some pieces with new or reworked versions. The changes to the libretto were done this time by Gaetano Rossi. Only the printed libretto and a few fragments of individual numbers of this version survive. The interpreters of Semiramide, Ircano and Sibari were the same as in Turin. There was another production in the town of Senigallia (near Pesaro) where a small opera season used to be held: 18 performances were staged. Wider performance of *Semiramide* was curtailed because Bassi, who had obtained sole rights to the score, made little use of this privilege, intending to reserve this *cheval de bataille* for her foreign appearances in projected guest roles. (See Schuster 2003, 2: 71–4; Beghelli, Piana, Reinke and Schönleber, 2005.)

Thereafter the opera disappeared from history until revived at the Rossini Festival in Bad Wildbad in June–July 2005 (with Deborah Riedel as Semiramide, Fiona Janes as Scitalce, Philippo Adami as Arcano, Wojtek Gierlach as Mirteo, Olga Peretyatko as Tamiri, Leonardo Silva as Sibari, and Richard Bonynge conducting); and then at Martina Franca in August 2006 (with Clara Polito, Aldo Caputo, Eufemia Tufano, Federico Sacchi, Stefania Grasso, Roberto De Biasio, and Rani Calderón conducting). Both performances were recorded.

As in *Gli amori di Teolinda*, this opera is remarkable for showing just how pivotal Meyerbeer's work was at this stage, looking back to the previous century in the appropriation of Metatasio and the *opera seria* (Gluck and Mozart), looking forward in the exploration of form (in response to the Neapolitan Rossini), in the Romantic sensibility of the orchestral writing (conscious of Mayr's example), and in the sumptuous realization of the bel canto ethos, especially in the female duets (anticipating Bellini). The heritage of the past and the challenge of new expressiveness are thus in tension, a pull between the lyrical exploration of the old text with its essentially static action and a dynamic search for largeness and grandeur in extended forms and scenic conception.

4.3 *Emma di Resburgo [Emma of Roxburgh]*

Melodramma eroico in due atti [heroic melodrama in two acts]
Text: Gaetano Rossi, after Andrea Leone Tottola's *melodramma eroico-comico* libretto *Elena e Costantino* (Naples, 1814) for Giovanni Simone Mayr, based on Jean-Nicolas Bouilly's *opéra-comique* libretto *Héléna* (Paris, 1803) for Etienne-Nicolas Méhul
First performance: Teatro San Benedetto, Venice, 26 June 1819

Meyerbeer consequently had all the more reason for looking to his next opera for additional success: *Emma di Resburgo*, planned for the early season at the San Benedetto in Venice, with which the composer had already negotiated concerning *Romilda*. Rossi was once again the librettist. He held to his model in the chief features of the action, shifting the scene from Provence to Scotland. There was both chance and risk involved in the venture because *Emma* was to be preceded by the first performance of a new opera by Rossini, the pasticcio *Eduardo e Cristina* (Andrea Leone Tottola and Gherardo Bevilaqua-Aldobrandini after Giovanni Schmidt's libretto *Odoardo e Cristina* for Pavesi, Naples 1810). Later reports by German correspondents suggesting that Meyerbeer's success had put Rossini's opera in the shade, and had thereby caused the Italian to resent the German, are not substantiated. Nonetheless, *Emma* appears to have made a considerable impression, and it became Meyerbeer's first international success.

Plot
Early medieval Scotland.

Act 1. Count Edemondo of Lanark, falsely accused of the murder of his father, Roggero, has escaped the subsequent threat to his life by fleeing. His wife, Emma, followed him, but has been unable to track him down. Previously she abandoned her son at the castle of the friendly Olfredo who has taken the child into his care. The new lord of Lanark, Norcesto, is feverishly trying to capture the fugitive Edemondo, and, through his herald, summons the people to join in the search. In order to see her child, Emma, disguised as a bard, enters Olfredo's castle. At the same time, Edemondo, pretending to be a shepherd, also appears in the castle. The couple recognize each other, and are also identified by Olfredo. He, convinced of Edemondo's innocence, does not betray them. Both take part incognito in a banquet arranged by Olfredo when Norcesto appears with his followers. The latter remarks on the likeness of the child to the fugitive Edemondo, and by questioning establishes the origins of the child. When Norcesto wants to drag him away, Emma throws herself between them, identifying herself as the mother of the child and Edemondo's wife. Only Olfredo's efforts prevent Edemondo from also giving his identity away.

Act 2. Norcesto redoubles his efforts to find the fugitive, now believed to be in the vicinity, but without success. When, however, the knights and the people begin preparations to kill the child in vengeance, Edemondo comes forward. Even though he proclaims his innocence, he is condemned to die on the grave of his father. Emma, in despair, denounces Norcesto as the real murderer, now trying to hide his guilt through the death of an innocent. Just moments before Edemondo's execution, however, Norcesto breaks his silence. Not he, but his late father Duncalmo, whose reputation he has sought to protect, committed the deed. Emma rejoices in being reunited with her husband.

TERZETTO

Ah! tu vivi

Nell'Opera Emma di Resburgo

DEL SIG.ʳ MAESTRO

Giacomo Meyerbeer

Eseguito in Venezia dalle Sig.ᵉ Morandi, Cortesi e dal Sig.ʳ Luc.° Bianchi.

Dedicato dall'Autore

All' Ill.ᵐᵒ Sig.ʳ Marchese.

COSTANTINO MARUZZI

MILANO

Proprietà dell'Editore
N.º 639.

Deposto alla C.R. Bibl.ᵃ
Prezzo Lir 3. Ital.°

Pʳᵉˢˢᵒ GIO. RICORDI Negoziante di Musica, Editore del C.R. Conservatorio, e Proprietario della Musica del R. Teatro alla Scala, che tiene Stamperia, Archivio di Spartiti e Magazzino di Cembali di Vienna e Monaco, nella Contᵃ di Sᵃ Margherita N.º 1118

Illustration 4.3   *Emma di Resburgo:* the printed title-page of the Act 1 trio (Milan: Ricordi, 1819)

More than with any of the proceeding operas, *Emma* opened discussion of
Meyerbeer's personal style. However much contemporary judgement linked
this with Rossini, there could be no doubt about an unmistakable tone which
now distinguished the composer of *Emma* from the usual run of Rossinian
imitators. This work demonstrated a new musico-dramatic idiom. To speak of
a mere mixing of Italian and German elements would be to deny something
specific about the style. The matter was more closely described by the critic
of the *Gazetta privilegiata di Venezia* (*BT*, 1:667) who, in his account of the
premiere, linked his praise for the composer's technical mastery and richness of
invention with a cautious reproach of the elaboration of the writing, and pointed
out that art should accompany nature and not be her master ('l'arte dev'essere la
scorta e non la tiranna della natura'). This discussion in fact anticipates a central
tenet of later Meyerbeer criticism: the striking characteristic of the composer's
musical–dramatic conception, already decisively evident in his early operas.
This is particularly so in relation to the treatment of the Romantic subject. The
new musical colours, apparent even before similar developments in Rossini's *La
donna del lago* (1819), are not used in the depiction of nature, but in the realistic
situational transposition of the drama.

The tyrant Norcesto announces in the Introduction that he wishes to spread terror
among his enemies. He is driven to this by his fear of noble Edemondo and his
wife Emma whom he exiled from the land. He indicts Edemondo of parricide, an
accusation reinforced by the herald who announces that if Edemondo should ever
return, he will pay with his life. The chorus react with horror (fortissimo, on an
emotive diminished chord): 'Edemondo, such a name, o traitor!' (ex. 4.3a).

Example 4.3a   *Emma di Resburgo*: Edemondo's motif in the introduction to Act 1

The child of the proscribed in the meantime is growing up, unbeknown to the tyrant, in the house of the loyal Olfredo. Emma returns, disguised as a bard, and sings of her sorrow to her harp, while a chorus of peasants try to encourage rather than pity her. Emma's entrance cavatina ('Sulla rupe triste, e sola') (On the cliff, sad and alone), borrowed from *Semiramide*, conjures up a Romantic mood through the Ossianic cypher of the harp-accompanied song with effects *da lantano* as part of the scenic conception.

Edemondo, refusing to live in exile any longer, enters in a big Scena e Cavatina. The orchestral introduction is one of the most elaborately crafted pieces in the score, gathering together, as it does, Edemondo's conflicting emotions: his abandonment (the deep strings in unison), his hopelessness (the theme of the cavatina 'Ah ciel pietoso' [O merciful heaven]), and his determination (dramatic instrumental recitative—sharply pointed bass figures and tremolo chords in the high strings). The picturesque situation is translated into a virtuoso play on the pastoral topoi of echo effects whereby external events become recognizable correlatives of a mental process.

Emma's Scena e Rondo ('Ecco di morte l'ora...Il dì cadra') (This is the hour of death...The day will end), with its graveyard imagery of Roggero's tomb and its inscription accusing his murderers, provides visual reminiscence of Mozart's *Don Giovanni* (1787), and does not lose itself in mood-painting, but rather transposes the atmospheric into strict but effective musical form and language.

Döhring points out (1991, 4:115) that the historical ambivalence of *Emma* between reminiscence of Mozart and the older opera, as well as direct Rossinianism and occasional borrowing from French opera, is not the result of artistic indecision but more the consequence of a pluralistic aesthetic, even showing the characteristics of a decisive choice of style, which uses the available musical–dramatic vocabulary to bring about a new mode of expression. This is particularly forward-looking in the big tableaux: the Chorus of Judges, rightly admired in its day, through-composed as an integral part of the action, and the graduated Act 1 finale, dramatic in its contrasts, is as sublime as it is effective. At the beginning of Act 2 Emma tries to urge the nobles to rescue her son. But they refuse her pleas in a C minor passage reminiscent of Gluck, and call out Edemondo's name three times, as at the beginning of the opera, again fortissimo on a diminished chord supported by the whole orchestra (ex. 4.3b).

Example 4.3b   *Emma di Resburgo*: Edemondo's motif in the introduction to Act 2

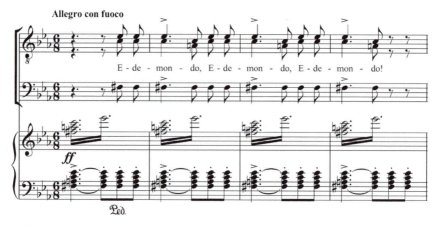

The restrained recurring use of such strong harmonic colour in such a dramaturgically important passage indicates a carefully considered structural ability. Edemondo is forced out of his disguise by the cries of the chorus, identifying himself: 'Ecco Edemondo'. His self-justification is not accepted, in spite of his urgent protestations of his innocence (in leaps of octaves and tenths). The Judges sentence him to death, and Emma pleads in vain for her spouse. She reveals the truth, accusing Norcesto of the death of her father-in-law, but the tyrant remains obdurate. Emma then resolves to join her husband in death. The hard-hearted despot is so moved by this moral greatness, that he capitulates and pardons Edemondo, admitting that it was his father who had the old Count Edemondo removed. All hail the happy couple, now reunited.

This *lieto fine*, or happy ending, belongs to the eighteenth century. The libretto is still infused with old Enlightenment ideals, embodied in the clemency shown in the end by the tyrant. Meyerbeer had learned to understand the spirit of enlightened Utopia so characteristic of the past epoch, carried over into the new times, and lending to art the bright illusion of a better world. He had the opportunity to learn how to formulate Utopia musically. Always in his later works, whenever real hope shines (even if it is invariably doomed) and those threatened by death believe themselves saved on an island of optimism, when that recurrent illusion or Utopia appears, the exalting swelling melodies he learnt to write in Italy make their appearance.

The triumphal premiere of *Emma di Resburgo* (with Rosa Morandi as Emma, Carolina Cortesi as Edemondo, and Eliodoro Bianchi as Norcesto) initiated a run of 74 performances and firmly established Meyerbeer's position in Italy. Many houses both inside and outside Italy took on the new opera, and for at least a decade it was part of the European repertory. Among the outstanding Italian productions were those at the Teatro della Pergola in Florence in 1820 (with Ester Mombelli, Cortesi and Carlo Cardini) and at the Teatro Nuovo in Padua (with Carolina Passerini, Fanny Eckerlin and Bianchi). Performances in Germany began in 1820: in Italian in Dresden directed by Carl Maria von Weber; in the German translation of Joseph von Seyfried (as *Emma von Leicester oder Die Stimme des Gewissens*) first at the Theater an der Wien (with Mme Pfeiffer, Julie Schwarz and Franz Jäger); in the translation of Christoph May (as *Emma von Roxburgh*) in Berlin (Karoline Seidler, Josephine Schulze and Heinrich Stürmer). For the Berlin performance Meyerbeer revised *Emma* and added some new numbers, including a new conclusion. The opera reached Warsaw in 1821 in a Polish translation by Ksawery Godebski. (See Loewenberg 1970: 664; Döhring 1991, 4:115; Schuster 2003, 2:133–60.)

4.4 *Margherita d'Anjou [Margaret of Anjou]*

Melodramma semiserio in due atti [semi-serious melodrama in two acts]
Text: Felice Romani, after the *mélodrame Marguerite d'Anjou* (1810) by René-Charles-Guilbert de Pixérécourt in the translation by Francesco Gandini
First performance: Teatro alla Scala, Milan, 14 November 1820

After the triumph of *Emma di Resburgo* (1819), Meyerbeer undertook his next work for the Carnival season of 1819–20 at La Scala, a step that involved a change of librettist. In place of the prolific Gaetano Rossi, the no less respected Felice Romani now appeared on the scene. The subject first proposed was *Francesca da Rimini*, a piece Meyerbeer regarded very highly, according to his letter to Franz Sales Kandler of 19 November 1819 (*BT*, 1:391). However, objections from the censor derailed the project (Romani was to realize it later for Feliciano Strepponi, Vicenza 1823). The search for new material required time, and since Meyerbeer's wish for postponement of the premiere necessitated a later date within the season which could not be granted, he withdrew from the contract. How a new subject was found and led to a new *scrittura* for La Scala in the autumn season of 1820 has not yet been established.

Plot
England during the War of the Roses, after the Battle of Tewkesbury (1471)

Act 1. King Henry VI's widow Margaret had fled to France together with her young son in the face of pursuit by the Duke of Gloucester, leader of the Lancastrian party. Once she has succeeded in raising support at the French court for her attempt on the throne, she returns to England at the head of a French army. The commander, the Duke of Lavarenne, has fallen in love with Margaret, and on her account has left his bride Isaura behind in France. The latter has nonetheless followed him secretly and, disguised as a youth called Eugenio, has joined the army as assistant to the doctor Michele Gamautte, in the hope of winning back her beloved. Michele becomes the only confidant to her secret. After initial successes, Margaret's troops have confronted difficulties: the Battle of Wakefield has been lost, and after fleeing to Scotland, Margaret is taken prisoner by the Highlanders who are fighting on Gloucester's side. Their leader Carlo, once banned by Margaret and since then her enemy, after meeting her personally, has renewed his support for the queen and now rescues her.

Act 2. Carlo has hidden Margaret with her son Edward in a small remote cottage. She is tracked down there by Gloucester who wants to kill her. Rescue arrives at the last moment from Lavarenne who disarms Gloucester. The Lancastrian troops are defeated in a decisive battle in which Isaura has distinguished herself in acts of bravery, saving the lives of Margaret and Lavarenne. Before this she had already revealed her true identity to the queen, who for her part renounces Lavarenne. He, after much irresolution, has slowly become aware of his enduring love for Isaura. Overjoyed, he throws himself at her feet, aware that he owes his life to her. Isaura's hopes are now realized, just as the wily Michele had predicted.

Between both premieres was a period of some 14 months which Mayerbeer used by Meyerbeer to imbue his score with new things without disturbing the public by speculation over novelties. These innovations were the manifestation of a self-understanding about his own artistic intentions, which increasingly were not being directed at an imitation of the Rossini style, but at the renewal of Italian *opera seria* generally. With *Margherita d'Anjou* Meyerbeer chose a historic topic for the first time, although it is not the actual subject of the action, as in his later works, but really the occasion for a private drama. It is nonetheless surprising to see just to what extent history influences the *couleur* of the work, and lends shape to the dramatic events. This national subject determines the mass military scenes as well as the characters. This is especially true of the comic figure of the doctor, Michele Gamautte, to whom the opera particularly owes its generic designation of *melodramma semiserio*; he appears here not so much as a buffo type, but rather as the personification of certain national characteristics. This libretto presented the composer with new challenges. Even more than in *Emma*, there is a tendency to formal integration, particularly in the big scenes. The unusually extended introduction, for example, not only develops the ambiance of the action, but also the central conflict, all within a single closed musical scene. This not only unfolds all the personal conflicts of Act 1, but also illuminates the social circumstances of the protagonists by detailed presentation of the historical and local colour—as already given in thematic compression by the rondo overture with its alternating military refrain and lyrical episodes.

Illustration 4.4   *Margherita d'Anjou:* the printed title-page of the overture (Milan: Ricordi, 1820)

Moreover in *Margherita*, and the two following operas, a big scenic complex was already being shaped that would later become known as *tableaux* in the French *grands opéras*. The Introduzione to *Margherita* begins typically of so many other first scenes in 6/8 time, and develops a genre picture, the stage filled with soldier and peasant types, gambling and hawking. But this introduction is characterized by a musical variety—by building up dramatic intensification in choral entries and by the strengthened deployment of trombones and the serpent—a deep, strong wind instrument made of wood covered in leather with a profound, but attenuated, tone. Usually the trombones would have been silent at the beginning of an opera, being reserved for dramatic high-points, but Meyerbeer tried their effect as a new interesting colour, just as his colleague Weber was doing in Hosterwitz with the orchestration of *Der Freischütz*. For both composers, the standard size of lined musical manuscript paper would no longer suffice, and they would have to append a special addendum, *trombone, tympani, piatti al fine*, at the end of each number. So the instrumental palette was slowly being expanded, the general use of such instruments, first tried after 1789 by the French composers (like Méhul and Le Sueur), was reaching for a new standard culminating in an explosive disposition of the wind instruments in 1830 with Berlioz's *Symphonie fantastique*. Several genre choruses depict the activity in the French camp, while Margherita's entrance aria is both contrasted and integrated by the *a parte* commentary of Carlo, who is reconnoitring the camp in disguise. The stretta (in fact, the cabaletta of Margherita's aria) initiates an additional intensification at the moment of resolution through the approach of the stage *banda* which announces the arrival of the victorious Lavarenne and prepares the way for his later entry. The first finale unfolds in a comparable audio-spatial way, with the sounds of the band behind the scene heralding the dramatic turn of events with the advance of Gloucester's troops.

The many Romantic and picturesque situations are not merely occasions for the application of local colour, but, as already the casein Romani's libretto, are consciously used as elements in a process employing idyllic and pastoral topoi, sometimes with ironic application. This is the underlying situation of the extended matinal rustic chorus in Act 2 ('Che bell'alba') (What a lovely morning) when the Highlanders stress their closeness to nature in negative comparison with the ignorant city dwellers ('sciocco cittadino') (ex. 4.4a).

Example 4.4a   *Margherita d'Anjou*: the Pastoral Chorus (Act 2)

The simple cottage where Margherita finds refuge as a disguised peasant is stylized into a Virgilian *locus amoenus* (place of safety and delight) surrounded by danger, a situation underlined by the composer: the decorative writing of Margherita's big scene and aria with obbligato violin ('Dolce albergo di pace') (Sweet refuge of peace) lends it a delicate otherworldliness, the atmosphere established by the extended instrumental prelude.

The comic character of Michele is of special importance to the novel nature of this opera. He functions as a comic counterpoint to the action, as illustrated early in Act 1 when he smugly comments on Isaura's pathetic love complaints in sparkling parlando (in the duet 'Ah! Tu non sai com'io l'adoro' [Ah, you do not know how I love him]). Michele's part is the first instance in which Meyerbeer uses the special tone and style of French comedy which would become an important element in his later operas. Through him the whole musical fabric of the opera takes on an unusual elegance and suppleness, as well as a latent irony and preciousness of expression that gives this work a special place among the operas of its day. At the same time, Meyerbeer created his own models which would be used again in his French operas in comparable dramatic situations. Thus in this duet Isaura, sorely tried, sings of her love for her faithless husband in great, ranging melodic arcs, typical of Meyerbeer's bel canto of yearning and hope, while Michele Gamautte proffers his comfort in muttered bass buffo ruminations, short semi- and demisemiquavers declamation, almost clumsy and stumbling. It is the forerunner of a similar dramatic situation for Valentine and Marcel in Act 3 of *Les Huguenots*.

This tendency to develop models becomes even clearer when the similarities are drawn between the bass trio 'Pensa e guarda amico' (Think and take care my friend) in Act 2 of *Margherita* (ex. 4.4b [a]) and the hymn in the famous Blessing of the Daggers from Act 4 of *Les Huguenots* (ex. 4.4b [b]). The first is, of course, meant to be a piece of musical comedy, and the later is in deadly earnest, in more ways than one. The Italian melody is rather less fluid, and the counterpointing of the theme more a virtuoso embellishment than a dramatic commentary. In the French scene, sharper punctuation changes the melodic structure into something more declamatory and syllabic, making it loftier and serious. The harmonic feel is altered by a regular stressing of the tonic E and its part in the syncopated and echoing emphases of the commenting accompaniment. The triplets in the final phrases of the hymn also provide an innate stress and a gathering of energy for further propulsion. It is interesting to see just how Meyerbeer's creative instincts were developed and refined over the 15 years that separate these two numbers (Zimmermann 1991: 116–17). Building on the foundations of his Italian repertoire, a piece written along the lines of certain traditional expectations is transformed by the simplest but most telling means into a piece of cogent musico-dramatic theatre.

Example 4.4b   *Margherita d'Anjou*: from a) the trio (Act 2) and b) *Les Huguenots*:
                 the Blessing of the Daggers (Act 4)

Whether or not Meyerbeer understood his work at this time as something preparatory to further development is not known, but he did work with some plan of his future career in mind, always seeking out the musical environment right for his stage of development, seeking out the effective elements, analysing their uses and experimenting with their capacities. The Italian years were very much more than a period of Rossinian imitation, but rather a deep appropriation and personal adaptation of a whole style, culture and ethos.

Margherita d'Anjou was 'given with great success, and on the first three evenings, the maestro...was called on stage after each act' (*Leipziger Allgemeine musikalische Zeitung*, 3 January 1821). A brilliant ensemble of singers moved amidst the striking stage designs of Alessandro Sanquirico: Carolina Pellegrini as Margherita, Rosa Mariani as Isaura, Nicola Tacchinardi as Lavarenne, Nicolas-Prosper Levasseur as Carlo and Nicola Bassi as Michele. In the orchestra, directed by Vincenzo Lavigna, Alessandro Rolla was the concert-master, who had a special role to play in this opera with the lengthy violin solo. Even more significant was Meyerbeer's first meeting with the important singer Levasseur who, later in France, would become his most outstanding bass soloist.

Among the most notable productions in Italy were those in Bologna in 1824 (with Fanny Corri-Paltoni as Isaura), and the revival at La Scala in 1826 (with Luigia Boccabadati as Margherita, Isabella Fabbrica as Isaura, Giovanni Battista Verger as Lavarenne and Vincenzo Felice Santini as Carlo). The opera found almost greater favour outside Italy: in Munich 1822; Dresden 1824 (with Friderike Funk, Costanza Tibaldi, Giuseppe Fink, Alfonso Zezi, Gioacchino Benincasa, with Carl Maria von Weber conducting); Barcelona 1825; London 1828; Königstätisches Theater, Berlin, 1831 (with Betty Spitzeder-Vio, Amalie Haehnel, Eduard Holzmiller, Wilhelm Fischer and Josef Spitzeder); Prague 1831 (with Katharina Podhorsky, Marie Emmering, Joseph Derska, Karel Strakaty and Franz Feistmantel); Madrid 1836; Lisbon 1837.

The work had a special reception in France. Soon after the production of *Il crociato in Egitto* (1824) at the Théatre Italien in Paris in 1825, the Théatre de l'Odéon presented the successful *Margherita* as an opera with dialogue. During the 1820s the repertoire of this theatre consisted almost entirely of *opéra comique* adaptations of Italian and German operas. The free French adaptation of *Margherita* in three acts was by Thomas-Marie-François Sauvage, the music was directed by the house conductor Pierre Crémont, and the scenery was painted by Pierre-Luc-Charles Cicéri (with Mlle Lemoule, Mme Montano and Lecomte). The French *Marguerite d'Anjou* was received with enthusiasm, and a series of productions followed: in Brussels 1826 (with Laure Cinti-Damoreau as Isaura), Amsterdam 1835, and The Hague 1839. (See Loewenberg 1970: 669; Döhring 1991, 4:117; Schuster 2003, 2:207–31.)

The first revival in modern times was the concert performance by Opera Rara at the London Festival Hall on 2 November 2003 (with Annick Massis as Margherita, Bruce Ford as Lavarenne, Daniella Barcelona/Patricia Bardon as Isaura, Alaister Miles as Carlo Belmonte, Fabio Previati as Michele Gamautte, Pauls Putnins as Riccardo, Colin Lee as Bellapunta, Roland Wood as Orner, with David Parry conducting). This version had been recorded prior to the performance. The opera was then staged at the Leipzig Oper (27 May–3 July 2005) (with Eun Yee You as Margherita, Robert Chafin as Lavarenne, Marina Prudenskaja as Isaura, Felipe Bou as Riccardo, Tuomas Pursio as Carlo Belmonte and Herman Wallén as Michele Gamautte, with Frank Beermann conducting).

4.5 *L'esule di Granata [The Siege of Granada]*

Melodramma serio in due Atti [serious melodrama in two acts]
Text: Felice Romani, after Gaetano Rossi
First performance: La Scala Milan, 12 March 1822

A few weeks after the first performance of *Margherita d'Anjou* (1820), Meyerbeer signed a contract for a new opera for the Carnival season at the Teatro Argentina in Rome: *L'Almanzore* to a libretto by Gaetano Rossi, with Carolina Bassi Manna proposed for the leading role. When Meyerbeer began composing is unknown, and why he never finished it has never been explained. The triumph of *Margherita d'Anjou* resulted in a second invitation to the composer to provide another opera for La Scala Milan. Likewise, it is not clear whether the libretto by Felice Romani, *L'esule di Granata*, which he took up a year later, entailed a reworking of the lost Roman material. The recurrence of the hero's name in the new work makes some connection between them very likely.

Plot
Granada, Moorish Spain, *c*.1490.

Prehistory. In Granada the two powerful tribes, the Abencerages and the Zegris, are in conflict since Boabil, the previous ruler of the Zegris, had banned the Abencerages. The new ruler Almanzor recalls the exiles because he would like to win for himself the daughter of the Abencerage prince Suleman. This is a crime in the eyes of the rest of his clan, who now conspire to dethrone him.

    Act 1. Scene 1. A riverbank near the gardens of the Alhambra, close to a mosque. Ali and other adherents of the Zegris who deplore Almanzor's policies of tolerance, gather secretly. Led by Alamar, they enter into a conspiracy against Almanzor. They pull back as a group of Abencerages women, first inside then outside the mosque, and pray for heaven's protection on Almanzor in his fight against the Spanish. Omar, the leader of the Abencerages, appears at the head of the troops and announces Almanzor's victory. When all have departed, Suleman comes down from the mountains and greets his homeland. He hears a group of girls singing the praises of Almanzor's bride, and is horrified to learn from Fatima, Azema's maid of honour, that the bride is none other than his daughter. Without revealing his identity, Suleman tells Azema that her mother and brother were killed by the Zegris when she was a child, and upbraids her for agreeing to marry one of this hated tribe. After Azema has gone, Suleman asks Fatima to help him see his daughter again.

    Scene 2. In the throne-room of the Alhambra a throng of people await Almanzor's imminent return. He appears with his courtiers, who carry in the booty of war, and declares that it is more important to have peace than the palm of victory. Azema crowns him, and the two prepare for their marriage.

    Scene 3. In the Court of Lions in the Alhambra Suleman, looking for Fatima, meets Azema. He weeps, revealing himself to be her father. Their mutual joy ends when he forbids her to marry a Zegris, swearing otherwise to kill Almanzor. Almanzor enters at this moment and is surprised to find a stranger in the palace. Azema tells him that

Almanzor is a relation of her mother. Azema is torn between her love for Almanzor and the demands of her father. Omar appears and announces that the time has come for the marriage ceremony.

Scene 4. A crowd has gathered for the wedding. Almanzor enters with Azema and wishes everyone a happy feast. The bride trembles when Almanzor leads her to the altar and asks her to be his bride. Azema, who has seen Suleman with a dagger, says no, to general consternation. As she will reveal nothing, all present believe her to have been unfaithful to Almanzor, who banishes her from his sight. All, apart from Suleman and Alamar, bewail the unexpected twist of events.

Act 2. Scene 1. A riverbank near the Alhambra. Maidens and warriors of the Abencerages bemoan the events, until interrupted by Omar who informs them that the wedding will take place after all. Omar tells them that Azema, distressed at news of her family brought her by an exile, had lost her composure. Now she has been comforted by the king. Alamar, who has heard the news, calls for bloodshed, but Ali tells him that among the Zegris there is no one prepared to kill the king. Alamar says that he has noticed an old man uttering threats against Almanzor and Azema, and has him brought for questioning. Suleman appears and says that he had intended to kill Almanzor. He and Alamar agree that the deed will be done at nightfall. Ali remains behind, pulled between his desire to protect the king and fears for his own well-being.

Scene 2. In an enclosure in the gardens of the Alhambra Azema bids goodnight to her handmaidens. Alone, she gives way to disturbing thoughts about her angered father. Fatima appears and tells her mistress that one of the Zegris wishes to speak to her. Ali enters and tells her of the plot to murder Almanzor. Warriors of the Abencerage are summoned, and Azema declares that she will be the first to fall prey to their swords. When she tries to leave, Almanzor comes in and learns from Ali about the attempt on his life. The king notices how uneasy Azema becomes when Ali describes the would-be assassin, and understands that this is her father.

Scene 3. In the throne-room Alamar and Suleman go over their plans for the murder of Almanzor, and then leave. Without disclosing his identity, Almanzor tells Suleman that Azema has revealed his secret, but that the king still offers Suleman his friendship. Suleman, who has suspected who Almanzor really is, poses to him a hypothetical situation: were I Suleman, I would not ask for the land of my fathers, but only for the return of my daughter. Disconcerted, Almanzor replies with an equally hypothetical answer: were I Almanzor, I would rather my throne be taken, as long as I were left my real treasure, the beloved Azema. As the tension between the two rises, Suleman tries to stab Almanzor, but fails in the attempt. He is led to prison, and Almanzor swears to punish him.

Scene 4. In the Court of Lions Almanzor regrets the harsh punishment he has imposed on Suleman. Omar appears with the news that the great court has signed the death warrant. Azema gives Almanzor the choice either to pardon her father or to let her die with him. Almanzor shows clemency to Suleman and the other conspirators, and allows the former monarch to leave with his daughter. Moved by Almanzor's noble magnanimity, Suleman embraces him as his son-in-law. All praise the power of love.

The sources are silent about the circumstances surrounding Meyerbeer's second *scrittura* for La Scala Milan (a stage esteemed by the composer as the first in Italy) and the genesis of this work. A letter from Michael Beer (13 August 1821) (*BT*, 1:433–5) reveals that the composer was still looking for a suitable subject. A letter of 29 December from Romani to Giuseppe Maria Franchetti, the government official responsible for theatrical spectacles in Milan, indicated that Meyerbeer had rejected an earlier subject, and that Romani was now pressed for time in completing *L'esule*. He also comments on the innumerable changes requested by Meyerbeer, revealing the composer as concerned and involved as ever in the genesis of the new work. The libretto was submitted for approval in various stages, and on 17 January appears to have been completed, since Romani asks for his payment. Meyerbeer probably began composing in December 1821 while work on the libretto was still in progress. The score must have been prepared with some expedition, because on 6 March 1822 he wrote to Franchetti detailing a schedule of rehearsals (7–11 March). The premiere on 12 March brought him nothing more the a *succès d'estime*—and this in spite of the spectacular stage designs of Alessandro Sanquirico (featuring the Court of Lions at the Alhambra in both act finales) and a brilliant company of singers (Benedetta Rosmunda Pisaroni, Adelaide Tosi, Berardo Winter and Luigi Lablache). The sublime musical–dramatic conception of the big scene (the introductory tableau), and indeed the level of composition in general, was acknowledged by the specialists, but seems to have been held at a distance by the public. Meyerbeer himself gave up any ideas of a future stage career for this opera, and used the score as a source of ideas for his next, and indeed several other of his later works. The work was produced only once after its Milan premiere, in Florence in 1826.

While Meyerbeer had embraced the innovations of Rossini, he increasingly remoulded Italian conventions to accommodate his own burgeoning musical ideas. The most significant to these was scale. This is clearly in evidence in the complex, multi-movement introduction which makes up the first scene of this opera. From the moment the curtain rises, it is clear that the composer was working on a larger canvas, employing all the effects at his disposal—choruses, stage bands, scenic devices and brilliant vocalism. The conspiracy hatched in the twilight of dawn (C minor – E flat major – C minor), the *preghiera* accompanied by a harp behind the scenes (which became the Children's Chorus in the Coronation Scene of *Le Prophète*) (F major – B flat major – F major), the fusion of both opposing parties with the gradually returning victorious troops and the stage band (C major – G major – D minor – G major – C major), presents a huge formal concept in terms of structure, sound (with highly organized key system), various timbres (male and then female voices) and orchestral hues (prominent solos for harp, horns and flutes, military band), and a dramaturgy of darkness and light, softness and loudness, in a consistently varying spatial dynamic (with various off-stage effects of recession and approach, underscored by the *banda*).

Illustration 4.5a *L'esule di Granata*: Luigi Lablache, the creator of Sulemano
(lithograph by F. Salabert)

The other piece to be especially admired was the Gran Duetto from Act 2,
in its four-part Rossinian structure (tempo d'attacco, cantabile, tempo di mezzo,
cabaletta). The expansive shape derives its interest from the formal representation
of hidden emotional states, since each character pretends not to know who the other
is for most of the duet. Both characters repeat similar phrases, but with different
implications and, in the cantabile, pose possible situations to each other which
reveal the truth of their real desires and intentions. Each punctuates their statements
with a little flurried declamatory phrase underlying the hypothetical nature of
the proposal. The cabaletta, after the assassination attempt during the tempo di
mezzo, is reflective, the F major posturing of the main staccato theme giving way
enharmonically to a more expressive legato aside in D flat major that reveals the
true emotional distress beneath the defiant surface. A duo of confrontation thus
takes the place of the usual love duet which is missing entirely. The only mutual
expressions of love take place as part of a trio, and in the presence of a third party
hostile to the love. The writing is lyrical but consistently eschews the sensuous.

Meyerbeer's sensitive instrumental exploration continues in this score. The
character of Azema comes to be associated with the cello (as used effectively in
Lavarenne's Act 1 solo in *Margherita d'Anjou*). The cabaletta of the Act 1 duet
with her father is introduced by a highly unusual concertante figure for the cello
(ex. 4.5 [a]), while her solo in Act 2 uses two cellos as obbligato, first in a long
atmospheric introduction in which the cellos play in unison, in thirds and sixths,

Illustration 4.5b *L'esule di Granata*: the printed version of the Act 2 duet (Milan: Ricordi, 1822)

in dialogue exchange (ex. 4.5 [b]), in commentary during the recitative ('Eccomi sola') (Here I am, alone), in unison with alternating woodwind figures during the cavatina ('Vieni nel sonno, amor') (Come while I sleep, love), and then, resuming the mood of the introduction, in a duet for the two instruments playing soli, with no orchestral accompaniment. What underlines this adventurous usage is the formal experimentation it initiates: a lyrical andante interpolation ('Se lo diffende amore') (If love is protecting him) after the cabaletta ('Si, miei fidi') (Yes, my loyal ones), and serving as an interlude before a second cabaletta ('Ma seguite, io vo primierà') (Follow me, I will go first), really a stretta to the cabaletta. Something similar happens in Almanzor's scena finale, where the introductory recitative leads into a full-scale aria in ternary form ('Oh! come rapida') (Oh, how swiftly). The tempo di mezzo follows, providing the denouement when Almanzor pardons Sulemano, the clemency flowering in another cantabile ('Cedi alla sorte') (Surrender to fate) before the advent of the cabaletta in rondo form ('Più bella vittoria') (A nobler victory). This experimentation with generic expectation and expansion would become a feature of the French operas.

Example 4.5 *L'esule di Granata*: from a) the Act 1 duet, b) Azema's Act 2 scena, c) the Introduzione

Example 4.5 *L'esule di Granata* continued

c.   **Allegro alla breve**

In all, this score represents a remarkable achievement, all the more so for its apparent lack of success. There is a melodic austerity, a grandiose but restrained formality, quite different from the serene limpidity of *Margherita d'Anjou*. A tendency to chromaticism and enharmonic modulation regularly disrupts diatonic openness (the introduction and Gran Duetto are typical), and sometimes an almost alienating curtailment of the satisfying expectation of cadential closure (as in the final bars of Azema's scena). An apprehension of grand gestures and forms instils a monumental quality, at the same time adding a forward-looking perspective. There are pre-echoes of the Risorgimento in the introduction ('Si, vendetta pera cada') (Yes, revenge, let him perish, let him die) and 'Alza, Granata, il cantico della tua gioia intorno' (O Granada, raise the hymn of your joy everywhere) (ex. 4.5 [c]), while the father–daughter duet suggests nothing less than other later such family encounters, like the Act 1 meeting between Verdi's Rigoletto and Gilda ('Dei or favella sventurata non trovai / Vive si lo fortunato, ma sventura orror la prema').

The first ever revival has been the Opera Rara recording of 2005 (with Manuela Custer as Almanzor, Laura Claycomb as Azema, Mirco Palazzi as Sulemano, Paul Austin Kelly as Alamar, Brindley Sherratt as Ali, Ashley Catling as Omar, and Giuliano Carella conducting. (See Schuster 2003, 2:251–5; Loomis 2005: 8–36.)

4.6 *Il crociato in Egitto [The Crusader in Egypt]*

Melodramma eroico in due atti [heroic melodrama in two acts]
Text: Gaetano Rossi, after Jean-Antoine-Marie Monperlier's *mélodrame Le Chevaliers de Malte* (1813).
First performed: Teatro La Fenice, Venice, 7 March 1824

During the winter of 1822–23 which Meyerbeer spent in Venice, plans were laid for a new opera to be written for the next Carnival season at La Fenice, with Rossi again as librettist. The composer proposed that the theme of the new opera be taken from Marie-Joséphine Cottin's novel *Mathilde, ou Mémoires tirés de l'histoire des croisades* (1805), but after several months of discussion, still nothing came of the project. Another Crusader subject was selected instead of the one Meyerbeer had suggested. By 26 September 1822 the librettist was preparing a text *Il cavaliere di Rodi* for Meyerbeer, again chosen from a French *mélodrame*, this time by Monperlier, *Le Chevaliers de Malte* (the title *Il crociato in Egitto* was selected only later). Matters of casting seemed to be the decisive element in this change of subject. After a period of uncertainty it emerged that Giovanni Battista Velluti (1780–1861), the last significant castrato of the Italian opera, would be available as the leading light of the ensemble. The role of Armando seemed made for him. Rossi's letters to Meyerbeer during the genesis of the work (*BT*, 1:519–80) document, like hardly any other contemporary source, the praxis and aesthetics of Italian opera in the early nineteenth century. This is particularly true of Meyerbeer's role as *spiritus rector*, something that distinguishes him from all the other composers of the period. New and forward-looking passages in the opera can be traced back to ideas and explanations emerging from proposals by the composer: most particularly the *magica scena della romanza* (the Act 1 trio for Felicia, Palmide and Armando) and the *scena classica del Gran Maestro* (Adriano's Dungeon Scene in Act 2). Meyerbeer and Rossi took their time: after sketching the *ossatura* (the theatre vocabulary for the bare skeleton of the opera) in July 1823, the work continued for another three-quarters of a year. The concluding phases were marked by discussions with the censor who took exception to mention of an 'illegitimate' son of the Crusader. The problem was obviated by the addition of a few verses of recitative making reference to a secret Christian betrothal between Armando and Palmide. This passage was, however, cut in productions in other places, such as Trieste in 1824.

Plot
In and around the Egyptian port of Damietta in 1250, during the Sixth Crusade.

Prehistory. A brigade of the Knights of Rhodes has fallen to an Egyptian ambush. All have been annihilated apart from Armando d'Orville, a young knight from Provence, who, by disguising himself in the armour appropriated from a fallen Egyptian, has taken his place in the enemy army. Under the assumed name of Elmireno he has won great respect for his deeds of bravery. After saving the life of the Sultan Aladino, he has become a confidant at court. There he has met and fallen in love with the Sultan's daughter, Palmide. She has secretly returned his love, and has taken on his faith. From their union a son has been born who has been secretly brought up in the harem.

Act 1. The port of Damietta with a perspective across the harbour. Christian slaves are seen at their wearisome labours, full of homesickness and despair. Palmide enters and distributes alms among them. Sultan Aladino announces to his daughter that he wishes to bestow her hand on Elmireno who has distinguished himself in battle, and will soon be arriving home. The occasion of the wedding will be marked by the imminent arrival of a delegation of the Knights of Rhodes, with whom a peace treaty is to be signed, and all remaining prisoners in Damietta are to be freed. Armando will be put into double jeopardy by this development, since he will appear to both sides as a deceiver and traitor. To Palmide, his devastated betrothed, he is obliged to reveal his knightly status and his earlier engagement to the Provençal maid Felicia. The Knights arrive in their great galley, and Armando is recognized by his uncle, Adriano di Monfort, the grand master of the Knights of Rhodes, and the leader of the delegation. He accuses Armando of breaking his betrothal, and challenges him to a duel. Felicia has come with the Knights to Damietta, disguised as a man, to look for her missing beloved. In conversation with Palmide she pretends to be Armando's brother, but lets all pretence fall when she realizes that Palmide is his lover and the mother of his child. Although she is bitterly disappointed, for the sake of the child she is prepared to forego her love of Armando. The latter, for his part, has decided to renounce his love for Palmide and comes to bid her farewell, but loses his resolve when he finds Palmide with Felicia who sticks to her decision about him. Things come to a flashpoint when Armando appears before the assembled court at the feast for the invited Crusaders in the garments of a Knight of Rhodes, acknowledges his faith and origins, and refuses the hand of Palmide. The Sultan is deeply offended and draws his dagger on Armando, but he is saved by Felicia, still pretending to be his brother. When the Sultan orders Armando to be thrown in prison, Adriano responds with a declaration of hostilities. From the mosque comes the signal for holy war. Amidst general tumult the Egyptians and the Crusaders rally around their respective banners.

Illustration 4.6a   *Il crociato in Egitto*: design for Act 2 (watercolour from Alessandro
Sanquirico's *Raccolta di Varie Decorazioni Sceniche, Inventate
ed Eseguiti per l'I. R. Teatro alla Scala*, Milan 1827)

Act 2. The gardens of the Sultan's palace. The intriguing vizier Osmino, who
himself aspires to Palmide's hand, reveals to the Sultan that his daughter has a
child by Armando. The raging Aladino now wishes to kill the child, but relents to
Palmide's pleading. He gives Armando his freedom, his blessing on the union with
Palmide, and offers reconciliation to Adriano. When the latter learns of the existence
of the child, he again covers Armando with reproaches, and is mollified only when
Palmide agrees to become a Christian. In the presence of Felicia and the Knights,
Adriano witnesses their betrothal and calls the blessings of heaven down on the
couple. This secret ceremony is betrayed by Osmino and the emirs, and the Sultan,
feeling that his magnanimity has been betrayed, has them all arrested and threatens
them all with death. In the dungeon Adriano and the Knights pledge themselves to
accept martyrdom. Osmino has in the meantime conspired to overthrow the Sultan,
and looks to the Knights for help. He secretly arms them and, just before their public
execution, gives the signal for the uprising. He throws himself on Aladino, intending
to murder him. Armando, however, anticipating the plan of action, overpowers
Osmino and places his co-religionists under the Sultan's protection. The conspiracy
collapses and the Sultan, moved by these demonstrations of loyalty, sets Armando
and the Knights free, and blesses the union between his daughter and the man who
has again saved his life.

More than hardly any other opera of the first third of the nineteenth century, *Il crociato in Egitto* appears as work standing between the epochs. In its engagement with the traditions of the *melodramma*, Meyerbeer exploited here to the full all the possibilities offered by the form, without actually questioning its nature. Whereas Rossini in his Neapolitan operas had undertaken a transformation of the genre, moving it in the direction of French grand opéra, Meyerbeer, on the one hand, continued a heightened development of the generic tendencies, while, on the other, affecting a deliberate resumption of older forms, already obsolete at this time (such as simple romance structures and the use of recitativo secco, especially to mark the closure of scenes). The disparate medium of presentation spans isolated individual numbers and highly integrated tableaux of solo and chorus, traditional lyrical virtuosity and the dramaturgy of modern instrumental colour, melodic models from the eighteenth century, and anticipation of middle Verdi, integrated only by the strongly imprinted force of Meyerbeer's individual style. Even more than in *Margherita d'Anjou* and *L'esule di Granata*, the *Crociato* opens up to the historical opera. The personal conflict still determines the dramaturgy, but this is projected onto historical circumstances and given a philosophical component through the figure of the religious fanatic Adriano. Throughout the whole opera the antagonism between the Crusaders and the Egyptians, until their final magnanimous reconciliation, is depicted in contrasting dramatic terms as the confrontation between two cultures and religions. The formal structures for such a dramaturgy also shape the tableaux in this opera.

In their detailed collaboration Meyerbeer and Rossi had planned that every move on the stage should be dramaturgically motivated, every entry carefully considered, especially in connection with the 44-year-old castrato Velluti, one of the last of a dying tradition. He needed an entry of brilliant virtuosity which would nonetheless relate to his performing abilities and not tire him too early. The other figures are grouped around him with similar entries and demands made upon them. Big ensemble scenes were carefully put into place. The dramatic flow was not to be sacrificed to the interests of the singers, as was all too often the case at the time in Italian opera. Great, subtle concern was taken to lend the work dramatic truth that would leave Meyerbeer space for the unfolding of his ever-expanding musico-dramatic ideas.

The introduction was especially developed in a most personal manner. It occurred to the composer that the first scene retained the dramatic potential of presenting the subject in such a way that the social context of the action could emerge out of and over any depicted private conflict—with considerable possibilities for local and historical colour adding to the theatrical context. This procedure can be understood as the preliminary stage of the expositional dramaturgy of his later grand operas, where the entire first act is conceived as an introduction. In this respect the composer was, even then, regarded as an innovator—borne out in a comment by Rossi who, in a letter of 28 October 1822, reported to his colleague that he had written an introduction *alla* Meyerbeer for Rossini's *Semiramide* (1823), where the various entries of the characters are highlighted in the context of a *quadro imponente* (imposing scene).

Illustration 4.6b *Il crociato in Egitto*: Giovanni Battista Velluti as Armando (watercolour by Chalon)

As in the big introductions to *Margherita* and *L'esule*, the chief female protagonists become the dramatic focal points of the tableau. The same applies in the *Crociato* with Palmide. Here also, the private conflict is fixed in a historical panorama that gives credibility to the religious and political motivation of the action (the forced labour of the Christian slaves at the court of the Sultan). These events are not only depicted chorally, but also visually as pantomime, in which the music minutely illustrates the prescribed movements of groups and individuals busy with their labours, the exchange of news among the prisoners and the activities of the overseers. One of the principal ways in which this new dynamic dramatic plasticity was implemented was through the large number of scenic directions, prescribing entries and placements precisely—something most unusual in an age of relatively unregulated movement on stage. The singularity of the undertaking is evident from the very beginning of the opera:

All is still at the break of dawn. Shortly after one hears three trumpet calls. Guards come and open the cells for the slaves from the different European nations; they emerge, eyes raised to heaven, greeting each other, embracing, and then going about their labour. Some drag huge blocks, others work on pillars and pediments, and erect columns. A youth helps his aged father who suffers from the weight of the chains. A guard mistreats the old man because he is not working properly. The youth offers to take his father's place. The latter falls on his knees, blessing his noble son with tears. One of the slaves steals a moment of rest, pulls a little portrait from his garments, stares at it, kisses it, and secretes it quickly, fearing to be discovered. Another reads and kisses a letter, pressing it to his breast. The guards withdraw, and on the instant the slaves gather hurriedly in groups, and begin to sing powerfully [of their homesickness and captivity].

There is no overture: the work begins with this Pantomima e Coro d'Introduzione. The violins intone a two-part song—a dream of freedom—that is roughly broken by the trumpet calls before the plight of the slaves is depicted in a rushing bass line and powerful chords. A serene melody for the clarinets distils pathos and prayerful hope. Some five different musical ideas are unfolded before the chorus comes in with great power. This plenitude of ideas is what distinguishes the introduction from comparable works of other composers and from Meyerbeer's earlier achievements. Here is manifested a tendency discernible throughout the opera: a theory of effective contrast, to elevate the drama and the vitality of musical forms in a hurried succession of contrasting elements (ex. 4.6a).

Example 4.6a   *Il crociato in Egitto*: from the opening Pantomima

The plastic conception of the scenic proceedings is supplemented by the sonic extension of the stage space. For example, the fanfares towards the end of the introduction that announce the arrival of ship carrying Knights of Rhodes are positioned in no less than four different positions (six trumpets in the formation 1–1–2–2, with two in the orchestra). In the first finale Meyerbeer handles the three drums in a similar manner: their sounding makes the highpoint of the confrontation between the Egyptian and Crusader forces. Each party is further identified tonally by an appropriate band (the Egyptian one made up of shrill Janissary instruments). The stretta combines both bands with the regular orchestra, the soloists and the chorus, and, in spite of the massed sounds, is characterized by tonally clarity ('All'armi vi chiama la gloria, la fede') (Glory and faith call you to arms). The finale can be understood as a theatrical transformation, for very large forces, of a four-movement classical symphony. Rossini, but also Mozart, Haydn and Beethoven, can be discerned in its contents and construction. (Beethoven's *Wellington's Victory* symphony was an influence here: at the premiere in 1813 Meyerbeer had played the bass drum.) In the directness of dramatic attack and the steeliness of the musical structure, this finale heralds a new era in opera. By contrast, the most extraordinary passage in the ensemble is 'Sogni ridenti' which combines canonic writing with subtle chromatic harmony and displays Meyerbeer's assured technique of juxtaposing a cappella vocal timbres with instrumental ones.

The bel canto tradition, moreover, is triumphantly epitomized: the demands on the virtuosity of the singers are carried to the heights. Lyricism and drama are brought into a proportioned relationship, the borders of both extended outwards. Drama is strengthened by a wealth of contrast, while lyricism sometimes exceeds even Rossini in luxuriousness. The work is built around the soloists, from whom much is demanded. Indeed, vocal accomplishment was the prerequisite condition of the structure of the new aria with its elegiac beginning and virtuoso cabaletta. The developed thematic–motival work that Meyerbeer learned from the Abbé Vogler was not possible in this type of aria, and he replaced it with exquisite orchestration, often entailing demanding solo contributions.

Meyerbeer devised a singular dramatic resolution for the central scene in Act 1 where Armando meets his two women in the trio 'Giovinetto cavalier'. This piece turns the story of a tragic love in the past into the story of the present. First, Felicia affirms her former love (first strophe, solo) as she sings the romance to Palmide, which Armando, whom she believes dead, once performed for her in Provence, and which stretches even further back into the past since it is a song recounting the story of a faithless knight. Her new friend Palmide joins in the song (second strophe, duet) since her heart was also captured in the same way by a strange knight singing this very song. Suddenly one hears his very voice, and right afterwards he himself appears (third strophe, trio). Armando, once Felicia's lover and now Palmide's, is the incarnation of that faithless lover from the romance. The musico–dramatic realization of the story entails the interaction of four different levels of time (the knight of the romance, Armando and Felicia's love, Armando and Palmide's relationship, and then Armando, Felicia and Palmide all together in the present). Narrated time and the present coalesce in the timelessly fulfilled moment which captures the memory in actual time. The melody of the romance, which made its way through all the salons of Europe, sustains an aura particularly by means of a concertante ensemble of seven instruments (cor anglais, clarinet, horn, harp, violin, cello and double bass). It was apparently inspired by the romance 'Ov'è la bella vergine' from Act 2 of Mayr's *Alfredo il grande, re degli anglo-sassoni* (Bergamo 1819, libretto by Bartolomeo Merelli). The solo instruments combine with the three female voices in a sublime amalgam of sound, in which the barcarolle melody of the romance strophes trails away in an alienating sfumato.

Melodic patterns are frequently cut to eighteenth-century models, even if in new formal or harmonic contexts. So, in the Act 1 duet for Palmide and Armando ('Ah! non ti son più cara') (Ah you must no longer love me), the overflowing of feeling in the dramatic situation unfolds from the overlapping linearity of the voice parts; the movement as a whole, however, is subjected to the supposedly modern montage principle evident in the truncated cabaletta. Palmide's big Act 2 aria ('D'una madre disperata') (Of a despairing mother) begins as an exaggeratedly virtuoso paraphrase of 'Fuor del mar' from Mozart's *Idomeneo* (1781), but dissonant orchestral accents soon superimposed on the demisemiquaver scales lend an additional dimension of expression to the whole context. Conversely, other elements look forward to later developments in Italian opera. Take, for example, the virtuoso female duet, introduced by Rossini into *Tancredi* (1813), and used by Meyerbeer in *Romilda e Costanza* and *Semiramide*. He developed this even further in the *Crociato*, as in the middle section of Act 1 duet for Palmide and Armando ('Non v'è per noi più speme') (There is no more hope for us) where it assumes a whole new specific sound dimension which Bellini could later develop in similar pieces.

Adriano's Dungeon Aria ('Suona funerea l'ora di morte') (The hour of death tolls mournfully) in Act 2 created the prototype of the big tenor scene that would remain statutory until middle Verdi; the three-part unfolding of form, with the decisive arc of emotion rising from the dark minor to the soaring major ('Speriamo in te, Signore') (We hope in you, O Lord), would become the model for innumerable slow arias of Donizetti and Verdi (ex. 4.6b [a]). Further, in the Act 2 Conspiracy Chorus of the emirs ('Nel silenzio fra l'orrore') (Silently, here in the darkness) the *Crociato* provided the model for many choruses in Risorgimento operas, with its characteristic melodic slancio of dancing-like tension (ex. 4.6b [b]).

The attention Meyerbeer devotes to the chorus is new and forward-looking in his creative work. The chorus to date had invariably served as a scaffolding for the soloists, usually to strengthen the harmonic background for their coloratura displays; but here, building on the developments in *Emma*, *Margherita* and *L'esule*, the chorus receives a precise dramatic role as slaves, emirs, Crusaders and conspirators. While the emirs sing in a light, friendly and attractive tone, realized in chromatic half-tones, the Crusaders, on their numerous entries (as with the arias of their leader Adriano) always begin on a piercing brass and drum device, like soldiers marching on the turn of C and G major. Nothing less than military machinery is set in place, something maintained throughout the opera. The reveilles of Berlin must have found their enduring resonance in the composer's memory. The *banda*, so much a part of the Italian operatic tradition, finds a sort of apotheosis in Meyerbeer with his intuitive Prussian background. In both *Margherita* and *L'esule* the stage band occupied an increasingly important role: in *Crociato* two are used at the same time.

Example 4.6b   *Il crociato in Egitto*: from a) the Inno di Morte and b) Chorus of
                Conspirators (Act 2)

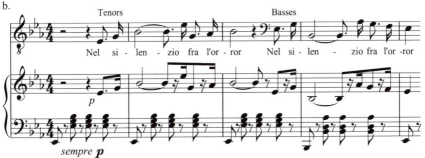

Among those works that supposedly made a strong impression on Meyerbeer,
two pieces by Rossini that appeared in 1819 should be mentioned. First is *Ermione*,
an attempt at producing an Italian *tragédie lyrique* after Racine's *Andromache*. This
work was never produced outside of Naples, and was not plundered by Rossini
for other works. Rather, this self-imposed task, both in tonality and theme, was a
carefully involved musical tragedy of conscientious workmanship rarely found in
Rossini. Second is the *azione sacra*, *Mosè*, which accorded the chorus an unusually
large role. The first appearance of the slaves in the *Crociato* is modelled on that of
the captive Hebrews in *Mosè*. These were high compositional standards by which
Meyerbeer rightly wanted to measure himself (Zimmermann 1991: 132).

Meyerbeer was known in Italy as the *maestro-dilettante* since he composed without professional necessity: now he experienced the greatest triumph of his career. At the premiere and the following performances he was feted in the midst of a brilliant ensemble, with Velluti (Armando), Henriette Méric-Lalande (Palmide), Brigida Lorenzani (Felicia) and Gaetano Crivelli (Adriano). The enthusiasm with which the opera was received everywhere was described a few years later by Heinrich Heine: 'If ever I saw human madness, it was at a performance of the *Crociato in Egitto* when the music suddenly changed from soft melancholic tones into exultant sorrow. In Italy such madness is known as *furore*' (*Reisebilder*, 3. Teil: *Reise von München nach Genua* [1828], Kapital 27).

The enthusiastic reception of the *Crociato* did not keep Meyerbeer from undertaking many adaptations in the period following. Some of these changes related to new demands of casting; others, however, had effects on the dramaturgical structure of the work itself:

1. In the production for the Teatro della Pergola in Florence on 7 May 1824 (with Velluti as Armando, Tosi as Palmide, Domenico Reina as Adriano), the entrance of the protagonists in Act 1 was newly ordered. Armando's arrival in Scene 2 was moved (his aria and the following duet with Palmide falling away) to Scene 3 (with a new *sortita*, 'Caro mano dell'amore' [Dear hand of love] with chorus and ballet in place of Felicia's entrance aria). For the advent of the Crusaders with Adriano and Felicia (minus her aria), a new fourth scene (the equivalent of Act 2 Scene 3 in Venice) was inserted. In what was now the fifth scene (the earlier fourth), the romance trio was arranged in a new version. In Act 2 Scene 1 the aria of Felicia was exchanged for one by Alma ('D'un genio che l'ispira' taken from *Semiramide*, and written for Teresa Ruggieri); in Act 2 Scene 2 Palmide's aria 'D'una madre disperata' was made tauter; the whole of the fourth scene in the dungeon was missing. In the closing fifth scene Armando's final aria was reduced to the introductory recitative and the tempo d'attacco part of the double chorus of Egyptians and Crusaders, and replaced with a final duet for Armando and Palmide ('Ravvisa qual alma') (Behold what virtue).

2. Meyerbeer arranged the work differently for the production in Trieste on 10 November 1824 which placed Nicola Tacchinardi as Adriano at the centre (with Bassi Manna as Armando and Katharina Wallbach-Canzi as Palmide). Armando's entry was shifted back to Act 1 Scene 2, and the duet with Palmide restored (but not his aria). Adriano's new aria compensates for this: his entry in Act 1 Scene 3 is given sharp profile by a new heroic aria with *banda* ('Queste destre l'acciaro di morte') (These hands the murderous sword), and supersedes the new fourth scene devised for Florence. In Scene 4 the older structure of the romance trio is restored. Act 2 Scene 1 is transferred to the inside of the palace, and the aria removed; Scene 4 in the dungeon is restored, and through a new version of Adriano's cabaletta gains in lyrical as well as dramatic impact. To add to the complication, and as concessions to the singers, various substitutions were made for arias that had been cut: Palmide's aria in Scene 2 was replaced by 'Dolce albergo di pace from *Margherita d'Anjou*; Armando's

final aria was substituted by either 'Oh! Come rapida' from *L'esule di Granata* or 'Col piacer la pace scenda' from *Semiramide* (Bassi's choice). Despite a certain lack of unity, these changes collectively resulted in shift of emphasis from a private to the political-religious conflict, especially the demotion of Felicia and the revaluation of Adriano within the hierarchy of roles. This strengthened a tendency already present in the work. Although Meyerbeer himself thought the work benefited immeasurably by these interventions (see his letter to Heinrich Baermann of 6 March 1828), he never actually fixed the final form of the *Crociato*. He undertook an attempt at this when he began revising the work as a grand opera for Paris, before his interest was taken up with other matters, most especially *Robert le Diable* (1831).

In the meantime the *Crociato* was performed on many stages, usually in unauthorized mixed editions. There was particular historical significance in the 1825 productions in London and Paris, cities that in the future would become centres of Meyerbeer's fame. In the King's Theatre in London Velluti appeared again, with the young Maria Malibran as Felicia, and Rosalbina Caradori-Allan, Alberico Curioni and Ranieri Remorini. At the Théâtre-Italien in Paris, where Meyerbeer had been invited by the director Rossini, success was guaranteed by the exceptional cast of Giuditta Pasta, Ester Mombelli, Adelaide Schiasetti, Domenico Donizelli and Nicolas-Prosper Levasseur. Outstanding productions in Italy in 1826 were in Milan (Bassi Manna, Teresa Melas and Crivelli), Naples (as *Il cavaliere Armando d'Orville*, with Lorenzani, Méric-Lalande and Winter), Bologna (Francesca Festa, Santina Ferlotti and Tacchinardi), and in 1827 in Venice (with Tosi and Crivelli). In 1826 the *Crociato* appeared in Dresden (Schiasetti, Matilde Palazzesi, Alfonso Zezi, conducted by Francesco Morlacchi), with a new production in 1828 London (at Covent Garden, with Velluti, Henriette Sontag, Marietta Brambilla, Curioni and Carlo Ottolino Porto) and at the Théâtre-Italien (with Pisaroni as Armando), 1829 in Vienna (in the German text of Josef Kupelweiser, with Amalie Haehnel as Armando), again in 1838 (with Sabine Heinefetter), in 1832 in Berlin at the Königstädtischen Theater (Haehnel, Katharina Kraus-Wranitsky). In Prague the opera was first performed in 1828 (as *Der Ritter von Rhodus*, with Katharina Podhorsky, Marianne Katharina Ernst, Sebastian Binder and Josef Wolfgang Kainz) and again in 1836 when it was brilliantly produced as a festival opera for the coronation of Emperor Ferdinand I as king of Bohemia (with Wilhelmine Schröder-Devrient, Jenny Lutzer, Friedrich Demmer and Josef Pöck).

Until the middle of the century the work was frequently performed in Europe and overseas (Havana 1826, Mexico 1837) before falling in the shadow of Meyerbeer's French operas. The opera was revived at La Scala Milan in 1859 (with Barbara Marchisio) and in the Théâtre-Italien in 1860 (with Adelaide Borghi-Mamo), but by then not even these illustrious interpreters could conjure up the former magic. The disappearance of Rossini's serious operas from the stage meant that these performances, given against Meyerbeer's wishes, served simply as reminiscences of a bygone era.

Only in recent decades have a series of concert performances brought the historical significance of the *Crociato* back into consciousness: at Queen Elizabeth Hall, London in 1972 (Opera Rara with Patricia Kern, Janet Price, William McKinney, Christian du Plessis, conducted by Roderick Brydon); Carnegie Hall, New York 1979 (with Felicity Palmer, Yvonne Kenny, Rockwell Blake and Justino Diaz, conducted by Gianfranco Masini); Montpellier 1990 (Radio France, with Martine Dupuy and Rockwell Blake, conducted by Massimo de Bernart); London 1991 (Opera Rara, with Diana Montague, Yvonne Kenny, Bruce Ford and Ugo Benelli, conducted by Davis Parry), a bicentennial performance that was recorded—the original 1824 score and all the other variants; Dresden and Ludwigsburg 1991 (with Ning Liang, Elena Brilova, Rockwell Blake/Ken Hicks, Volker Horn, conducted by Jörg-Peter Weigle). (See Loewenberg 1970: 692; Döhring 1991, 4:121–2; Schuster 2003, 1:125–218.)

The first full production in modern times, using the original score, was at La Fenice, Venice, 14–21 January 2007 (with Florin Cezar Ouatu, a counter-tenor, Patrizia Ciofi, Laura Favaron, Fernando Portari, Marco Vinco, and Emmanuel Villaume conducting). Pier-Luigi Pizzi's staging was minimal but true to the dramatic intentions of the scenario.

By 1836 *Il crociato in Egitto* had been produced some 30 times: on all the big Italian stages, in London, and in Paris. This was followed by *Margherita d'Anjou* (14 productions until 1857), *Emma di Resburgo* (ten productions by 1829), *Romilda e Costanza* (six productions by 1822), with three productions of *Semiramide* and two productions of *L'esule di Granata*.

The *Crociato* raised Meyerbeer to the foremost representative of Italian opera after Rossini. It is interesting to speculate what further developments in the genre would have occurred if Meyerbeer had further pursued in Italy the course laid out in this opera. However, reform of the Italian opera was not his aim, but rather Paris, which, from the beginning of his career, had seemed to him the very Mecca of dramatic music.

Chapter Five

French Operas: *Grand Opéra*

With the success of *Il crociato in Egitto* (1824) at the Théâtre-Italien in Paris on 25 September 1825, Meyerbeer saw the partial realization of his long-cherished aspiration to succeed as a dramatic composer in the musical capital of Europe. Indeed, he still held Italy open as an artistic option, and engaged in negotiations on various possible topics for a new opera, with one of them reaching the stage of a contract (*Ines de Castro*, with a libretto by Gaetano Rossi, planned for the San Carlo in Naples, 1824). But any interest in pursuing his Italian career diminished in proportion to the emergence of new projects in Paris. It was increasingly obvious that he sought an entrée into French opera. He worked intensively on preparing a French version of the *Crociato*, and after *Margherita d'Anjou* had been produced as an *opéra comique* at the Théâtre de l'Odéon in 1826, he began on another work in this genre, *La Nymphe de Danube*, with a text by Thomas-Marie-François Sauvage, after Kauer's story *Das Donauweibchen* (1798), which he envisaged as a pasticcio using music from his Italian operas. All these Parisian projects slipped into the background, however, when Meyerbeer received from René-Charles Guilbert de Pixérécourt, the director of the Opéra Comique, the contract for a new work, *Robert le Diable*.

5.1 *Robert le Diable [Robert the Devil]*

Opéra en cinq actes [opera in five acts]
Text: Augustin-Eugène Scribe and Germain Delavigne
First performance: Opéra, Salle de la rue Le Peletier, Paris, 21 November 1831

It is in the heady context of Meyerbeer's new life in Paris, his careful study and assimilation of French operatic culture that the plan took shape to make his debut there in the genre of *grand opéra*. This type of opera, after a long period of stagnation, had once again rung a chord in contemporary aesthetical thinking with the stirring premieres of Auber's *La Muette de Portici* (Scribe 1828) and Rossini's *Guillaume Tell* (Jouy and Bis 1829)—the former for its dramaturgical, and the latter for its musical innovations. For a while Meyerbeer appears to have hesitated over whether to choose a new subject, or to rework *Robert*. The librettist was to be Germain Delavigne, who delivered a preliminary draft. At the beginning of 1827, however, Augustin-Eugène Scribe was drawn in, and soon after took over the principal authorship.

Inspired by the quality of the material, Meyerbeer immediately began composing, and made rapid progress. A long entry in his pocket calendar for the second half of

1829, in the nature of series of dramaturgical notes (*BT*, 2:593), indicates that he was rethinking the whole project: a new concept was emerging that did not fit in with the original contours of the envisaged genre of *opéra comique*. These *Taschenkalender* observations are starting points for discussions with the librettists, a fascinating glimpse into the composer's involvement in the every detail of the genesis of his works, his preoccupation with detail and *couleur locale*:

> Viganò's *Bianca di Messina* as [model for] a dance piece. Likewise a dance piece for Taglioni and Montessu as they struggle against the magic sleep in the Act 2 finale and make powerful leaps in an attempt to revive themselves, and are the last to fall asleep. - In Act 3 a big recitative for Bertram in which he recounts the story of his fall from heaven etc: it should contain only a small arioso which recurs from time to time. Lots of rhythmical changes. Since it captures the whole of Robert's history, all the main themes of the opera must recur in the orchestra. - I must have Hartmann bring *La pachianella* (Sicilian dance) and other Sicilian melodies from my trunk; Michael must likewise write to Cattereau in Naples. - Fata Morgana - Wilhelm must take down all the data from Mödler. - *Bianca di Messina*, ballet by Ayblinger.- *Terzetto buffo* or quartet for Bertram, Alberti and Raimbault instead of the quartet in Act 2, in which the two curiously question Bertram who mocks them. - Bertram has too little to sing. - Aria for Alberti. - The action happens in Sicily, and yet apart from the Princess there is not a single other Sicilian, not even a chorus to bring out the Sicilian *couleur*. The conspiracy must be different. There are no comic pieces, not even a comic chorus. - 4 acts - The opera is a little bare and people will say it has the *baguette en main* and does not know how to eat it. Perhaps Fata Morgana is therefore the solution. In Act 1 after the quartet, a journey through the air. At the end of Act 2 Bertram takes Robert through the air. – Alberti's role. - Perhaps one could see the procession to the tournament on horseback on the heights in the background, perhaps even a little of the tournament itself. - Perhaps in the conspiracy scene there could be a *conseil des diables* as in *Manfred*. - *Pèlerinage de Sainte Rosalie*. Alice could be called Rosalie, or perhaps Robert's mother, and she must have been a Sicilian princess. Perhaps Alice is making the pilgrimage *en son honneur*. Where could the Devil hold his sabbath in a place where it could be seen? Only by an independent coincidence (like Fata Morgana) could Alice interrupt the conspiracy without some *niaiserie* by the Devil, but the crucifix would not be allowed. Already in Act 1 and also in the new introduction, the *Maître des Ceremonies* should have something to sing. The action should be shifted to Palermo. There should be demonic laughter at the words 'hell is as bad as they say'. - Flares in the *tableau des vices*. - One must speak earlier about the *Procession de St Rosalie*. The whole of the Hell scene must be without singing until he picks the branch which is attached to a solitary tree. Then the chorus comes in with *il est à nous*. The tree goes up in green fire.

The contract Meyerbeer signed with the Opéra on 1 December 1829 mentions no title; soon after that he decided to stick with the old material. The July Revolution upset all his plans, but already in the following year the new director, Louis-Desiré Véron, an astute businessman and an inspirational organizer, determined that *Robert* would be the first big opera premiere of his tenure. For this production Véron contracted the elite of the French theatre to his house. For the *chef du service de la scène* there was Edmond Duponchel, who shared the stage management with Scribe the librettist and Adolphe Nourrit, the tenor who would create the title role. The scene designer was to be Pierre-Luc-Charles Cicéri, the choreographer Filippo Taglioni, the conductor

François-Antoine Habeneck. Added to this was a first-class ensemble of singers and dancers, and what was at the time the best opera orchestra in the world.

During the rehearsals over many months Meyerbeer, in close consultation with the artistic team, undertook many conceptional changes. The medieval legend of Robert le Diable had survived in many literary genres, and since the late eighteenth century had become widely known, had been taken into the Bibliothèque bleue, and had appeared in various melodramas and pantomimes. The opera libretto in fact shared only the character of the eponymous hero and the *couleur* of the epoch in common with the medieval sources. The dramaturgical structure of the libretto and its central motifs actually derive from the German Gothic novel *Das Petermännchen, Geschichte aus dem dreizehnten Jahrhunderts* (1791) by Christian Heinrich Spiess which appeared in 1820 in a French translation by Henri de Latouche as *Le Petit-Pierre ou Aventures de Rodolphe de Westerbourg*. Other motifs and scenes are taken from the English literature of dark Romanticism, especially Matthew Gregory Lewis's novel *The Monk* (1796) and Charles Robert Maturin's play *Bertram* (1816). The development of Bertram into what is essentially the central role of the opera appears in the reworking of the subject, and can be traced back to Meyerbeer himself.

Plot
In and around Palermo, *c.*1250.

Preliminary history. Berthe, the daughter of the Duke of Normandy, succumbs to the black arts of a demon knight, who, in the service of Satan, can buy time on earth only by leading others to hell. A son, Robert, is born of the union; he so much takes after his father that he is given the soubriquet of 'the Devil'. Because of his many crimes he is banished from his homeland, and eventually on his travels arrives in Sicily, where he falls in love with the Princess Isabelle. She responds to his love, but his uncontrolled behaviour has led to his being challenged by the local knights. In conflict he would have been overwhelmed by the enemy force if he had not been rescued by the timely intervention of an unknown knight who saved him from death. This stranger, called Bertram, is actually Robert's father, who does not, however, reveal his identity to his son. Even though Bertram loves Robert above all else, he is relentlessly required to seduce his son into evil, and can be united with him only in common damnation.

Act 1. Camp of the Norman knights on the beach of Palermo, with a view of the harbour. Several elegant tents stand in the shadow of trees. It is morning. The knights are drinking while waiting for the beginning of a tournament ordered by the king. The victor is to receive the hand of Princess Isabelle in marriage. Among the knights is Robert who must rehabilitate his name in the eyes of the princess by success. The minstrel Raimbaut, who has just arrived from Normandy, entertains the knights with a song. He sings them the Ballad of Robert the Devil, telling of his macabre origins and his many misdeeds. Infuriated by this public affront, Robert reveals his identity and is determined to hang Raimbaut. He is mollified when he hears that the minstrel is accompanied by his bride. Determining to exercise his right as overlord, Robert has her summoned, and is amazed to recognize in her his foster-sister, Alice, who has come to Sicily to find him. She presents to Robert the will and dying blessing of his late mother. The shocked Robert feels unworthy of touching the testament, and asks Alice to safeguard it for him. He tells her of his unhappy love for Isabelle, and Alice resolves to go to the princess in order to arrange a reconciling conversation between Robert and Isabelle even before the tournament. The capricious Robert, however, gives way to the temptations of his dark alter ego. Induced by Bertram to play dice with the other knights, he loses all his possessions, including his arms. After sadly reflecting on his unfortunate destiny, he turns in fury on the mocking knights and risks being killed. Bertram's magic holds them petrified.

Act 2. A big hall in the palace. In the background is a gallery which looks out onto the landscape. It is midday. Isabelle muses on her sad fate and love for Robert. Alice enters with other petitioners and brings the princess Robert's message. Isabelle receives the waiting penitent, grants him pardon, and provides him with new weapons for the imminent tournament. The people gather for the occasion. Bertram, in order to foil any possible success, exercises his demonic powers. A herald appears and presents to Robert the challenge of an alleged rival, the Prince of Granada, who is awaiting him in a nearby wood. He is actually a phantom demon in Bertram's service. Robert follows the herald, so breaking the code of chivalry by accepting a rival outside the lists. When Isabelle signals the beginning of the tournament, Robert does not appear, to her consternation. In his place comes the Prince of Granada who sweeps to victory.

Act 3. Scene 1. A dark rocky landscape near the cavern of St Irene. To the right are the ruins of an antique temple, and in the background the entrance to a cave. On the other side stands a great stone cross. It is afternoon. Alice and Raimbaut have agreed to marry in an isolated chapel. Raimbaut is intercepted by Bertram on his way there, and induced by gambling to abandon his bride. This easy success does not lessen Bertram's anguish since Satan now demands Robert's soul. The voices of demons are heard calling Robert's name from the cavern. Bertram goes into the cavern from where the fires of hell glow. Alice, who is wandering about the valley looking for Raimbaut, prays to the Virgin. A tempest breaks, and Alice becomes the unwitting witness of events. Bertram emerges from the cavern; he has sought in vain to extend the period of temptation: if he has not won Robert's soul by midnight, he will himself be called to hell and lose his son forever. He espies Alice, and compels her silence by threatening death. The bewildered Robert now enters. The three reflect on this decisive moment, before Bertram's menaces cause Alice to flee. Bertram offers Robert a final means to dispose of his rival. All he need do is pluck a magic branch from the grave of St Rosalie, situated in the ruins of a neighbouring monastery once notorious for its dissipation. By theft of this talisman, which bestows absolute power, Robert will finally give himself over to evil. As night falls Robert makes his way to the abandoned place.

Scene 2. The cloisters of a ruined abbey. On the left is an overgrown cemetery, on the right several tombs with effigies of nuns, and among them the statue of St Rosalie with a spring of green cypress in its hand. It is evening and the moon is shining. Bertram arrives before Robert. In the fullness of his diabolic majesty he summons the spirits of the debauched nuns from their graves for a short appearance of life, and requires them to cause Robert to pluck the branch. Will-o'-the-wisps shimmer on the gravestones. The nuns rise from their tombs, and united in the guise of seductive women, and led by their Abbess Helena, dance a bacchanal in the moonlight. When Robert appears, he draws back, recognizing in the statue of the saint the features of his own mother. Before he can flee he is held in thrall by the nuns, who try to seduce him with drinking, gambling and finally love. Blandished by the beautiful Helena, he picks the branch. Demons emerge triumphantly and dance around Robert, while the nuns are transformed back into ghosts.

Act 4. The bedchamber of Princess Isabelle. In the background are three large doors opening on to a long gallery. It is later in the evening. Isabelle receives the good wishes of the court on the eve of her marriage to the Prince of Granada. Robert appears, and through the power of the talisman causes the assembly to fall into a deep sleep. He frees Isabelle from the magic and seeks to abduct her by force. She falls to her knees and implores heaven for mercy—for him and herself. Deeply moved, he breaks the magic branch and power of evil. Awoken from the enchanted slumber, the assembly throw themselves on Robert who escapes only with Bertram's help.

Act 5. Forecourt to the Cathedral of Palermo. In the background a curtain which hides the nave. It is close to midnight. A procession of monks sing of immortality. Fleeing from his pursuers, Robert seeks sanctuary in the church. Bertram is at his side and promises Robert the opportunity for vengeance if he would only sign away his soul to him [Bertram]. Robert is affected by the sounds of the organ and the pious hymns coming from the cathedral: he is filled with memories of childhood. As he considers Bertram's black parchment, Bertram plays his trump card and reveals to Robert that he is his father: he explains the deception with the phantom rival and begs Robert to sign the pact, otherwise at midnight the two will be separated for ever. Robert is just about to agree when Alice enters with the news that the Prince of Granada is not able to cross the threshold of the church, and that Isabelle, freed of the evil magic, is now waiting for Robert at the altar. He is torn, not knowing what to do. Alice now hands over to him his mother's testament: she warns Robert against the evil tempter, and assures him of her prayers. As the earthly representative of the heavenly intercessor, Alice now struggles with the infernally aligned Bertram for the soul of the wavering Robert. She is able to delay the signing of the pact until the midnight hour strikes, and Bertram, his power broken, is taken down to hell amidst flames and tempest. The curtain at the back is raised to reveal the brilliantly illumined interior of the cathedral. Heavenly voices reaffirm the beneficence of providence as Robert leads Isabelle to the altar.

Illustration 5.1a   *Robert le Diable*: card depiction of the Gambling Scene in Act 1
(Edition de la Chocolaterie d'Aiguebelle)

Criticism that the libretto lacks dramatic logic has followed from a fundamental corruption of the whole concept of the drama, deriving in its turn from an ever more careless theatrical praxis. Damaging abridgements and the disregard for important scene directions have resulted in two important elements of the action being ignored: the unity of time and the phantasmal nature of the Prince of Granada. The fact that the action unfolds in the course of a single day has little to do with the classical rules of dramatic poetry. The theatrical visualization of the times of day generates an undercurrent of tension that underscores the passage of time leading to the mythical moment of reckoning at midnight. Further, it is crucial to Bertram's intrigue that Robert's rival, the Prince of Granada, is not a real person but, as Bertram's creature, a malign ghost: from his first appearance this generates the all-pervasive atmosphere of the uncanny and the ambiguous. The apparently real events are shaped by and are contingent on Bertram's phantasmagorical web of deception.

   Neglect of the thematic implications of the drama can undermine the fundamental symbolic unity of the fictional universe depicted. In *Robert* we see a mythological and Romantic view of religion in a bygone age in which demons are confronted in a very direct way and defeated by an uncomplicated faith mediated through the Church and the actions of key individuals. Here, heaven and earth act together to defeat the powers of evil with a pure communion symbolized through the intervention of Robert's dead mother and her agent Alice interceding on his behalf.

In the figure of the demonic Bertram heaven and hell are linked in a character at once bizarre and contradictory, yet at the same time psychologically developed. His attempts to seduce and destroy Robert are paradoxically an act of love, indeed of passion. This love is tragic insofar as it is fatefully constituted, and can find its fulfilment only in the destruction of its object. This is exactly analogous to the plight of Dr Frankenstein and his monster in Mary Shelley's masterpiece of Romantic horror *Frankenstein* (1818). The Act 5 aria for Bertram directed to his son ('Jamais c'est impossible') (Never, it is impossible), already cut before the premiere, develops at length the mythological explanation that is otherwise only hinted at: the unquenchable love for his son is a penance imposed by God on the fallen angel. As one who loves, despite hell and his status as *ange revolté*, he, unlike Robert, has no real choice, since his remonstrations against hell can never bring him closer to heaven. It is this very unholy bifurcation of character that raises this character above the sphere of melodrama and the popular horror novel, and reveals a deep-rootedness in dark Romanticism, most especially Maturin's late Gothic masterpiece, *Melmoth the Wanderer* (1820). In the opera, as in the novel, the burden of deathlessness, an ironic inversion of life everlasting, is related to damnation, and the fusion of the two becomes a mythological cipher for stricken existence, tragically thrown back on itself in unresolvable and inescapable contradictions.

Against this, Alice does not possess a profile of similar relief, although her appearances retain a dramatic–symbolic function in confrontation with her counterpart in Acts 1, 3 and 5. The character of Alice is reflected in the forms and style of her music. Her Act 1 narration is a simple romance, not a more elaborate cavatina. Nonetheless, the musical thought is developed symphonically, with all the tributary themes deriving from a common source—in this case a rising fourth that will characterize Alice's musical personality throughout the score. The opening of the romance underlines the *naïveté* of the messenger sent by a dying mother, but *naïveté* soon passes into an elevated serenity as the narration becomes a prayer, the harmonies and orchestration investing the whole with a luminous, 'spiritual' quality. In Act 3 she enters to the same type of high woodwind writing. Her characteristic form is again of the simplest type, a ballad (*couplets*), as she tells her story, the account of the hermit's predictions passing once again from narration into prayer, with increasing rhythmic and harmonic modifications at each of the strophes indicating the presence of dark forces. She becomes the overt agent of heaven in Act 5, and her contribution from the very first is a prayer—an ever-rising, hovering and soaring melodic arc.

But the passive title-hero is differentiated in a very different way. Robert's wavering between Good and Evil can plausibly be understood in terms of a psychological indecision between the maternal and paternal components of character. And when he does decide, this is not so much out of his own volition, but rather as the result of the beseeching and intercession of others: Alice, Isabelle, his sainted mother, and beyond them all the Virgin herself. Because he does break the magic talisman obtained through black magic and crime, there is an element of personal decision in his renunciation of the power of evil, and he shows himself open to the grace bestowed on him at the end. Important for Meyerbeer and Scribe is the figure of the repentant sinner, drawn from both the medieval legend of Robert the Devil and the Romantic Rudolf of the Spiess/Latouche novel. Striking features of the character also correspond with the recurrent literary figure of the amoral seducer that goes back to Don Juan, with its more contemporary manifestation of Zampa in Hérold's and Mélesville's eponymous *opéra comique* (1831) which found popular entrée into the French musical theatre at the time. It is in comparison with Zampa that another, bigger dimension emerges with regard to Robert: this relates to the psychology of the character and is also bound up with an overarching context of ideas. For the title of an opera to be that of an anti-hero was hardly less novel and bold as the concept of Bertram's role. It both fascinated and repelled contemporary aesthetic opinion. Heine's rather forced interpretation of Robert's character in political terms, as the mirror of the moral uncertainty of the times (*des moralischen Schwankens damaliger Zeit*) did not reflect Meyerbeer's intentions (see Heine 1976, 5:344), but nonetheless illumines the effect of the opera on the public of the time (Döhring 1991, 4:126).

The most competent contemporary music critics, however, were at one in the conviction that dramatic music had reached a new stage of development in *Robert*, and it heralded nothing less than a change of epoch. Something of the nature of this judgement is suggested by the letter of congratulation that Jean-François Le Sueur wrote to Meyerbeer after the premiere (*BT*, 2:156): at the end of the current artistic period, whose exponent was embodied in Rossini, dramatic music espoused a hedonistic principle (*l'âge de plaisir*), but now, led on by Meyerbeer, has been exposed to new shaping forces and thereby reinvented itself (*cet âge actuel de force, d'energie, de maturité de l'homme* [the current age of power, energy and human maturity]). Thoughts about the change of era determined and stimulated many musical and literary *feuilletons*. Discussion with direct reference to this opera are reflected in Giuseppe Mazzini's *Filosofia della musica* (Paris, 1836), Heine's *Neunter Brief. Uber die französische Bühne* (1837, and apparently influenced by Mazzini), and Honoré de Balzac's *Gambara ou La Voix humaine* (1837). Franz Liszt, writing a little later in 1854 from the distance of Weimar but with the authority of historical witness, persuasively depicted the intellectual climate of the time, whose leading representatives acknowledged in *Robert* not so much a loved and successful opera as a complete work of art, full of ideas. Although not a historical opera as such, *Robert* contained *couleur locale* and *couleur de temps* in rich measure, and especially a conflict of ideas that embraced the totality of human existence: tragic and comic, sublime and grotesque, good and bad, heaven and hell. If the adaptable Scribe had used the religiously tinctured pathos of the subject as a concession to the trends of the age, this certainly did not apply to Meyerbeer who was noticeably moved and artistically inspired by these features.

The new musical language of *Robert* can be characterized as a fusion of elements derived from the *tragédie lyrique*, the *opéra comique*, *mélodrame*, *Singspiel* and pre-Romantic ballet into an independent, eclectic and cosmopolitan style. This is actually a further development of existing elements and tendencies in the composer's *oeuvre* rather than a reaction to Rossini and Auber. The unprecedented pictorialism with which Meyerbeer's music conjured up people and situations grew out of a powerfully driven interaction of form, sound colour, motif and melody, pursued to the extreme. This was especially to do with the subject, where the novel configuration of ideas suggested a concise musical dramaturgy. This is most especially obvious in the development of the tableau—in *Robert* the governing principle shaping the musical dramatization. As far as the exposition is concerned, Meyerbeer needed only to carry forward the techniques that he had already perfected in his Italian operas. The *introduzione* is now broadened out to incorporate the entire first act. Two extensive complexes (the Bacchanale and the Gambling Scene), expansively structured, musically as well as scenically, constitute the frames of a single picture, each containing an interpolated solo number (Raimbaut's Ballad and Robert's Sicilienne), enclosing a central episode (Alice's Romance which in turn is the centre of her duo-colloquy with Robert).

This tableau unfolds the nature of the chief characters, exposing the underlying conflict of ideas as well as incorporating the important narrative pre-history, all the while presenting a contrasting and colourful picture of medieval chivalry. If the expositional dramaturgy of *Robert* represents the continuation of a development, then the elaboration of a corresponding dramaturgy of the finale broaches new ground. The impressionable effect of the conclusion is not built on the obvious *colpo di scena* of Bertram's descent into hell, but rather on the progressive preparatory stages of events as they unfold in Act 5, with the big trio for Alice, Robert and Bertram ('Que faut-il faire?') (What should I do?) providing both the highpoint and closure of the drama. The musical process unfolds out of the situation and brings the conflict of ideas in the piece to a highpoint, with the contrasting of the three protagonists (first presented in relation to each other in Act 1, and again in Act 3), peaking for the last time in what is almost pictorial symbolism, and imparting to the scene an irresistible undercurrent.

The social background to the action is depicted in Acts 2 and 4. Often criticized, these actually form the backbone of the work to which the individual holds fast, is soothed or invited to take up counter-positions. There is a dominating concept of norms in each act, forcing the individual into specific frames of reference: *Mars et l'Amour—Dans la noble carrière il faut vaincre ou mourir* (Mars and Amor—where the banner waves there is only victory or death). The alternatives are love or violence. The tournament (*tunier*) in Act 2 (Mars) is an image of latent aggression, of controlled violence, that dominates this medieval society—war games that at any time could suddenly turn into actual violence. The second finale is controlled by the devil and his delusions, present in the necromantic Prince of Granada and his motif, and growing out of that melodic germ, the tournament theme itself, 'La trompette guerrière' (Let the war trumpets sound). If correctly realized musically and dramatically, the conclusion to the act can seem like a vortex into the abyss.

Illustration 5.1b *Robert le Diable*: costume designs for Robert, Alice, Isabelle and
      Bertram (engravings by Alexandre Maleuvre)

In Act 4 (Amour) the panorama of society is widened and complemented in a mixture of fairytale and the grotesque, confusing nightmare and clear consciousness. The choruses of ladies and courtiers that open the act are in opposition to the demonic *choeur dansée* that closes Act 3. The latter represents chaos, the former closed rituals of marriage. The conforming female type (Isabelle) is tacitly juxtaposed with the rebellious (the Abbess Helena). In Act 4 the authors went further than ever in devising grotesque situations. State and court process in with gifts for the princess, the formalities reducing the wedding rituals to a mechanical process. The devil and his delusion are again the controlling feature in Robert's magic branch which causes the assembled society to fall into sleep, leaving Isabelle open to abduction and rape, the violation of all social norms and rituals. The branch becomes an object for action, a catalyst opening up psychological and social circumstances. Through it, all the courtiers, concerned with appearance and position, are put into a new and strange perspective. With the breaking of the branch, the destructive potential in society bursts forth. The circle of their order and ceremony is destroyed, and all press down on Robert. The music of the extended ensemble finale depicts how each strikes against the other. Uncontrolled mass hysteria ensues, unorganized and discharged randomly (Möller and Berg 1989).

Meyerbeer is the master of scenic dialectic. In this Act 4 finale, the peripeteia of the drama, Robert must count Isabelle as lost by logical, earthly law, but he receives her back through grace, since he renounces black magic and breaks the enchanted branch. By using the branch, he had wanted to force what was no longer available to him without violence. The conjuration by the magic branch (the petrification of the festive gathering and the rule of law), and the breaking of the branch (the release from the magic slumber and the onslaught of the outraged social tumult that breaks over Robert) are the impulses driving the action forward. And the contrasting tableaux of the surface action—the opposition between immobility and uproar—correspond to the deep dialectic of the inner structure: Robert loses Isabelle when he tries to take her by force, but wins her back when he appears to lose her by the renunciation of violence (Döhring on the dramaturgy of Grand Opéra in Zimmermann 1991: 174). The advent of grace in the enacted parable of a Gospel teaching (cf. Mark 8: 35) make the underlying analogy of the morality play both a determinative structural and thematic principle of the opera.

The search for greater dramatic coherence and musical continuity means that recitative takes on a fuller, independent life of its own, with the orchestra providing a continuous and pointed punctuation and commentary. This is nowhere better seen than in the treatment of Robert himself. He is present in all the acts, but does not have a single extended aria of his own. Nonetheless, his feckless, ambiguous, impulsive and fated personality emerges immediately in Act 1, and nowhere more memorably than in his words about Bertram: 'Je lui dus la victoire et perdue le bonheur' (I owed my victory to him but lost all my happiness), where an exultant fanfare is abruptly cut short by a theme of sadness underscored by the diminished fourth. In these seven bars about victory and loss, Meyerbeer succinctly presents the whole theme of the opera: the conflict between heaven and hell, light and darkness, society and individual, the public and private realms and their demands (ex. 5.1a).

Later, when Robert is tempted to gamble away even his armour, his sense of doomed helplessness is captured in his sad observation with its wistful oboe commentary

('Dans mon destin funeste') (Into my dismal fate). Similarly, Bertram reveals his sinister yet ambiguous relationship to Robert, and his own anguished consciousness, in the words 'Tu ne sauras jamais à quel excès je t'aime' (You cannot imagine how much I love you), the eight bars charged with tenderness and distress. The characterization is continued in the trio of the Valse infernale, where Bertram alone sings of his satanic anguish at his unrealizable love for his son whom he must damn. The phrase is ample, ardent and luminous ('De ma gloire éclipsée, de ma splendeur passée, toi seule me consolais c'est par toi que j'aimais') (You alone consoled me for my eclipsed glory, for my faded splendour, it is through you that I have loved).

The legendary Cloister Scene of Act 3 Scene 3 made opera and ballet history. The dance here is not an interpolation extraneous to the action but an essential element of the drama and not detachable from the scenic context without loss of dramatic coherence. Robert, like Bertram at the beginning of the scene, sings some recitative on his entry, but has a miming role for the rest of the act. The message of Romanticism (according to Ivor Guest 1966: 112) transmitted through this scene lies in the totality of the fantastic, brought about through the perfect cooperation of all the theatrical elements. Meyerbeer devised a glassy, alien, elfin music of diabolical elegance (with its recurrent downward runs) and langour (especially in the Séduction par l'amour with its voluptuous cello solo), which moves on points, piano/pianissimo for long stretches, until the spectacular final choral attack when the dance is revealed for what it is, the demons emerge and the nuns become phantoms again.

Example 5.1a   *Robert le Diable*: Robert's recitative (Act 1)

Illustration 5.1c *Robert le Diable*: the Cloister Scene in Act 3 at Her Majesty's Theatre (from the *Illustrated London News*, 1847)

In envisioning the crucial Cloister Scene, the Wolf's Glen episode in *Der Freischütz* (1821) must have presented itself as a model. In this opera the young hero and his evil genius confront the powers of darkness while forging the magic bullets: the satanic seems to infuse and control nature itself, as at each casting, some natural phenomenon takes place, always with incremental intensity, until eventually all the elements seem caught up and convulsed, as a great tempest breaks out at the appearance of the Black Huntsman. Nature and local mythology are fused in the process of exploring a psychological process. Meyerbeer, in depicting his confrontation, eschewed a direct presentation of hell, preferring initially to elicit *frisson* through the acoustical impression of distance and depth (from the cavern of St Irene). The invisible chorus of demons make present the dark forces (like those at the beginning of the Wolf's Glen), but their otherness is emphasized by the spatial dimension, as they sing through speaking-trumpets positioned under the prompter's box where they produced an eerie, undefined sound. In *Freischütz* the forces of darkness seem to gradually infest the natural world; in *Robert*, despite the tempest that erupts when Bertram descends into the cavern, nature remains essentially a neutral playground, and horror is found in people themselves. In this way the companionable popular dance of bourgeois society becomes the vector of inverted values, deformed into the Valse Infernale (ex. 5.1b).

Example 5.1b   *Robert le Diable*: the Valse Infernale (Act 3)

The Valse is built quite regularly, with main theme and trio as appropriate to the correct form, but begins with the twofold repetition of an obsessive and intransigent four-note rhythmical motif that announces something new: a sound gesture that, through colour, motif and instrumentation, takes the place of hitherto pleasing formal and melodic expectations of the classical movement. The muffled stage band of trumpet, horn and trombone, with skirling piccolos, provides the alienating sound, while the formal unfolding is suddenly curtailed with brutal force by the tempest that accompanies Bertram's descent. In Weber's opera, wild Romantic nature, almost anthropomorphized, can be either an invitation to the transcendent (as in Agathe's two arias) or the locus of dark forces (as in the Wolf's Glen). In Meyerbeer's it is not so much nature as the desolated monastery that carries the symbolic burden: here are the ruins of history, the wreck of human endeavour and idealism. The confrontation with the powers of darkness is about the dissolution of the socially and spiritually proven, whole and reassuring, the questioning of an entire set of historical and metaphysical presuppositions (Zimmermann 1991: 178–9).

Sound colour also becomes a dramaturgical agent, not just providing the *couleur* of the scene, but also clarifying the central conflict. Here Meyerbeer could also relate to Weber's *Der Freischütz*, although the task for Meyerbeer was more difficult. One cannot simply present the conflict of ideas in the piece as a light–dark antithesis. It was necessary to differentiate a basic colour for the demonic in multifarious ways, analogous to the dramatic dominance of Bertram. This happens through a spectrum of sound that amounts to a *Leitklang* (leading sound) (clarinet and bassoon in the lower registers, horn, trumpet, trombone, ophicleide, drums, tamtam), whose differentiated combinations precisely characterize the varying manifestations of the demonic in form of the *chevaleresque* (Raimbaut's ballad, the entrances of the Herald and the Prince of Granada) or the spectral (the Cloister and Slumber Scenes). Opposed to this is the *ton céleste* pertaining to Alice (flute, oboe, clarinet in higher register, strings), which in Act 5 (the Church Scene) receives a sacred dimension through the use of the organ.

Illustration 5.1d *Robert le Diable*: Marie Taglioni and Adolphe Nourrit in the Ballet
of the Nuns (contemporary engraving, 1831)

Specific moods characterize the world of knights and ladies, affirming a Romantic dream of the Middle Ages in the choruses and dances, and especially in Isabelle's melancholically inflected entrance aria in Act 2 ('En vain j'espère') (In vain do I hope). The dramaturgy of sound colour is concentrated into two motifs, both belonging to Bertram's sphere of action, and whose appearances at decisive moments in the action indirectly evoke the power of evil working in secret. One springs from Raimbaut's Ballad in Act 1 ('Jadis régnait en Normandie') (Once there reigned in Normandy), which develops a portrait of the demon in the chromatic tincture of hell. The recurrence of this theme at key moments in Acts 1 and 5 (the first meeting of Alice and Bertram; Bertram's confession to Robert) gives the dramatic idea a concrete perspective. In this respect the piece appears as the direct harbinger of Senta's ballad in Wagner's *Der fliegende Holländer* (1843) with which it also shares similar musical details (a three-strophe layout with resolution on the last strophe; the melodic-rhythmical structure of the beginning of the theme). A further accentuation of the demonic colours is achieved through the theme of the Prince of Granada (Acts 2, 3, 4), whose pointed instrumentation (four kettle drums and double-bass) effectively underscores the phantasmal manifestation. The overture, based on the fanfare theme of Bertram's Evocation, anticipates the dramatic leading thought and fundamental colour of the work in its knotted counterpoint and cold atmosphere, and established the type of the short monothematic prelude so popular in the nineteenth century.

Also markedly forward-looking was the creation of several melodies which unfold their specific effectiveness only in the context of a musical movement structured by a dramatic idea. Melodic structure widens from the recitative and develops into free arioso, as in Bertram's Act 3 Evocation ('Nonnes qui reposez' leading to 'Roi des enfers') (You nuns who rest...king of the underworld), or sees the lyrical line emerging from heightened declamation into impassioned lyricism, as in Isabelle's Act 4 cavatina ('Robert, toi que j'aime' leading to 'Grace pour toi même') (Robert whom I love...mercy for yourself).

One can hardly overestimate the influence of *Robert* on nineteenth-century opera. This ranges musically from early Verdi up to the *nuova scuola italiana*, and dramaturgically from Wagner's *Tannhäuser* (1845), Gounod's *Faust* (1859) and Bizet's *Carmen* (1875) to Korngold's *Die tote Stadt* (1920). Certain aspects of the score introduced a new dramatic orchestral language that later became common operatic currency. An instance is provided by the Gambling Scene in the Act 1 finale where the throwing of the dice is represented in an orchestral figure where the tremolando strings and pianissimo trombones hold the chord of the diminished seventh, followed by a shrill wisp of a rising chord on woodwind, a silence then a pizzicato comment from the strings (ex. 5.1c [a]). Such effects are found throughout the rest of the century—as in the storms in *Macbeth* (1847) and *Rigoletto* (1851), or the Card Scene in *Carmen*. The same is true of the chorus of monks that opens Act 5 of *Robert*: a mixture of heavy chordal dotted rhythms and triplets, mounting octave phrases of the basses in unison with the voices, and a climax on the dominant seventh. This was so much imitated as to become a theatrical mannerism, found in the Miserere of *Il trovatore* (1853) and Violetta's death in *La traviata* (1853), or in the priests who condemn Radames in the last act of *Aïda* (1871) (ex. 5.1c [b]).

Example 5.1c   *Robert le Diable*: a) the dice motif from the Act 1 finale,
          b) the Monks' Chorus (Act 5)

The trio in the last act of *Robert* is the model for many others, most especially in Wagner's *Der fliegende Holländer* and Gounod's *Faust*. The role and music of Micaëla in Bizet's *Carmen*, in relation to Don José and Carmen, echoes that of the saintly Alice, standing between Robert and Bertram. Meyerbeer's opera concludes that phase of operatic history leading to the final formulation of *grand opéra*. It also constitutes, in its thematic and dramaturgical aspects, the link between *Der Freischütz* and *Der fliegende Holländer*. The thematically crucial ballad is the most obvious aspect of this, especially for the Wagner opera, but so is the wider symbolic action of the quest for redemption. This influence is palpable in the whole movement of *Tannhäuser* (1845), but also in *Parsifal* (1882) where the hero and the Flower Maidens in Klingsor's Garden is exactly analogous to Robert and the Nuns in the Cloister Scene—even down to the choice and symbolic alignment of changing tonalities (see Keller 1971).

Illustration 5.1e   *Robert le Diable*: painting by François-Gabriel Lépaulle of the Act 5 trio

Even technical breakdowns on stage could not compromise the successful premiere of *Robert*. The fantastical equipment, the *mise en scène* with new lighting effects in the Cloister Scene, and the extraordinary casting (with Laure Cinti-Damoreau as Isabelle, Julie Dorus-Gras as Alice, Adolphe Nourrit as Robert, Nicolas-Prosper Levasseur as Bertram, Marcelin Lafont as Raimbaut, and Marie Taglioni as the Abbess Helena) resulted in a theatrical experience that propelled the genre of opera into the centre of contemporary artistic discussion in France and soon all over Europe. The continual run of 758 performances, which, with breaks only in 1869, 1875 and 1880, lasted until 1893, resulted in a distancing from the aesthetic presuppositions of its creation, at first hardly noticeable, but later ever more obvious. After only a few performances there were changes in the casting with the role of Helena: the ethereal Marie Taglioni was replaced with Pauline Duvernay, technically just as perfect but lacking the aura of her predecessor. Marie-Cornélie Falcon's assumption of Alice in 1832 imprinted a more dramatic interpretation on future assumptions of this role. The tenor Mario's debut as Robert in 1838 brought a more Italianate interpretation to the part. Meyerbeer moreover composed expressly for him a Scène et Prière ('Ou me cacher...Oh! ma mère ombre si tendre') (Where shall I hide...O my mother, gentle spirit), an interpolation (for the beginning of Act 2) that significantly altered the idiom of the character. When Gilbert Duprez, with his favoured promotion of the chest register, assumed the part in 1840, he introduced a more dramatic but rougher type of character. There were other outstanding debuts in the following decades: as Isabelle—Constance Jawureck 1832, Maria Nau 1836,

Anne-Caroline Lagrange 1848; as Alice—Mlle Treillet-Nathan 1842; Emma La Grua 1852, Jeanne-Sophie-Charlotte Cruvelli 1854; as Robert—Lafont 1835, Italo Gardoni 1845; as Bertram—Prosper Dérivis 1832, Hippolyte Brémond 1842, Adolphe Alizard 1847; as Helena—Amélie Legallois and Louise Fitzjames 1832, Flora Fabbri-Bretin 1845, Célestine Emarot 1847.

A spectacular new production was prepared in 1860, for which Meyerbeer sanctioned a series of cuts. The cast included Caroline Duprez, Marie-Constance Sass, Louis Gueymard and Belval. In 1865 Marie Battu and Eugénie Mauduit made their debuts as Isabelle and Alice respectively—roles they maintained over many years. Another fresh production appeared in 1876 in the new Salle Garnier: by now the singers embodied types of voices that were not appropriate for the roles: Caroline Carvalho (Isabelle) was a light coloratura soprano, Gabrielle Krauss (Alice) a dramatic soprano, while Marius Salomon (Robert) and Auguste-Acanthe Boudouresque (Bertram) represented the heavy tenor and bass types. Laure Fonta danced Helena. Among the more notable interpreters at the Opéra towards the end of the century were Adèle Isaac (Isabelle 1884), Marie-Lureau Escalaïs (Isabelle 1883, Alice 1884), Josephine de Reszke (Alice 1878), Léon Gresse (Bertram 1886), and especially Léonce Escalaïs (Robert 1884) who once again brought to the title role a virtuoso vocal brilliance cognizant of the original traditions.

Robert rapidly spread over all the stages of the world. In the productions sanctioned by Meyerbeer himself in 1832 for London (the Haymarket Theatre) and Berlin, Meyerbeer accepted both musical and scenic changes which found some reflection in the printed score. London had the same casting as the Paris premiere (with the exception of Joséphine de Méric as Alice and Thérèse Heberle as Helena). In Berlin the outstanding Pauline von Schätzel (as Alice) and Taglioni (as Helena) provided the strongest interpretations. The success of the Berlin production saw the first sharp opposition of nationally-minded critics who denounced the cosmopolitan nature of the composition as 'immoral'. Other important regional productions followed: Vienna 1833 (with Sophie Lowe, Marianne Katharina Ernst, Hermann Breiting and Joseph Staudigl); Prague 1834 (with Jenny Lutzer, Katharina Podhorsky, Friedrich Demmer and Karel Strakaty); Florence 1840 (with Sophie Méquillet, and later, Mariana Barbieri-Nini as Isabelle; Maschinka Schubert, and later, Teresa Brambilla-Ponchielli as Alice). The latter production by Alessandro Lanari marked the beginning of the Italian reception of Meyerbeer's French operas and was a catalyst in the contemporary aesthetical debate on the reform of the *melodramma*. Other productions were also notable for their casting: Her Majesty's Theatre in London in 1847 (with Jenny Lind as Alice and Staudigl as Bertram); St Petersburg in 1848 (Teresa De Giuli Borsi, Erminia Frezzolini); Covent Garden, London in 1850 (Giulia Grisi, Jeanne-Anaïs Castellan, Enrico Tamberlik and Karl Johann Formes); Genoa in 1852 (Marcella Lotti Dalla Santa as Isabelle); Madrid in 1853 (Clara Novello as Alice); Vienna in 1854 (Mathilde Wildauer, Therese Tietjens, Joseph Erl, Staudigl, with Leopoldine Brussi as Helena) and 1870 (Maria von Rabatinsky, Marie Wilt, Georg Müller, Carl Schmid, with Guglielmina Salvioni as Helena); Deutsches Theater, Prague, in 1891 (in the context of Angelo Neumann's Meyerbeer Centenary Cycle, with Betty Fink, Marie Rochelle, Adolf Wallnöfer, Georg Sieglitz, and Marie Diem as Helena).

At the turn of the century, with post-Wagnerian music drama and verismo determining public taste, understanding of the qualities of style needed for *Robert* disappeared in tandem with the inability to meet the demands of casting. Nonetheless, productions at this time could still impress with good singers, even if they were not the authentic vocal types required, as can be seen from the Berlin staging of 1902 which aimed at recovering something of the original intention (Emilie Herzog, Ida Hielder, Wilhelm Grüning, Rudolf Wittekopf, with Richard Strauss conducting). After 1900, productions of *Robert* became rare events: Théâtre Gaité-Lyrique, Paris, in 1911 (with Escalaïs as Robert); Hamburg in 1917 (with Martha Winternitz-Dorda, Vera Schwartz, Richard Schubert, Max Lohfing, conducted by Karl Alwin); Volksoper, Vienna in 1921 (with Hedwig von Debicka, Rena Pfiffer, Albin von Rittersheim, Leo Kaplan, conducted by Felix Weingartner). (See Loewenberg 1970: 736–8; Wolff 1962: 184–6; Döhring 1991, 4:128–9.)

Revival began only towards the end of the century: Maggio Musicale Fiorentino, Florence 1968 (with Renato Scotto, Stefania Malagù, Giorgio Merighi, Boris Christoff, conducted by Nino Sanzogno) was a significant event, but was vitiated musically and dramaturgically by disfiguring cuts. The 1980s continued this revival with a production at Reading University in 1981. The return of *Robert* to the Opéra in 1985 occurred as part of a slow re-evaluation of Meyerbeer, and was characterized by an ensemble who showed themselves understanding and capable of the stylistic and technical demands of the roles (June Anderson, Michèle Lagrange, Alain Vanzo/ Rockwell Blake, Samuel Ramey, with Thomas Fulton conducting). The effects of a lavish stage conception were consistently undercut by parody, especially in the famous Cloister Scene. A scholarly reconstruction of Taglioni's Ballet of the Nuns was undertaken in 1985 by Knud Arne Jürgensen for the London Studio Centre. A concert performance followed in New York 1988 (with Chris Merritt as Robert and Samuel Ramey as Bertram, conducted by Eve Queler).

Three important revivals marked the turn of the millennium. The first was at the State Opera in Prague in 1999 (with Valerij Popov as Robert and Ulf Paulsen as Bertram)—a badly cut version but in richly evocative sets like a medieval tapestry. Then the opera was staged at the Staatoper Berlin in 2000/2001 (with Nelly Miricioiu as Isabelle, Marina Mescheriakova as Alice, Jianyi Zhang as Robert, Kwangchul Youn as Bertram, conducted by Marc Minkowski), using a critical edition of the score, but in an alienating production by Georg Quander in which any attempt at exploring the underlying symbolism was beset with gimmickry. A full version of the printed score and a more conventional staging characterized the production at Martina Franca, also in 2000 (with Patrizia Ciofi as Alice, Annalisa Raspagliosi as Isabelle, Warren Mok as Robert, Giorgio Surjan as Bertram, conducted by Renato Palumbo). None of these productions fully realized the vocal requirements of these roles, and hardly evinced a deeper understanding of the thematic issues.

5.2 *Les Huguenots [The Huguenots]*

Opéra en cinq actes [opera in five acts]
Text: Augustin-Eugène Scribe and Emile Deschamps (with additional ideas, revisions
and words by Gaetano Rossi, Adolphe Nourrit and Giacomo Meyerbeer)
First performance: Opéra, Salle de la rue Le Peletier, Paris, 29 February 1836

Soon after *Robert le Diable* (1831) Meyerbeer turned to his next operatic project.
Several plans were considered and rejected, among them *Le Brigand* (text by
Alexandre Dumas and Scribe) and *Le Portefaix* (Scribe). Eventually, plans for a
five-act *grand opéra* focused on the historical events surrounding the massacre of St
Bartholomew's Night: *Léonore ou La St Barthélemy*, the first panel of Meyerbeer's
Reformation diptych, again by Scribe. A contract was signed with the director of the
Opéra, Louis-Désiré Véron on 23 October 1832, with production scheduled for the
beginning of 1834. After reading Act 1, Meyerbeer raised objections to the text on
the grounds that it lacked the evocation of the authentic atmosphere of the chosen
epoch (*BT*, 2:232). Already at the planning stage he had begun textual and musical
studies of the historical milieu, an indication of the new qualitative way in which
he intended to realize a historical opera. In the certainty that Scribe's text did not
offer the requested options, he decided to break the composition, incurring thereby
the financial penalty stipulated in the contract, and in October 1833 travelled to
Italy. In Milan he met up with his old friend and colleague, the librettist Rossi, in
order to think through the whole project very thoroughly. The most important result
of their common deliberations was the transformation of the role of Marcel, whom
Meyerbeer raised to the actual protagonist and idealist of the action. In this context
he decided to employ Martin Luther's famous Reformation chorale *Ein' feste Burg
ist unser Gott* (1528) as the musical emblem of the epoch and its religious issues
(Becker 1981: 84).

On his return to Paris, Meyerbeer was silent about Rossi's collaboration and,
with Scribe's permission, had the new Italian passages (which he presented as his
own) translated into French by Emile Deschamps. Meyerbeer continued to work
further on the text with Deschamps, and an extant copy from the middle of 1834
indicates the composer's many changes, insertions and comments. Act 3 received a
new first scene (that would be cut later) set in Saint-Bris's Paris hotel from which
Valentine observes an attempted assassination of Admiral Coligny in the streets (see
Böhmel and Zimmermann 1973). After signing a new contract with the Opéra on
29 September 1834, other alterations were made in response to suggestions from
Edmond Duponchel who was to be responsible for the *mise en scène*. Because of
the length of the work Meyerbeer was obliged to cut out some three-quarters of
an hour of music from three acts (cuts reflected in the autograph). Other changes
were necessitated by the objections of the censor and by the suggestions of
Adolphe Nourrit, the creator of Raoul, for the duet in Act 4. While Meyerbeer,
after initial hesitation, went along with Nourrit's suggestion for a new version of
the middle part of the duet, thereby deepening important musical and dramatic
elements, he saw the intervention of the censor as threatening to the work. After
wearying discussions, the censor insisted on a change of title and on cutting

Catherine de Medici's part in the Blessing of the Daggers. Meyerbeer was obliged to redraft the role for a bass voice (Saint-Bris) (Döhring 1982: 48).

The events of St Bartholomew's Eve had received several literary treatments over the centuries. In these earlier presentations interest was focused on the psychology of the characters, but, later, concern for the social and political constellation of the conflict came more to the fore. During the 1820s the topic became almost a literary fashion. Novels, dramas and essays were written about the event as an example in the controversy about the nature of the state and the issue of religious tolerance, so characteristic of the last days of the Restoration. Neither Scribe nor Meyerbeer made any precise allusion to the origin of the material. Scribe certainly used historical presentations as sources (Walter 1987: 22–46). Typical of the contemporary practice of librettists, he also drew inspiration for certain characters and situations, as well as ideas for the *couleur* of the epoch, from literary sources, most especially Prosper Merimée's novel *Chronique du temps de Charles IX* (which first appeared anonymously in 1829). The complex process of revision, however, increasingly distanced the opera from any historical and literary models, characterizing it as a deeply individual work of art in its own right.

Plot
Touraine and Paris, August 1572.

Act 1. A hall in the chateau of the Comte de Nevers in Touraine. In the background a view of the gardens. The count has invited a group of friendly nobles to a banquet on the eve of his marriage. Among the guests still expected is a young Huguenot, Raoul de Nangis. In response to sceptical questions from the Catholic gentlemen, Nevers tells them that this invitation is intended as sign of reconciliation, echoing what is happening at the highest level with the forthcoming marriage between Marguerite de Valois and Henry of Navarre. The gentlemen remain doubtful of any peace. Raoul enters, full of admiration for the splendid assembly. The party then repairs to the table. As an entertainment, it is decided that each of the guests should speak of their love experiences, beginning with Raoul. He tells of his meeting with an unknown beauty whom he defended from the unwanted attentions of some unruly students. He has never been able to forget her. Raoul's old servant Marcel now appears, and upbraids his young master for consorting with the enemy. The stern old soldier takes exception to the loose talk of the hedonistic revellers and seeks comfort in prayer, intoning Luther's hymn as a statement of faith. He then provocatively sings an old Huguenot battle song about the siege of La Rochelle, to the amusement of the guests. Nevers is called away to see a veiled lady, while the gentlemen secretly observe the meeting through an oriel window. Raoul in consternation recognizes her as the mysterious lady of his adventure. All presume her to be Nevers's latest mistress. In a soliloquy Nevers reveals the actual situation: she is his betrothed, the noblewoman Valentine de Saint-Bris, lady-in-waiting to Marguerite de Valois, who has asked him to release her from their engagement so that she can assist in the royal plan for national reconciliation. Although in chagrin, he has magnanimously agreed, being a man of honour. He returns to his guests who congratulate him on his new 'conquest'. The page Urbain now enters with a message from a noble lady for one of the guests. To everyone's surprise it turns out to be Raoul, who is invited to attend a secret meeting, blindfolded. The knights have recognized the queen's seal and suddenly become obsequious and deferential towards Raoul, who is more mystified than ever. They send him on his way joyfully, assuring him that honours and riches await him.

Act 2. The chateau and gardens of Chenonceaux near Ambroise. On the right a broad staircase leads to the chateau. The gardens lead down to the River Loire. Marguerite de Valois, with her ladies, celebrates the idyllic beauty of the place and prays that all religious hatred be kept away. The queen receives Valentine who tells her of the positive outcome of her visit to Nevers. Marguerite, notorious for the amorous pleasures of her court, but politically concerned with finding compromise, is pursuing a plan to further reconciliation by arranging a marriage between scions of leading families from the rival parties: in this case the Catholic Valentine and the Protestant Raoul. This is in accord with Valentine's wish since she has loved Raoul since their first meeting. Marguerite reveals that she has summoned him here in pursuance of her plan. Raoul approaches, led blindfolded through the garden. When he meets Marguerite, he is entranced by her beauty and places himself at her service. Although the queen is herself attracted to Raoul, and would not be averse to a little amorous adventure, she has pledged him to marriage with Valentine. When the court and various Catholic and Protestant notabilities have assembled, she puts the proposal of marriage to him, and all swear a vow of peace. Marguerite's attempted compromise is, however, doomed to failure: when Valentine is brought out, Raoul recognizes his unknown beauty, and the apparent mistress of Nevers. To Valentine's consternation, Raoul, feeling dishonoured, insultingly rejects her hand, fervently supported by Marcel. A confrontation ensues, and only Marguerite's presence prevents an open battle between the parties.

Act 3. Paris, the famous Pré-aux-Clercs on the banks of the Seine. On the right is an inn; on the left is another inn, with a chapel. It is approaching evening. People are still promenading in their Sunday best. The Huguenot soldiery in Paris, with Admiral Coligny, enjoy a drink in their inn. A cortège of young Catholic women conduct Valentine to the chapel where she wishes to spend the evening in prayer after her marriage to Nevers, who had renewed his betrothal with her after her rejection by Raoul. When the drunken Protestant soldiery mock the Marian hymn of the Catholics, a street confrontation develops, and violence is again circumvented only by the distraction of a group of Gypsies who tell fortunes and dance. Raoul and Marcel are now retained in the service of the queen. Marcel appears to deliver a challenge to Saint-Bris for the insult Raoul has sustained. Saint-Bris conspires with Maurevert to have his opponent killed by an ambush. Valentine, hidden in the chapel, has overheard the plot, and in order to warn Raoul whom she still loves, overcoming her family and party loyalties, she approaches Marcel, who is keeping vigil outside the chapel until the duel, and warns him of the plot. He is initially inimical, but is so moved by Valentine's goodness that he blesses her. She disappears back into the chapel, and the contestants, each with two seconds, enter and confront each other. As the duel begins, Marcel is able to summon help from the Huguenots in the inn. The tumult brings the Catholics out from the other inn, and a street brawl ensues. Only the return of Marguerite to the Louvre stops the uproar. Both Raoul and Saint-Bris accuse each other of treachery, but Marcel's account of the strange woman's warning solves the dilemma. Saint-Bris pulls off her veil to reveal his daughter. Only now does Raoul realize the mistake he has made. Nevers arrives on the Seine, in a festive bark, to conduct his wife home. Under the general nuptial celebrations the Catholics and Protestants menace each other.

Act 4. A room in the city palace of the Comte de Nevers. Family portraits hang on the walls. In the background are a door and a Gothic window. To the left is the door to Valentine's room; to the right a fireplace and tapestry. Valentine grieves about her arranged marriage and her sorrow over Raoul whom she still loves. He comes secretly to seek her out and beg her forgiveness. They hear steps, and she hides him behind the Gobelin. Saint-Bris enters with great authority, accompanied by prominent members of the Catholic party. He is enjoined on command of the king and his mother to present a plan for the salvation of the land—the extirpation of the Huguenots—and to receive their vow of complicity. Only Nevers refuses to join the conspiracy and is taken away under arrest. Saint-Bris explains the details of the plot: at midnight the bell of St Germain Auxerrois will be the signal for the Catholics to begin a massacre of the Protestants. Monks enter and solemnly bless the weapons of murder, while identifying white scarves are distributed. After the conspirators have departed, Raoul, having overheard all the details, comes out of hiding, determined to warn his co-religionists. Valentine is determined to hold him back from death, and reveals the depth of her love. Raoul is caught up in ecstasy, and for a moment forgets his duty in the fervour of their mutual confession. Only the tolling bell brings him back to reality. They see the carnage beginning in the street, and, despite Valentine's desperate pleading, he leaps from the window into the night.

Act 5. Scene 1. A brilliant ballroom in the Hotel Nesle where the marriage of Marguerite de Valois and Henry of Navarre is being celebrated. The dancing is interrupted by distant pealing of bells, but resumes. Raoul, covered in blood, appears. He tells the shocked assembly of the massacre, and urges the Huguenots present to avenge the murder of Coligny. Aghast, the guests hurry from the hall.

Scene 2. A cemetery adjoining a Protestant church, with the entry to the left, and a grille on the right, looking on to the street. It is in the early hours. Raoul and Marcel enter in the wake of a crowd of fleeing women and children who seek sanctuary in the church. Valentine soon follows them, looking for her beloved. She is free, since Nevers has been murdered by his own party. She urges Raoul to take a white scarf and flee with her to Marguerite who will protect them if he changes his faith. After a brief struggle, Raoul rejects this escape plan. Valentine, in despair, says she will become a Protestant out of her love for him. In the hour of death Marcel blesses their union against the hushed prayers of the refugees. A group of Catholic assassins break into the church and begin shooting the women and children. Marcel, Valentine and Raoul decide to prepare for death as martyrs, and are wounded in volley of shots.

Illustration 5.2a *Les Huguenots*: costume designs for Urbain, Raoul, Valentine and
Marcel (engravings by Alfred Albert, 1836)

Scene 3. A Parisian street with starlit sky. Marcel and Valentine support the
wounded Raoul, but are challenged by another party of assassins led by Saint-Bris.
They declare themselves Huguenots, and are shot down. Saint-Bris recognizes his
own daughter, who in dying forgives her father. Queen Marguerite, returning to the
Louvre in her litter, tries in vain to stop the horror.

'...The fable is almost invented, and only the epoch and the actual conclusion of
the piece are historical.' Meyerbeer's description of the material on the basis of
the first draft of the libretto (see his letter of 10 October 1832) characterizes the
contemporary principles used in constructing historical novels and dramas. The
factual elements of history lend poetic fiction the appearance of authenticity, and
in this way raise their effectiveness. Mérimée's *Chronique*, like other novels and
dramas of the period, illustrates the point that the historical in a literary context
had achieved a wider, enriching function. The reconstruction of a past epoch was
no longer only the means, but the very aim of literary presentation. No longer, as
previously, was the fictional moment avoided, but on the whole it had become more
empirical, more scientific. The historical medium was moreover the context for a
more specific, if tacit, discourse on faith that is the consistent subtext to the surface
action. In *Les Huguenots* the Romantic simplicity of *Robert le Diable* is lost in the
turmoil of the Reformation and Counter-Reformation. Internal division and conflict
has compromised the ability of the Christian faith to confront evil and has made it a
source of many wicked acts. It has been left to the actions of individuals to overcome
prejudice and division—in this case the figure of the heroine Valentine, who is vital
in bringing about a change of heart in key figures. Ultimately, however, even the

noble and good individuals are swept up in the tide of hatred spawned by bigotry, and are killed in its violent consequences. Thus, religion in its organized expression has become a source of evil and the destruction of good rather than a means of grace as in *Robert le Diable*. This is conveyed powerfully by the contrasting use of the bell motif in the two operas. In *Robert* the tolling of the church bell is a sign of the breaking of enchantment and a source of grace for both the hero and those around him. In *Les Huguenots* the church bells have been transformed into a grotesque contradiction of their holy use in *Robert*: here they signal the start of the massacre of the Protestants.

With *Les Huguenots* a new historicizing tendency received its major realization on the operatic stage. The sources show that it was Meyerbeer, and not Scribe, who must be regarded as the creator of such a historical opera. His participation in the shaping of the libretto was aimed purposefully at the restructuring of the play of intrigue, as Scribe had originally planned it, into a historical drama of ideas. This method of structuring a musico-dramatic context according to an idea had already been developed to a degree of some perfection by Meyerbeer in *Robert le Diable*. But while the intrigue in *Robert* depends on a traditional sense of dramatic structure, the parallel action in *Huguenots* necessitates a structural mix of drama and epic. Meyerbeer's textual interference, especially in the first three acts, lays the ground for a new dramaturgy. The illustrative genre scenes as Scribe had originally conceived them become broad historical panoramas that provide a differentiated picture of social life in France on the eve of St Bartholomew's Night in which the forthcoming catastrophe is sketched and prefigured in threatening shadows (Frese 1970: 136). Private action (Queen Marguerite's failed marriage plan) is motivated by the historical conflict, and not the other way round. In the finales to Acts 2 and 3, where the political and private spheres first collide, the assumptions of the historical events are exposed, and their consequences are then explored in the last two acts. In order to finalize his conceptions, Meyerbeer did not hesitate to push back the private dimension of the action in the first three acts, something that must have rubbed against the grain of the theatrical conventions of the time. This is particularly noticeable in the role of Valentine. In Scribe's draft she was to have been introduced by a romance in Act 1 and be part of a trio in Act 2. In the final version she enters silently in the first, and has only a short recitative in the second, until the finale when she comes into her own ('Et comment ai-je donc mérité tant d'outrage?') (How have I deserved such outrage?). Apart from her supple and beautiful romance at the beginning of Act 4 ('Parmi les pleures') (Amidst my tears), which was not always part of the conception of the work, Valentine does not have her own solo number. The need for abridgements just before the premiere encouraged Meyerbeer to strengthen this approach. Eventually in the first three acts alone he cut prominent solo and ensemble passages, as, for example, in the third finale which was reduced by a third of its original dimension.

All parts of the work are related to the historical–philosophical idea. So the knightly and courtly scenes of the first two acts unfold with colour and brilliance, the splendid spectacle of a feudal society doomed to perish (Miller 1985: 7). From the 'Court of Love' at Chenonceaux Queen Marguerite spins out her plan of marriage and reconciliation: its failure exposes it as the enlightened liberal Utopia of a repressive society.

The process of dissolution is mirrored in the dwindling vocal presence of Queen Marguerite. Her role is pared away, from the coloratura poise of her entrance aria ('O beau pays de la Touraine') (O beautiful land of Touraine) with echo effects that affirm a romantic and mannered world of artifice in Act 2, through the words of admonitory recitative and her fraught participation in the finales of Acts 2 and 3, to her silent appearance in Act 5, first in the deluded celebration of the ball, and then finally as the stricken and helpless witness of the bodies of the murdered Raoul and Valentine. The fortunes of the lovers parallel this retreat from the idyll of Chenonceaux. Raoul's Act 1 account of his first meeting with Valentine (the romance 'Plus blanche que la blanche hermine' [Whiter than the whitest ermine]), to which the viola d'amore imparts an unusual, sensuous timbre, conjuring up the genre and sound world of the troubadours, and his chivalrous bel canto courting of the Queen in Act 2 (the duet 'Beauté divine, enchanteresse' [Divine beauty, enchantress]) reveal his idealistic and gentlemanly nature.

Illustration 5.2b *Les Huguenots*: stage designs for Act 2 at the Paris Opéra (lithograph by Deshaye)

Meyerbeer's scenic dialectic and use of irony as a shaping aesthetic are very much in evidence in the Act 2 finale when attention moves from the almost hidden Court of Love to the public domain of national politics with the unfolding of the queen's plans for reconciliation.

The Court enter, sweeping down the great staircase of the gardens to a grandiose tempo di minuetto, with Marguerite stepping forward as the chivalrous portentousness is succeeded by another ceremonial theme, elegant and yet showy. This is the kind of brilliant public music that looks forward to Meyerbeer's essays in Court ritual and protocol embodied in his four *Fackeltänze* for the Prussian Royal family. In retrospect it can be seen that these same tones and rhythms of courtly deportment become the métier of murderous intent in Act 4. (See further discussion of this ceremonial music under '*Das Hoffest zu Ferrara*', p. 203).

The mood of expansive gesture continues but in a more restrained vein in the ensuing vow of friendship. All attempts at peace were doomed in this period, and it is significant that the promise is couched in a modality that belies its professed optimism. The C minor timpani rolls that sound in hollow dullness, and the great solemn chords on the horns pertain more to the funeral march. The voices are initially joined in a sign of unanimity, with the orchestra silent: but the words 'éternelle amitié' (eternal friendship) are uttered almost menacingly, descending as they do, by an octave to the lower notes to settle on the dominant (ex. 5.2a [a]). The form belies the content. It is hardly surprising when disillusionment and outrage take the place of optimistic endeavour.

When Raoul rejects Valentine, the whole orchestra holds a note of G fortissimo, before the chorus, soloists and orchestra whisper a chilling unison that is anything but unifying (ex. 5.2a [b]). The huge fast-moving ensemble that follows, generated from the melodic cell of Valentine's despair (ex. 5.2a [c]), is a frozen moment of contemplated fury, the concerted rage of the Catholic party opposed to the solo *Schadenfreude* of the gleeful Marcel with his *cantus firmus* variations on Luther's hymn.

Example 5.2a   *Les Huguenots*: from a) the Vow, and b–c) the Act 2 finale

Although Meyerbeer never expressed himself systematically about the creative process, several of his private statements about his *ästhetische point de vue* and his *dramatisches System* indicate that he was conscious in this work of having created a new conception of opera. At the heart of it stands the development of the chorale *Ein' feste Burg ist unser Gott* and its relation to the character of Marcel. Meyerbeer was well aware of the historical inaccuracy of using this Lutheran hymn as means of identifying a Calvinist movement, but this consideration seemed less important than the symbolic power of this melody to represent the spirit of militant faith in the century of religious wars ('I went into the Protestant church and listened to the canticles, the noble anthems, the simple and valiant hymns, half-martial and half-mystical, sacred relics from the heroic days of a faith already as old and as waning as our own,' is how George Sand expressed it in the eleventh of the *Lettres d'un voyageur*, 1837). When the chorale is first sung by Marcel at Nevers's banquet in Act 1, it appears, especially in relation to the subsequent *Chanson huguenote*, as part of the banner of religious fanaticism. This is equally true of Acts 2 and 3 where the melody functions as Marcel's battle cry. Only in Act 5, when the fate of the Huguenots is sealed, and Valentine, Raoul and Marcel have opted for martyrdom, does it take on new meaning, which in the light of its textual and musical shape can be understood in terms of a progressive sacralization. This process takes place in the Grand Trio which becomes the dramatic summa of the work. The chorale assumes a new dimension as a dirge, a prayer in the hour of death, sung by the women who have sought refuge in the church, and as the scene develops and the murders break into the sanctuary, it is deformed, with the melody alienated and broken. The last section of this development is the *Vision*, the final part of the trio, where, in the coda, the opening of the chorale is transformed in ever briefer sections like a montage through sequencing, diminution, contraction, and splitting into a crisp and affecting phrase ('Je ne crains rien de vous') (I fear nothing from you). This three-tone fragment becomes a motif integrating the Assassins' Chorus into the whole musical fabric ('Oui, renégrats, abjurez ou mourez') (Yes, renegades, abjure or die).

This compositional procedure, dramatizing the technique of motival variation, gives the musical process a symbolic dimension. That new interpretation of the sacred citation relates to the central idea of the work is indicated in the overture where just such variations on the chorale encrypt this process proleptically. The determined use of the chorale as a coded critique of religion emerges in the treatment of Marcel. Meyerbeer was aware of the unsettling novelty of this character: 'Marcel's role is worth more than all the other music that I composed in my life, including *Robert*. Whether he will be understood I do not know, I fear that initially he will not be' (letter of 15 September 1835).

Marcel's first entry characterizes him as a fanatical soldier of deep religious conviction, who rises to demonic greatness in the bizarre expression of the Act 1 *Chanson huguenote* ('Pour les couvents c'est fini') (All is finished for the convents). A similar profile marks his entry in Acts 2 and 3: his triumphant glee at the failure of Queen Marguerite's plan of reconciliation and his refusal to show reverence to the Marian procession stirs up the latent tension between Catholics and Protestants to simmering open conflict. Only in the course of Act 3 does the character assume some nobility. Fear for Raoul's safety breaks open the carapace of hatred, and allows paternal love to characterize his nature ('Ah! quel chagrin pour ma vieillesse') (Ah, what worry for my age). This moment of spiritual transformation was originally planned by Meyerbeer as big a monologue ('Je veux ici l'attendre') (I want to wait for him here), and after its withdrawal was transferred to the duet with Valentine ('Dans la nuit où seul je veille') (In the dark where I watch alone). Finally, in Act 5 every dogmatic–aggressive attitude falls away from Marcel. His solemn questioning of Valentine and Raoul binds them to a humane love that transcends martyrdom and death ('Dieu nous donne le courage en donnant l'amour') (In giving us love God gives us courage). This trio, the Interrogatoire (three questions by Marcel, three unison answers from the couple), raises the proceedings from a sacred–Christian sphere to one of magic ritual. The whole, which is is accompanied by the dirge-like tones of a bass clarinet, heard for the first time in the opera orchestra, must have exerted a powerful effect on contemporary audiences, and invests Marcel with the aura of an Old Testament seer and prophet. Only from here on does the refashioning of the textual and musical structure of the Lutheran chorale acquire its purpose not so much as a critique of the Christian religion itself, but rather as its historical perversion, characterized by its subjection to the politics of power. For Meyerbeer this self-imposed problem of religion manifests itself in the historical role of Christianity, with the sixteenth-century Wars of Religion providing a bloody example.

As a subject of history, not only the leaders but also the followers play their part. By this is meant not the people (*peuple/Volk*) as an ideal community of individuals, but rather the mass (*foule/Masse*) as an anonymous collectively destructive whole.

In the social and artistic sphere of experience the masses entered with the French Revolution, and thereafter functioned in opera as the recurrent model for great choral scenes, from Le Sueur's *La Caverne* (1793), through Spontini's *Fernand Cortez* (1809) and Auber's *La Muette de Portici* (1828) to Halévy's *La Juive* (1835). In these works the chorus remain bound up with a dramaturgy determined by private conflict. In *Les Huguenots*, however, they first appear as representatives of social forces and parties, whereby the religio-political antagonisms of the historical process are viewed almost as from beneath. The action realizes this to perfection in the Pré-aux-Clercs scene where the very generic conventions which demanded an Act 3 ballet are harnessed to the new dramaturgy: thus when the pagan Gypsy troupe suddenly burst on to the scene, the danced interlude postpones the conflict temporarily by functioning as a distraction remote from all religious controversies for the hostile parties.

Döhring points out (1991, 4:135) that long before Gustav Le Bon's analysis of crowd mentality (*La Psychologie des foules*, 1895), the big choral scenes of *Les Huguenots* explained a psychology of the masses as a manipulable but, in the last degree, unaccountable force. For the loyal Jew, Meyerbeer, opinions were expressed in reserved private ways, but the collective racial memories are revealed in their true and diabolical character by the unpredictable masses, and implemented in the pogrom. This is what determined the key dramatic function of the great Conspiracy Scene of Act 4 (the Blessing of the Daggers). Saint-Bris's murderous words uttered privately in the name of the Royal house ('Pour cette cause sainte') (For this holy cause) release a bloodthirsty fanaticism of horrifying blasphemy. The demands of *realpolitik* show themselves as a Black Mass in which the demonic forces of history celebrate their mastery. The destruction of the individual through the masses inflamed into violence is precisely interpreted by the musical form, its principle realized in a successive series of aria- and ensemble-constructions until finally exploding in the huge, cumulative unison chorus.

The monks (a tenor and two basses), in a solemn and impressive manner, execute a stern religious piece (andante, A flat, 3/4), repeated in full chorus of male and female voices, with grand effect. The subject is at first instrumented for three trombones with the voices piano, swelling to crescendo, the basses joining at the climax with a pedal, the violins in two parts descending alternately in thirds and sixths, and each phrase terminating sotto voce. In the midst of this imposing ceremony, the chiefs hold out their swords and daggers, when the priests and Saint-Bris, slowly advancing, in one energetic unison 'consecrate' the deadly weapons by their 'benediction'(really a malediction). This unison is supported by two chords only, fortissimo and pianissimo, sustained principally by trombones, with the harmonies, through the force of the unison on particular intervals, imparting a unique atmosphere. It begins with a burst on E flat major, succeeded by a major chord on A flat; the first *ff*, the second *pp*, and the benediction delivered on the *third* of each chord. The orchestral treatment avoids the potential shock of this transition, the progression both rising and falling to major triads.

The Bénédiction des Poignards is followed by an allegro furioso (G sharp minor, 6/8), a chorus indicative of the ferocity of the multitude, incited by the leaders of the ostensibly 'holy' cause. The harmonies of this chorus are occasionally harsh, with vocal parts in syncopations and fragments of intricate intervals, difficult to execute, but well suited to expressing the inflamed bigotry and immensely overpowering. When 'all push forward' and with their upraised fists threaten 'Dieu le veut! Dieu l'ordonne' (God wants it! God orders it), fear-inspiring music is unleashed, which bears down on all resistance and carries all before it. Mass hysteria and fanaticism are conceptualized with frightening power, into which Meyerbeer adds the striking observation that brutality is often mixed with self-righteousness and sentimentality. Only 22 bars into this pogrom-inciting music appears the sudden softened and unctuous turn: 'et la palme immortelle dans le ciel vous attend'(the immortal palm awaits us). Since 1789 the new historical experience that the masses could be manipulated and induced to act as a single motivated social group, be it as the people, a party or as a religious or social grouping, was part of the ongoing social discourse in the light of the immediate historical past. There was something seductive in bringing the destructively blind power of the frenzied masses on to the stage, as happened at the Opéra. *Les Huguenots* was singular for pursuing this theme in terms of religious fanaticism and intransigence to its bloody end.

In the crescendo of this final chorus the allegro merges into common time with an emphatic unison on the dominant note to the tonic (E major), in crochets, accompanied by quavers in triplets. Then follows in unison (*ff*, by all the voices, probably 90 in the original production) the resumption of the melody 'Pour cette cause sainte'. Here the canto is delivered with increased energy (*avec exaltation*), with two-thirds of the power of the orchestra employed, slowly, majestically. The accompaniment is in full harmony, with the remaining instruments (the ponderous basses, wind and strings) ascending chromatically, in triplets, on each alternate bar, with a crescendo, the power of which is assisted by the trills of a side drum in powerful and rapid articulation at the third crotchet of each bar. The climax is reached by the addition of cymbals and large drum con tutta forza. The impression of the action is correspondingly striking: having knelt down to receive their benediction, the people, seconded by the monks and chiefs, rush forward to the front of the stage, at the moment of each crescendo, brandishing their poniards with savage gesticulation. The whole movement terminates with a diminuendo, the people retiring, all the voices exclaiming *ff*—'Dieu le veut', the basses ending *pp* on the dominant, falling to the E ('à minuit'). This concludes a most striking scene. Maria Malibran declared it made more impression upon her than any dramatic exhibition she had ever witnessed.

In the course of the action, and finally after the Blessing of the Daggers to which Valentine and Raoul become unwilling witnesses, the couple are plunged into a tension between feeling and reality, the waking dream of the fulfilled moment (*erfüllte Augenblick*) where the longing of love and the intimation of death are equally present, and are subjected to the most extreme intensification. In the awkward situation of the lovers the unison bel canto of thirds and sixths, the traditional hallmark of the love duet, is no longer possible. The couple express themselves in declamatory *durchkomponiert* exchanges and objections, while inarticulate masses and meshes of sound likewise sweep away the classical melodic–harmonic structures. The unreal circumstance of Raoul's famous Andante amoroso cavatina that follows on Valentine's declaration of her love is characterized by a harmonious, otherworldly musical phantasmagoria (ex. 5.2b [a]). Meyerbeer weaves his Italianate *melos* into a dream of love and bliss. No part of this duet has a regular closure through cadence, the endings subsumed into ostinato figures, musical synonyms for the inescapability of the lovers' situation. The dominant melodic pattern is appropriately adapted, with lines of recurrent and slowly rising efflorescence followed by a steep descent. The latent danger is conjured up in different ways: through disruption of the melting melodic flow, through affecting dynamic contrast of the moment, where Valentine takes over Raoul's phrases of love while giving them another meaning, expressing the intensity of her fear of death. The passage 'Tu l'as dit' has been described as 'Meyerbeer's immortal melody' and 'the melody of the century' and constitutes the centrepiece of the Grand Duo. Through loosening the traditional forms of the duet in a series of free episodes in dialogue, this piece authoritatively influenced the development of this form up to the big duets of Wagner (*Tristan und Isolde*, 1865) and Verdi (*Otello*, 1887).

In the stretta the typical rising–falling melodic gesture dominating this duet is rushed to death (ex. 5.2b [b]). The tempo allegro con moto finds its origins in the luxurious type of Italian cantilena, entirely inappropriate to the situation. But it is exactly in the tension generated between the lyrical theme and the breathless tempo, underscored by the reiterative obsessive falling staccato quaver ostinato of the accompaniment, that lends the stretta its unsettling greatness. There is a sense of entrapment, of running on the spot without being able to move. The tolling bells are replaced with alienating imitation by the horns and ophicleide. This recurrence and iteration of the tolling motif, the symbol of the approaching disaster, add to the emotional heightening, paralleling and sharpening the dramatic situation with boding menace, constantly constricting the space left to the couple for articulation until only cries and exclamations remain. Again, their exchange, the melodic discourse, is broken off, without cadence, by a harsh diminished chord for the whole orchestra, as Valentine, overcome by the horror of the massacre seen through the open casement, faints, and Raoul must face his agonizing decision alone, the love exchanged now only a broken phrase of memory.

Example 5.2b   *Les Huguenots:* from the love duet (Act 4)

Example 5.2b   continued

Nothing exemplifies Meyerbeer's and Scribe's shaping of the historical scenario more than the treatment of Act 5. The entr'acte to Act 5 (a gloomy 6/8 allegro in F minor) takes up the stretta and bell motifs of the Grand Duo, depicting Raoul's fraught passage through the bloody streets. At the rising of the curtain, the Huguenot nobility are dancing a minuetto maestoso in honour of the marriage of Marguerite de Valois and Henry of Navarre. The triviality of the dance is synonymous with the carefree unsuspecting mood of the Huguenots, a foil to the seriousness of the situation. The progress of this dance is suddenly arrested by the alarm-bell, to which all present listen with surprise, but are unconscious of its import; the minuet is resumed, finally leading to a gavotte. The repetition of the bell, striking the bar with the dominant sound, naturally leads one to expect an inquiry, but again the cause is unheeded, and the gaieties are resumed with the utmost unconcern. Meyerbeer has conjured up the dignified character of the age in these courtly dances.

At the final cadence of the gavotte, Raoul rushes into the ballroom, his garments stained with blood and, in a recitative, informs the affrighted nobles now crowding around him of the massacre ('Des assassins gagés; les hordes meurtrières, / Seront ici dans un instant!') (The hired assassins, the murderous hordes / Will be here any minute). Raoul calls vengeance over a flurry of diminished sevenths, and in an air, with an intermediate pedal dominant, the bass and melody moving in octaves, he describes in a sombre and suppressed tone of voice the attack of the assassins and the death of Coligny ('A la lueuer de leur torches funèbres') (By the light of their funereal torches). The music is dramatic in accompaniment and tone, with the gloominess reflected in the melodic astringency. Raoul then launches into an energetic allegro, the

" Reviens à toi! Que faire?"

Marguerite et Henri au bal de l'Hôtel de Nesle

" Par le fer et par l'incendie exterminons la race impie "

Illustration 5.2c *Les Huguenots*: engravings of the Act 4 love duet and scenes from Act 5 (from Théophile Gautier, *Les Beautés de l'Opéra*, Paris 1845)

nobles joining as chorus ('Aux armes! à la vengeance!') (To arms! for vengeance!).
The women pale with fright; the men exasperated, and with swords drawn, now quit
the apartment in the greatest disorder as the music dies away into silence. The scene
is remarkable for its dramatic pacing—a careful transition from the party mood to
military frenzy through hushed reactions to Raoul's description of the horror and the
evidence of his own wounds.

The scene changes to a view of the cloisters leading to a church in the background,
to which Protestant women and children are running in great consternation to seek
refuge. An appropriate ritornello (an agitated 6/8, in A minor) is played until the
arrival of an exhausted Marcel, followed by Raoul and Valentine. The three stanzas
of Marcel's solemn blessing of the couple are sung in E flat minor, common time,
Marcel's bass, beginning with a solo *d'une voix grave et sévère*, seconded by the other
voices in a lovely phrase in the major tonic, expressive of pure love and religious
humility. The termination of the third stanza is interrupted by a beautiful effect: the
chorale is heard *pp*, sung by the sopranos in the church in B major, the above three
sustaining throughout the primal key E flat (becoming a major third, D sharp), the
basses in the orchestra having the tonic B, tremolando, *pp*. This disposition occasions
an enharmonic transition sympathetic to the ear and, at same the time, strikingly new
in treatment and distilling a poetry of faith (ex. 5.2c).

Example 5.2c   *Les Huguenots*: from the Interrogatoire (Act 5)

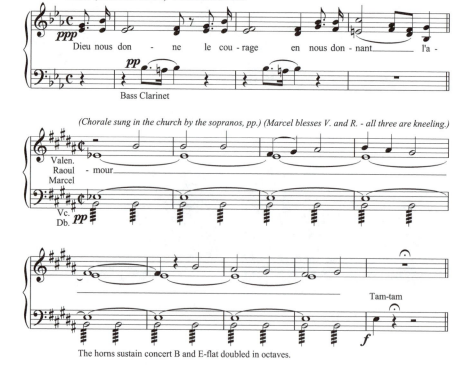

Illustration 5.2d *Les Huguenots*: an engraving of the massacre finale at Her Majesty's Theatre (from the *Illustrated London News*, 1859)

Now the work of slaughter proceeds with redoubled zeal. The Catholics launch an allegro feroce, with four crochets in each bar strongly accented, addressed to the affrighted people in the church, 'Abjurez, Huguenots, ou mourez!' (Abjure, Huguenots, or die). The people still chant, the attacks continue, and after a melange of fragments of the Catholic chorus with the chorale, the sounds die away, and the three Protestants in the cloisters mutter to each other in despair, 'Ils ne chantent plus' (They no longer sing). A profound silence now succeeds, which is broken by the declaration of Marcel's faith in the protection of heaven. A grand allegro in E flat terminates this trio, which Marcel opens with enthusiasm, expressive of the security of his faith; the other voices join in unison. The melody is flowing and continued with increased interest, with modulations both effective and natural, and two harps employed in the orchestra, intended to enforce the impression of the celestial sounds alluded to in the poetry. In the progress of this trio the assassins are heard to attack the grille leading to the cloisters, and, on forcing their entrance, they address their chorus 'Abjurez' in discords to each of the three Protestants, offering the Cross of Lorraine and white scarf, which are scornfully rejected. The soldiers become more infuriated, the Protestants more firm; and in reply to bursts of fury on a succession of discords, the Protestants boldly offer their lives, singing 'Dieu nous guide et marche avec nous' (God will guide us and walk with us) on the first two bars of the chorale *ff*, modulating half a note higher at each repetition. They are finally overpowered and dragged through the grille, at which point a rapid succession of gunshot reports are heard.

The Catholic chorus is concocted with trumpets supported by abrupt harmonies, crude and novel, depicting the savage ferocity of the assassins, beautifully contrasted by the zealous fervour expressed in the flowing canto of the Protestants. The melody, if that is what one can call this fanfare swinging between the tonic and the dominant, is like a breathless scream while running. The accompaniment is made up of a fundamental chord in A minor and the augmented subdominant, with recurrent augmentation of the submediant. There is no trace here of modulation in the classical sense. The determinative interval in this chord is A–D sharp, a tritone, not found in the usual major and minor tone scales. Harmonically this contradictory interval signifies the biggest distance between the two key signatures in the major–minor system used by Meyerbeer (ex. 5.2d). Berlioz was particularly struck by this passage: the augmenting of the sixth note in the minor scale (F) chiefly responsible for its gruesome effect, and 'a new proof of the decisive character of combinations, the occasion to which this note can give rise to, with and without alteration' (*Journal des Débats*, 10 November and 10 December 1836).

Example 5.2d   *Les Huguenots*: the Chorus of Assassins (Act 5)

The whole opera now spirals down in a process of growing negativity. The contrasts become sharper all the time. The warring parties are at first easily separated, then with difficulty, and finally not at all. Individuals can no longer control the situation: the Catholic leaders themselves can no longer prevent the bloodbath, even if they wanted to. This is symbolized by the helpless and speechless appearance of Marguerite de Valois at the end of the opera. The great emotional swings of the first two acts must give way to a hardening, even brutalizing, of the musical parameters that finally culminate in the Chorus of Murderers.

The opera ends in a roaring A major chord which drowns out the cries of the victims. A tragic opera closes without transfiguration. Valentine, Raoul and Marcel die, not as heroes in battle but shot by an anonymous murder squad, like any other victims of this night. For the first time in the history of the French theatre, the creators, Meyerbeer and Scribe, dared to cast a critical view on the deformation of the person, brought up in the bourgeois world, but disposed to mass murder with its calculated bureaucratic preparations in Act 4. This scene indicates how much care was entailed for Meyerbeer. The long genesis of this work cannot be ascribed to laziness or lack of inspiration, but to his minute calculation of all scenic and musical details. Meyerbeer's motto could have been: first think, then compose. The Blessing of the Daggers, and indeed Act 5, is a paradigm of his high dramaturgical intelligence, for which Scribe had provided a text that had correspondingly stimulated his compositional fantasy (Zimmermann 1991: 221).

Les Huguenots became a cultural event that influenced the discussion of artistic theories for years. More comprehensive than *Robert le Diable* because of its perception of history, it was viewed as the realization of the concept of the *Gesamtkunstwerk*, so favoured in contemporary philosophical and literary discourse. In words unpublished in his lifetime, Wagner summed up the tenor of this reaction: 'Meyerbeer wrote world history, the history of heart and feeling; he burst the bounds of national prejudice in writing deeds of music' (1911–16). The actual historico-philosophical message of the work remained largely uncomprehended, and Meyerbeer himself did nothing to repudiate the erroneous perception of his opera as the apotheosis of Protestantism, which privately he found quaint. This misunderstanding of the central religious concern meant that people did not grasp the deep pessimism Meyerbeer manifested in depicting the destruction of the idealistic idyll and the negation of any liberating role for the masses.

The premiere, surrounded by huge expectation, aroused a restrained approval but no great enthusiasm. The public had expected a second *Robert le Diable* and was somewhat disappointed with this completely different, new dramatic concept. Only the last two acts decided the success of the evening. But during the succeeding performances, growing enthusiasm prepared the way for a triumph that would prove to be one of the greatest and most significant of the nineteenth century. The reaction of the press was not unanimous. Mingled in the chorus of eulogistic approval were some dissenting voices, particularly among the representatives of the Italian party who had already raised criticism over *Robert*, regarding Meyerbeer's compositional style and apparently flawed dramaturgy, which they, on the basis of the official authorship of the work, ascribed to Scribe. Meyerbeer, nevertheless, must have found some consolation in the fact that 'even the opponents of this opera speak of it as one of the most important musical manifestations of the times' (letter of 6 March 1836). Meyerbeer's position as the leading opera composer received its definitive confirmation with *Les Huguenots*, and Heinrich Heine's prediction that every dramatic composer would have to study this work carefully would be proved prophetic.

For a long time to come the mounting of the opera, in the stage designs of Charles-Polycarpe Séchan, Léon Feuchère, Jules-Pierre-Michel Diéterle and Edouard-Désiré-Joseph Déspléchin, prepared over months of rehearsals, would also be the prototype.

Under the musical direction of François-Antoine Habeneck, the ensemble of performers showed themselves familiar with Meyerbeer's vocal style and able to fulfil to perfection the immense vocal and dramatic demands of the work: Julie Dorus-Gras as Marguerite, Marie-Cornélie Falcon as Valentine, Marie Flécheux as Urbain, Adolphe Nourrit as Raoul, Nicolas-Prosper Levasseur as Marcel, Jacques-Emile Serda as Saint-Bris, Prosper Dérivis as Nevers.

The performance history of *Les Huguenots* at the Opéra developed into a success story almost without parallel; it was the first work there to achieve 1,000 performances, a figure surpassed only by Gounod's *Faust* (1859). Among the singers at the Opéra who interpreted the leading role in the first decades were: Maria Nau, Claire Dobré (Marguerite); Mlle Treillet-Nathan, Rosine Stoltz, Kathinka Heinefetter, Eugenia Julienne-Dejean (Valentine); Gilbert Duprez, Félix Mécène Marié de l'Isle, Fort-Arthur Espinasse, Gustave-Hippolyte Roger (Raoul); and Dérivis, Serda, Luciano Bouché (Marcel). For the revival in 1853 (with Rosalie-Henriette Laborde, Mlle Poinsot, Louis Gueymard and Louis-Henri Obin) Meyerbeer agreed to a series of cuts and expanded the ballet in Act 3 with some new numbers (choreographed by Joseph Mazilier). The opera featured in the opening year of the Salle Garnier (1875) in a new production (with Caroline Carvalho, Gabrielle Krauss, Pierre-François Villaret and Belval). Another fresh staging took place in 1897 (with Lucy Berthet, Lucienne Bréval, Albert-Raymond Alvarez and Léon Gresse).

The enduring popularity of the work could not prevent a rapidly diminishing understanding of the composer's intentions. Robert Schumann's and Richard Wagner's polemic against the cosmopolitan nature of *grand opéra* had developed in a few decades from an outsider position to the ruling opinion. Furthermore, the routine of the theatre which sought refuge from the technical challenges of production in senseless cuts, encouraged a misconception of *Les Huguenots* as a spectacular show and singers' opera. Apart from in Paris, where the authentic working concept of the opera was maintained for a relatively long time, in practice on most stages the historical opera was transformed into a romantic drama. Extensive cuts of dispensable genre scenes in Acts 2 and 3, the omission of Act 5 Scene 1, and then the whole of Act 5, reduced the political action to the barest scaffolding for a tragic love story whereby the manipulation of the conclusion of the Act 4 duet (with Raoul jumping from the window to his death) provided a superficially effective end to the opera. Since the dramatic system of the historical opera is determined in Act 5, this amputation irrevocably falsified the vision of the work. Added to this were innumerable other abridgements that damaged, if not destroyed, the subtly balanced musical–dramatic *tableau* structures.

Further hindrance to the understanding of the actual aesthetic dimensions of the opera came from the interference of the censor in many places. This meant that in Catholic countries performances were, for many years, allowed, if at all, only in arrangements which eliminated, or at least dulled, the religious–political themes. Thus the work appeared in Munich in 1838 as *Die Anglikaner und die Puritaner* in a textual adaptation by Charlotte Birch-Pfeiffer, which shifted the action to England in the time of Oliver Cromwell. This text was also used for the first Italian production in Florence in 1841, as *Gli Anglicani* (translated by Francesco Guidi). An even freer arrangement, with massive consequences for the musical structures, was prepared by Georg Ott for the Theater in der Josefstadt in Vienna in 1839 as *Die Gibellinen in Pisa*; later in the same year this version was given at the Kärntnertortheater (with Jenny Lutzer, Wilhelmine van Hasselt-Barth, Joseph Erl and Joseph Staudigl). This bowdlerization into a chivalric drama from the times of the Northern Italian War of the Leagues of the twelfth century remained obligatory in the Habsburg lands until 1848 (Pest and Brünn 1839, Prague 1840), and was also played in other cities (Cassel 1839, St Petersburg 1850, where it was called *I Guelfi ed i Ghibellini* in the translation of Calisto Bassi).

The Protestant parts of Europe in general kept to the original form: Leipzig 1837 (in the German translation of Ignaz Franz Castelli), Dresden 1838 (in German, with Maschinka Schubert, Wilhelmine Schröder-Devrient, Joseph Tichatschek and Carl Risse), Stockholm 1842 (in the Swedish translation of Pehr Westerstrand, with Mathilda Gelhaar, Julius Günther and Giovanni Belletti), Copenhagen 1844 (in the Danish translation of Thomas Overskou). But the reception of *Les Huguenots* was not without problems in these countries as well. Militant Protestantism (which took exception to the use of Luther's chorale) and latent anti-Semitism banded together in resentment against the successful opera. In Berlin it came to production only in 1842 when Meyerbeer, as a sign of the liberalization of the cultural climate in the wake of the accession of King Friedrich Wilhelm IV, was made Generalmusikdirektor (the cast featured Leopoldine Tuczek, Schröder-Devrient, Eduard Mantius and August Zschiesche). In Covent Garden in London the work was performed by the guest artists of German (1842) and French ensembles (1845), and in a house production only in 1848 (in the Italian translation of Manfredo Maggioni, with Jeanne-Anaïs Castellan, Pauline Viardot-Garcia, Mario di Candida and Ignazio Marini). For this production Meyerbeer transposed the role of Urbain for the contralto Marietta Alboni, and provided her with a new rondo for insertion into Act 2, later known in its French translation ('Non...vous n'avez jamais, j'gage') (No, you have never, I wager).

In the middle of the century, and partly because of a relaxation of censorship, performance was in full flood, with *Les Huguenots* now regarded as a model for the modern music drama. In Prague, Vienna and Munich, the opera could now be performed in its original form for the first time (1848). The great stages of Italy followed: Teatro Canobbiana in Milan 1855, Venice 1856 (with Joséphine Médori as Valentine and Emilio Pancani as Raoul), Genoa 1857 and finally, also in 1857, La Scala (with Giuditta Beltramelli, Maria Spezia-Aldighieri, Antonio Giuglini and Alfredo Didot). Of the plethora of productions at this time, some were remarkable for their casting: London 1858 (with Albine Maray, Giulia Grisi, Mario and Henri-Charles-

Joseph Zelger, with the local practice of Urbain as a contralto—Constance Nantier-Didiée and, later, Sofia Scalchi). Later London performances saw the first assumption of Valentine by Therese Tietjens (1860), Pauline Lucca (1863) and Adelina Patti (1863). Another important performing tradition was established in Russia. The first production there (in the translation by Piotr Kalashnikov) was at the Maryinsky Theatre in St Petersburg in 1862 (with Iossif Setov as Raoul and Ossip Petrov as Saint-Bris). It was given at the Bolshoi Theatre in Moscow in 1879 (with Anton Barzal as Raoul) and in 1895 (with Mariya Deischa-Sionizkaya as Valentine and Lawrenti Donskoi as Raoul). There were new productions in Vienna in 1869 (with Maria von Rabatinsky, Amalie Materna, Gustav Walter and Hans von Rokitansky), as well as 1876 in the new house on the Ringstrasse (with Emilia Tagliana, Marie Wilt, Georg Müller and Rokitansky). In Prague the work appeared in 1891 as part of Angelo Neumann's Meyerbeer Centenary Cycle (with Leonore Better as Valentine, Sarolta von Rettich-Pirk as Urbain and Johannes Elmblad as Marcel).

With the ongoing specialization characteristic of this development of the vocal types during the later nineteenth century, there was a simplification of the complex role profiles and their adaptation to new types that had emerged in the meantime. This was the case with many operas of the Italian and French repertoires, and particularly so with *Les Huguenots*. Marguerite became a coloratura soprano, Valentine a dramatic soprano, Urbain a soubrette (occasionally a mezzo-soprano), Raoul a dramatic tenor, Marcel a deep bass and Saint-Bris a high bass and Nevers a baritone. With this type of vocal distribution, at the turn of the century the opera (as with Gounod's *Faust*) settled into a singers' opera *par excellence*, particularly at the Metropolitan Opera House in New York. Here performances attained a legendary status as 'the Nights of the Seven Stars': in 1894 with Nellie Melba, Lillian Nordica, Sofia Scalchi, Jean de Reszke, Edouard de Reszke, Pol Plançon and Victor Maurel; in 1905 with Marcella Sembrich, Nordica, Edyth Walker, Enrico Caruso, Marcel Journet, Plançon and Antonio Scotti.

The decisive consequence of this modern development of the vocal types and its effect on the stage history of this opera related to the penetrating power and mobility of the voice required for the part of Raoul. The tendency to cast this role for a heavy tenor trained in Wagner and the verismo school guaranteed the first of the conditions, but led to the cutting of the leggiero passages in Acts 1 and 2, as well as to transpositions and the omission of high notes in the other acts. Thus in the twentieth century the casting of this role was the biggest problem for any production. Even for the most important tenors some virtuoso passages had to be omitted, with the cuts thereby necessitated cobbled over. Nevertheless, the prevalence of tenors with the stamina to sing Raoul meant that the twentieth century up to the Second World War was a popular period for the opera, especially in the provincial houses of South America and France:

- with Enrico Caruso: New York 1905; London 1905; New York 1912; Philadelphia 1913; New York 1914
- with José Palet: 1911: Valencia, Bergamo, Madrid; 1912: Barcelona; 1914: Buenos Aires, Rosario, Cordoba, Rio de Janeiro, São Paulo, Montevideo; 1915: Turin, Barcelona, Madrid; 1916: Madrid, Santiago; 1918: Havana, San Juan, Ponce, Caracas, Lima, Valparaiso; 1919: Mexico City; 1920: Genoa; 1922: San José, Bogota; probably also Quito and Guayaquil; 1923: Medellin;

1928: Amsterdam; probably also The Hague and Rotterdam; 1929: Budapest
- with Giovanni Martinelli: 1915: Atlanta; 1916: Buenos Aires, Montevideo; 1921: Buenos Aires
- with Hipolito Lazaro: 1922: Barcelona; 1923 Havana; 1932: Barcelona.

Some exceptional voices, with a characteristic 'ring' or *squillo*, determined by a steely power in the high register, were to be found in John O'Sullivan and Giacomo Lauri-Volpi. The Irish tenor, whose voice found a literary echo in the work of his admirer James Joyce, counted Raoul as his speciality and sang the role during the 1920s and 1930s on many European and international stages—1910: Grenoble; 1911, 1912: Geneva; 1914: Paris; 1918, 1920: Rouen; 1920: Paris (with Josefa Gozatégui as Valentine, and Albert Huberty as Marcel); 1922: Lisbon, Milan, Bologna, Parma; 1923: Piacenza, Rome; 1924: Trieste, Madrid, Barcelona; 1925: Brescia, Cairo, Alexandria, Rosario, Cordoba, Buenos Aires, Montevideo, Rio de Janeiro, São Paulo, Barcelona; 1926: Venice, Seville; 1927: London, Covent Garden (with Bianca Scacciati and Alexander Kipnis); 1929, 1930: Paris, Algiers, Marseille; 1931: Naples, Toulouse, Perpignan, Montpellier, Marseilles, Toulon; 1932: Nice, Algiers, Vichy, Bordeaux, Rouen, Nantes; 1933: Toulouse; 1934: Lyons, Grenoble; 1936: Paris, Nancy, Nice.

Lauri-Volpi's interpretation, described as phenomenal, was the vocal crown of the legendary performance at the Verona Arena in 1933 (with Adelaide Saraceni, Rosa Raisa, Gianna Pederzini, Tancredi Pasero, Giacomo Rimini, and Antonino Votto conducting, and the production directed by Pericle Ansaldo). In older age he participated in a studio performance by Radiotelevisione Italiana Milan (3 June 1956) (with Anna De Cavalieri, Antonietta Pastori, Jolanda Gardino, Nicola Zaccaria, Giorgio Tozzi, Giuseppe Taddei, and Tullio Serafin conducting). Despite the diminution of his gifts, it remains a valuable document.

However, some attempts were also made to free this much performed work from the conventions of the singers' opera and to rediscover its musico-dramatic qualities ,lost in theatrical routine. Arturo Toscanini succeeded in doing this spectacularly in a model production at La Scala Milan in 1899 (with Adelina Padovani, Hariclea Darclée, Emilio De Marchi and Francesco Navarrini), when he reinstated innumerable cuts and also restored a great part of Act 5. The Court Opera in Vienna staged the work in 1902 as a testament to a nostalgically affirmed tradition (with Frances Saville, Sophie Sedlmair, Selma Kurz, Leo Slezak and Vilém Heš), and the opera was given in Berlin in 1908 (with Frieda Hempel, Emmy Destinn, Karl Jörn and Paul Knüpfer). Both productions were of the highest quality, musically as well as scenically, and set a standard for the interpretation of Meyerbeer in the German-speaking countries for years. These productions received special attention because of the outstanding personalities of their conductors: in Vienna, Gustav Mahler; in Berlin, Leo Blech. The latter established himself as Meyerbeer's advocate in the following years—the one who really understood Meyerbeer's effectiveness. Indeed, the first attempt to produce *Les Huguenots* with all the means of a modern theatre of movement was undertaken by the Berlin Staatsoper in 1932, with musical direction again by Blech. Gustaf Gründgens was the producer and choreographer, assisted by the endowment of Rochus Gliese. Blech presided over an outstanding ensemble: Margherita Perras, Anny Konetzni, Marcel Wittrisch and Emanuel List. Despite distorting interference in the working material by the musicologist Julius Kapp, who was anxious to cover over the features of *grand opéra*, the production as a whole left behind a deep impression, according to the critics, and strengthened the cautious tendency discernible since the 1920s to correct the received image of Meyerbeer.

If in Germany, after the shift in the paradigm from music drama back to opera, attention had been focused particularly on the musical qualities of these works that had been underestimated for so long, so in the early years of the young Soviet Union interest was manifested in the revolutionary flair of the opera. It appeared in the leading houses in ambitious new productions: at the Bolshoi Theatre in 1925 (with Xenia Derschinskaya as Valentine, Nikolai Oserov as Raoul, Vassili Nebolsin conducting and staging by Vladimir Losski), and at the Kirov Theatre in Leningrad in 1935 (with Valentina Pavlovskaya as Valentine, Georgi Nelepp as Raoul, Vladimir Kastorski as Marcel, Vladimir Dranishnikov conducting, staging by Nikolai Smolitsch). Following from this, it was proposed to devise a new text called *Dekabristi* which was not realized.

Another production of great historical interest, and committed to the dramatic realization of the opera was undertaken by the Palestine Opera Company in Jerusalem, 1926–27 (with L. Golinkin as Valentine, S. Krieger as Urbain, G. Giorini as Raoul, M. Konstantinovsky, J. Har-Melach and M. Ernstein).

The last performance at the Paris Opéra (the 1,120th) took place on 22 November 1936 (with Germaine Hoerner as Valentine, Solange Delmas as Marguerite, Renée Mahé as Urbain, Raoul Jobin as Raoul, Albert Huberty as Marcel, Arthur Endreze as Nevers, Henri Etcheverry as Saint-Bris, conducted by François Ruhlmann).

If the production history of the opera can be seen as a pull between the poles of singing and dramatic concept, then things took a new turn with the revival of old singing techniques and voice types which made it possible to achieve a more appropriate casting and a narrowing of the opposing positions. Even if Meyerbeerian *grand opéra* was not created for vocal exhibitionism, it is nevertheless true that, without the cooperation of singers qualified technically as well as stylistically, the opera cannot be convincingly realized. *Les Huguenots*, as a singers' opera with the usual big cuts and sometimes a fragmentary Act 5, made several appearances after the Second World War.

In the 1950s performances were given in Leningrad 1951; Birmingham 1951; Vienna 1951 (concert); Ghent 1955 (with Huberte Vécray as Valentine and Guy Fouché as Raoul); Milan 1956 (concert, with the aging Lauri-Volpi as Raoul, conducted by the veteran Tullio Serafin); Hamburg 1958 (with Clara Ebers, Kurt Ruesche and Sigmund Roth, and Albert Bittner conducting—a remarkably successful production).

In the 1960s performances were given in London (Scala Theatre) 1960, Milan 1962; Lille 1964; Rouen 1964; Verviers 1964; Chelyabinsk 1964; Ghent 1964; Marseille 1967; Verviers 1967; Dijon 1967; Toulon 1967; Nîmes 1967; St Etienne 1967; London 1968 (concert); New York 1969 (concert). All these French performances featured the powerful tenor Tony Poncet who also sang at Carnegie Hall with Angeles Gulin, Beverly Sills and Justino Diaz.

The most important were the legendary production at La Scala Milan 1962 (with Joan Sutherland, Giulietta Simionato, Fiorenza Cossotto, Franco Corelli, Nicolai Ghiaurov, Giorgio Tozzi, Wladimiro Ganzarolli, conducted by Gianandrea Gavazzeni), and the concert performance in the Albert Hall, London, 1968 (Joan Sutherland, Martina Arroyo, Huguette Tourangeau, Anastasios Vrenios, Nicolai Ghiuselev,

Gabriel Bacquier and Dominic Cossa), which led to the first proper recording of the opera under Richard Bonynge in 1970.

Productions staged in the 1970s were Vienna 1971 (concert) (with Nicolai Gedda, Enriqueta Tarres and Justino Diaz); Barcelona 1971 (with Diaz again as Marcel); Toulouse 1972; Los Angeles 1973; Leipzig 1974; Kiev 1974; Gelsenkirchen 1974; New Orleans 1975; Paris 1976 (concert) (with Alain Vanzo, Jules Bastin and Robert Massard).

Hitherto the most fundamental scenic exposition of the intellectual context of the historical opera was the production by Joachim Herz for Leipzig in 1974. The singers' contribution here did not match the scenic realization, however (with Jika Kovariková, Hildegard Bondzio, Ruth Asmus, Armin Ude, Paul Glahn, Rolf Tomaszewski and Achim Wichert). The production was based on a new German translation and edition undertaken by Böhmel and Zimmermann, including material not published by Meyerbeer (including the cut first scene of Act 3 and Marcel's monologue at the centre of Act 3). The same edition was used at Gelsenkirchen in 1976 (with Sabine Hass as Valentine and Ljubomir Romansky conducting).

In the 1980s another attempt at realizing the pre-eminent theatricality of this work was made by John Dew for the Deutsche Oper Berlin in 1987, although the cuts to Act 3 meant that this production was less successful (with Angela Denning as Marguerite, Pilar Lorengar as Valentine, Richard Leech as Raoul, conducted by Jesús López Cobos). This was revived in 1991 (with Lucy Peacock as Valentine, and Stefan Soltesz conducting). Richard Leech, after Nicolai Gedda, emerged at this time as the tenor best suited vocally for Raoul, with an understanding of the correct singing tradition.

Other performances were in Sydney 1981 (with Sutherland, Amenda thane, Austin, Grant and Suzanne Johnson); Montpellier 1988 (with Françoise Pollet as Valentine, Ghylaine Raphanel as Marguerite, Leech as Raoul, Nicolai Ghiuselev as Marcel, and Cyril Diederich conducting); Essen 1988 (with Gabriele Lechner as Valentine and Robert Durné as Raoul).

In the 1990s productions were staged in Sydney in 1990 (Sutherland, Amanda Thane, Austin, Grant, and Suzanne Johnson); San Francisco 1990; Montpellier 1990 (with Nelly Miricioiu, Leech); London 1991 (with Miricioiu and Judith Howarth, Leech, Gwynne Howell, Richard Van Allen, conducted by David Atherton); Berlin 1991; Novara 1993 (with Katia Ricciarelli as Valentine and Giuseppe Morino as Raoul); Ljubljana 1997; Dubrovnik 1998; Litomyšl (Czech Republic) 1998; Berlin 1998 (with Elisabeth-Maria Wachutka as Valentine, Chris Meritt as Raoul, conducted by Soltesz); Bilbao 1999 (with Ana María Sánchez as Valentine, Marcello Giordano as Raoul, Philippe Kahn as Marcel, conducted by Antonello Allemandi).

In the 2000s the work was performed in New York in 2001 (concert) (with Krassimira Stoyanova as Valentine, Marcello Giordano as Raoul, conducted by Eve Queler); Martina Franca 2002 (with Annalisa Raspagliosi as Valentine, Warren Mok as Raoul, Soon-Won Kang as Marcel, conducted by Renato Palumbo); Regensburg 2002 (concert); Frankfurt 2002 (concert) (with Annalisa Raspagliosi and Marcello Giordano); Metz 2004 (with Aleka Cela as Valentine, Rockwell Blake as Raoul, conducted by Jeremy Silver); Liège 2005 (with Annick Massis as Marguerite, Barbara Ducret as Valentine, Gilles Ragon as Raoul, Branislav Jatic as Marcel, conducted by Jacques Lacombe). (See Loewenberg 1970: 777–9; Wolff 1962: 115–18; Döhring 1991, 4:136–9; Kaufman 2001: 8–12.)

Centrepiece: Giacomo Meyerbeer in later years (lithograph by Maurou)

5.3 *Le Prophète [The Prophet]*

Opéra en cinq actes [opera in five acts]
Text: Augustin-Eugène Scribe and Emile Deschamps
First performance: Opéra, Salle de la rue Le Peletier, Paris, 16 April 1849

Already during the first series of performances of *Les Huguenots* (1836) at the Opéra, Meyerbeer expressed the intention 'of planting my dramatic system on immovable pillars through a third work' (letter of 20 May 1836) (*BT*, 2:527). The draft of a letter by Scribe of 23 April 1836 gives the first clue to the new opera and its theme: the original title of *Les Anabaptistes*. It could not have been foreseen that the work would appear only 13 years later. A scenario was prepared by December 1836, since at this time Meyerbeer wrote to Scribe with his detailed thoughts about related dramaturgical and production matters. Perhaps it was because of these reservations that the Anabaptist opera was held back in favour of another new project, *L'Africaine* (1865), for which a contract was signed. But dissatisfaction with the libretto, as well as the vocal difficulties of Marie-Cornélie Falcon, who had been envisaged in the title role, meant that in the summer of 1838 Meyerbeer decided to give *Le Prophète* immediate attention.

He began the process of planning and rejecting proposals that would lead right up to the premiere. For the composer this period presented a heavy tribulation, made worse by the expectations attendant on his public reputation, especially in Paris. Performances planned for the winter season of 1841–42, with Rosine Stoltz and Gilbert Duprez considered as the interpreters of Fidès and Jean de Leyde, undoubtedly came to nothing since Meyerbeer had difficulty preparing his score (and largely only in provisional form) by the stipulated contractual delivery date (27 March 1841). All further efforts by the director of the Opéra, Léon Pillet, to conclude a contract for the premiere came to nothing because in June 1842 Meyerbeer was appointed Prussian Generalmusikdirektor and was consequently tied to Berlin most of the time. He completed other compositions because of these duties, like *Ein Feldlager in Schlesien* and *Struensee*. In December 1843 Meyerbeer further had the opportunity to convince himself that Duprez was no longer suitable for the title role. Several letters between Meyerbeer and his Paris confidant Louis Gouin over the next few years reveal that Pillet apparently was no longer prepared, or in the position, to meet the composer's wishes for another tenor. By October 1845 Meyerbeer therefore decided to set aside both *Le Prophète* and *L'Africaine* and to busy himself with a new subject, *Noëma ou Le Repentir*, with a text by Scribe and Jules-Henri Vernoy de Saint-Georges. By November 1846 this new project was abandoned, and he again worked on the problems besetting the casting of *Le Prophète*, but nothing came of it. Only on 1 July 1847, with the departure of Pillet and the advent of the joint new directorship of Nestor Roqueplan and Edmond Duponchel, was the stasis at last resolved, and contact with the Opéra resumed.

Negotiations with the new directors continued to be complex because of the continuing search for appropriate singers, and then clearing the obstacles in the way of the engagements of Pauline Viardot-Garcia as Fidès and Gustave-Hippolyte Roger as Jean. For the first time in four years, in September 1847, Meyerbeer read through the score of his opera again. Scribe began to revise the libretto, and in early 1848, without Scribe's knowledge, Deschamps, who was sworn to secrecy, began putting Meyerbeer's latest requirements into verse. Meyerbeer himself composed new pieces for the opera, and then began a thorough overhaul of the score. The revolutionary events in Paris in February 1848, which provided the genesis of the opera with an unexpected actuality, were recorded in his diary by the composer, who observed the unfolding situation as reluctant participant: 'Spent the whole day on the streets in order to observe the course of events which in the course of the day developed into a formal revolution...In the evening and morning I worked on the stretta of the *Prêche* [of the Anabaptists in Act 1]' (24 February 1848) *(BT,* 4:368). The rehearsal period, which lasted for months, also inspired the composer to make various alterations to the score: many of the pieces received final shape only now. And because of the necessity of curtailing the performance length, further decisive cuts were made just before the premiere.

The action of this second panel of Meyerbeer's Reformation diptych depicts the highpoint of the history of the Anabaptist movement, the founding and fall of their Kingdom of Zion in the city of Münster in 1534. The Anabaptists did not conquer the city by attack from without, but through manipulation of internal civic politics. Their defeat followed on from a long siege. Johann van Leyden did not commit suicide but was brutally executed. The opera reworks the historical material in a free and novel way that provides a specific reference to the many earlier literary adaptions. Voltaire's *Essay sur l'histoire générale et sur les moeurs et l'esprit des nations depuis Charlemagne jusqu'à nos jours* (1756) provided some points of historical fact for Scribe, who also might also have used Carl Franz van der Velde's popular novel *Die Wiedertäufer* (1821) as a source, although the French translation by François-Adolphe Loève-Veimars appeared only in 1843, five years after Scribe's first version of the libretto.

Plot
In the Netherlands and Westphalia in 1534–35.

Act 1. A pastoral landscape in the region of Dordrecht. In the background is the River Meuse; on the right a castle; on the left some peasant cottages and a mill. At daybreak the peasants and millhands assemble for work. Berthe, a poor orphan, is looking forward to her wedding with Jean, an innkeeper from Leyden. Jean's mother, Fidès, has come to bring Berthe her ring, and to support her in requesting permission to marry from the local lord of the manor, Count Oberthal. Suddenly three men in black appear; Berthe recognizes them as Anabaptists, who for some time have been going about the land preaching social upheaval. Jonas, Mathisen and Zacharie, through prayer and fiery preaching, stir up a sense of injustice and hatred in the peasants, who pick up pitchforks and threaten to storm the castle in revolutionary zeal. Their courage deserts them when Oberthal suddenly emerges from the castle with his retinue. He orders the troublemakers to be driven off. Supported by Fidès, Berthe now comes forward to request the permission from Oberthal, telling how Jean once saved her from drowning. The tyrannical Oberthal refuses and has both women taken forcibly into the castle, to the dismay of the peasants. They turn to the Anapabtists who reappear menacingly.

Act 2. An inn in a suburb of Leyden. In the background are a door and a window. Other doors are on the left and right. Townspeople are drinking and dancing. The sun is setting, and Jean the innkeeper is concerned that his mother and bride have not returned. Among the crowd are the three Anabaptists, who comment on the likeness the innkeeper bears to a portrait of King David in Münster Cathedral. As the guests leave at nightfall, the Anabaptists engage Jean in conversation. He asks them as men of God, to interpret a dream that has troubled him of late. He has seen himself in the midst of splendid temple with a crown on his head, receiving the acclamation of the crowd who hail him as the son of God. Letters of fire appear on the walls, and his throne is swept from its pedestal by a wave of blood. Amidst satanic blood and fire, he is carried to the feet of God and thrice damned. But a voice from the depths answers with 'mercy', and thereafter he wakes, filled with horror. The Anabaptists assure him that it is a prophecy of his future destiny as ruler. Jean, however, wishes only for the love of Berthe, and turns from the prospect of power and glory. Hardly have the Anabaptists left him when Berthe rushes in, fleeing from Oberthal. Jean has only just hidden her when the count enters with Fidès, and threatens to have her killed if Berthe is not handed over. Jean is forced to relinquish his fiancée, and Oberthal leaves in triumph. Jean's mother tries to console him, and prays heaven's blessings on his sacrifice. The Anabaptists return and now have no difficulty in recruiting the outraged Jean to their cause. Jean is thirsting for vengeance and vows to struggle against tyranny. After an anguished farewell to his sleeping mother, he leaves with the Anabaptists.

Act 3. Scene 1. An Anabaptist camp in a forest in Westphalia near Münster. In the foreground is a frozen lake; on the right and left the surrounding forest. To one side are the tents of the Anabaptists. It is twilight. After several military successes under the charismatic leadership of Jean who has become their 'Prophet', the Anabaptist campaign has ground to a halt. They have besieged the city of Münster, but it is now winter. They drag in prisoners and celebrate their bloodlust, urged on by Zacharie. Peasants come across the frozen lake bringing provisions and entertaining the besiegers with dances. Night falls, and Zacharie sends the soldiers to their tents.

Scene 2. Zacharie's tent, with table and stools. Unknown to Jean, the Anabaptist leadership have begun their own political manoeuvring. Mathisen brings the news that the commander of the defenders, the father of Count Oberthal, will not surrender the city. Zacharie gives orders for the city to be attacked. Jonas appears with a stranger who has been apprehended in the camp. It is Oberthal in disguise, trying to reach the city. He pretends to be a sympathizer of the movement, and they invite him to drink with them, revealing cynically all the while their amoral principles. They strike a light and recognize Oberthal, and have him taken for execution. Jean comes into the tent, filled with sad reminiscences of his mother and bride. He forbids the execution of Oberthal, hoping to speak with him a last time. The count tells him that Berthe has escaped again and is in the city. Jean spares Oberthal, reserving his fate for Berthe to decide and resolves to redouble the effort to take the city. News comes of the defeat of the Anabaptist sortie and of mutiny spreading among the troops.

Scene 3. The camp, as in Scene 1. It is the early hours of the morning. The disappointed troops rail against the 'false prophet' and demand his death. Only by the power of his personality is Jean able to calm them and instil new determination. He leads them in prayer, asking forgiveness for their disobedience. Trumpet calls announce the time for the decisive onslaught on the city, and as the dawn breaks, Jean, as the new David, intones a marching song, calling on the King of Heaven to lead them to victory. The rising sun floods the camp with light as he leads them on.

Illustration 5.3a   *Le Prophète*: gouache by the Grieve family for Act 4 Scene 1 in Covent Garden

Act 4. Scene 1. A marketplace in Münster, dominated by the cathedral; on the right the city hall; various streets lead into the square. In the besieged city of their occupation the Anabaptists have initiated a reign of terror. Among the frightened townspeople the rumour is spreading that the Prophet will be crowned king of the Anabaptists today. Fidès, reduced to penury, goes through the streets begging for alms in order to have a Mass said for her dead son. To her astonishment she meets Berthe who, disguised as a pilgrim, has gained access to the city. Berthe greets her with rapture, but Fidès is forced to tell her that Jean is dead, supposedly murdered by the Prophet. Berthe frenziedly swears to be avenged on the tyrant in his palace.

Scene 2. The interior of the Lamberti Kirche, the Cathedral of Münster: a side angle, with a view of the central nave rising to the steps of the sanctuary. A great crowd watch the entry of the Prophet and his entourage. While his coronation is taking place off-stage at the high altar, Fidès, who has joined the congregation, curses the Anabaptist king, amidst the praise of the people who hail him as 'son of God' and do him homage. Just as Jean is marvelling at the fulfilment of his dream, Fidès recognizes him as her son. Her cry menaces all the plans of the Anabaptists, and they threaten to kill Jean unless she recants her error. Jean undertakes to save himself, his mother and the situation. The Prophet forces her to kneel, prays over her, and by the power of his personality induces her admit her mistake. The people hail this as a miracle wrought by the Prophet, and the coronation procession sweeps out of the cathedral in triumph. Fidès realizes that she must stop Berthe putting her plan into action.

Act 5. Scene 1. A subterranean vault in the palace of Münster. To the left is a staircase; in the middle a stone slab; to the right an iron grid. The three Anabaptists are conspiring against Jean. A message from the emperor, whose forces have surrounded the city, has granted them immunity if they will betray the Prophet.

Scene 2. Fidès is brought in by soldiers, and left alone. She is torn between love for her son and anger over his treachery. She prays for guidance, and that the Holy Spirit will change Jean's heart. The Prophet is announced, and mother and son are at last alone with each other. He begs for forgiveness, and she is gradually able to persuade him to give up his public role and flee with her. Berthe enters through the side door, carrying a torch. She has set fire to a slow fuse that will ignite the store of explosives in the vaults and destroy the palace with the Prophet and his followers. She is overwhelmed at finding Fidès and her betrothed whom she believed dead. The three are caught up in a dream of future domestic happiness together. But all is shattered when an officer enters to tell the Prophet of the plot against him, and how the Anabaptists intend to betray him during the banquet for his coronation. Horrified at learning that Jean and the Prophet are one, Berthe stabs herself fatally and dies. Jean is heartbroken; he resolves to let Berthe's revenge take its course and perish in the midst of his enemies. He commits his mother to the faithful soldier and goes to join his enemies.

Scene 3. The banqueting hall in the palace; in the middle a podium with a long table. In the background an iron gate. The Anabaptists are celebrating with the Prophet in their midst. Jonas, Mathisen and Zacharie mutter of their treachery. Jean whispers his orders to his faithful troops to close the portcullis. Amid scenes of profligate pleasure, Jean toasts his enemies. As Oberthal leads the imperial troops into the hall, the gate is closed and a vast explosion shakes the palace. Fidès appears in the midst of the tumult, smoke and flames to join her son. Together they hail the advent of expiatory death in the cleansing fire.

In *Le Prophète* Meyerbeer's dramatic language shows further evolution in refinement. The music, in the richness of harmony, the sophistication of orchestral colour, the vitality of rhythm and the expressive flexibility of melody, seeks to explore a complex scenario.

On first appearances it would seem that *Le Prophète* emphatically revisits the dramaturgy of *Les Huguenots*. But unlike the earlier work, where political and private events are seen working independently of each other, here they are identical with each other, insofar as Jean's personal destiny from beginning to end also determines the fate of the Anabaptists. So it appears that Jean's three decisions, on which depend the rise and fall of the Anabaptist Kingdom of Zion, are the results of a conflict between personal desire (his unfulfilled love for Berthe) and public demands (the consequences of his role as Prophet) that Jean always resolves by using political action for the furtherance of his own private aims. His decision to place himself at the disposal of the revolutionaries as leader springs from his wish to avenge Oberthal's crime against Berthe (Act 2); his order to storm Münster, whose capture represents the highpoint of the Anabaptists' quest for power, follows from his learning of Berthe's presence in the city (Act 3); his decision to be blown up with the traitors, which also marks the end of the movement, is his immediate reaction to Berthe's cursing of him and her suicide (Act 5). These private motivations of the political appear so obvious as to be a pulling back from the historical facts, and as determinants of action seem forced rather than plausible (with Berthe's crucial presence in Münster the result of 'hidden' events learnt only through narrative recounting). The uncompromising tendency of this system, which does not even eschew absurdity, leads to one conclusion: the private motivation of the political is part of the context of ideas in *Prophète* insofar as the concrete historical events become a paradigm for the relationship of the individual to history. If *Les Huguenots* is a historical opera, then *Le Prophète* follows as an opera about history. The private motivation of the political does not support the concept of the historically powerful individual, but unmasks it as ideology. This moment of ambiguity is expressed in the title: the original *Les Anabaptistes* would have been a historical opera closer to the mode of *Les Huguenots*; the ironic–polemical *Le Prophète*, at once apotheosis and dismantling, approaches more closely the idea of the historical 'pamphlet' (as perceived by Théophile Gautier 1858–59, 4: 82).

The original title also alerts us to the discourse of faith that is a crucial subtext here, as in all of Meyerbeer's four principal operas. The progressive unfolding establishes a definite thematic dialectic that is consistently commenting on the surface action in its direct handling of religion and power. In the third stage of consideration, depicted in *Le Prophète*, the focus has shifted from the grand scale of metaphysical struggle in *Robert*, and socio-political conflict in *Les Huguenots*, to an examination of the impact of corrupted faith upon the individual and its consequences for those around him. Once again, an organized faith fails to bring peace. Indeed, it brings the most abhorrent conflict and abuses of personal liberty. Once more the ultimate redemption of the hero is mediated through the actions of individuals, his mother and fiancée. Powerful biblical images are used in this process, drawing strongly from the story of Solomon and the contested baby (Fidès denies her son to save his life, cf. 1 Kings 3:16–28) and also Gospel passages (Jesus' apparent rejection of Mary, 'Who is my mother?' in Matthew 12: 48, and his words to her, 'Woman, what have you to do with me? My hour has not yet come', in John 3: 4). These show the theme of the Messiah potent in this scenario.

The radicalism of Meyerbeer's historical pessimism strikes one fully only against the background of the idyllic discourse. The morning twilight over the Dutch landscape at the beginning of the opera, developed through the pastoral cypher of the echo duet for two clarinets and then through the morning chorus of the peasants, presents the peace of nature whose effects in the human sphere is rendered delusory by the entry of the Anabaptists. Their symbolic self-expression sees the negation of the idyll, extended into the paradox that the love between Jean and Berthe (its only dramatic manifestation), never reaches a fulfilled relationship (conventionally expressed in the love duet), but is reduced to two chance meetings that both end in catastrophe. The only time they have to sing together in unison is at a moment of anguish in Act 2—and even here they have to share it with the menacing Oberthal, the nemesis of their love (ex. 5.3a).

Illustration 5.3b *Le Prophète*: stage design for Act 1 at the Paris Opéra (contemporary photograph)

Example 5.3a   *Le Prophète*: the thwarting of romantic love (Act 2)

Disappointed and tragically defined, Jean's feelings determine not only his love relationship, but his political career, until at the end he loses both love and power in equal measure. With the changeable personality of the Anabaptist king, Scribe and Meyerbeer created a further incarnation of the special type of the vacillating hero. To acknowledge this ambivalence as a characteristic of the personality was something difficult for contemporary German critics to accept. Even Richard Wagner, hardly to be suspected of a provincial judgement, felt he had erred here when he initially hailed Jean as 'the prophet of a new world' (*der Prophet der neuen Welt*) (letter to Theodor Uhlig, 13 March 1850), only later to ridicule him as an unworthy weakling (*Oper und Drama*, 1851) whose character is not adequate for the grandiose theatrical ambience created for him. The Camp Scene with the sunrise, to which Wagner's criticism was especially directed, contradicts this in the most convincing way. Jean's appearance before the mutinying soldiers does indeed reveal a charismatic figure, while at the same time demonstrating the modus operandi and the consequence of charisma in politics. It turns the leader into the seducer, who controls the masses like an actor controls his public.

For Döhring (1991, 4:148) the intoxication Jean generates does not spring from inspiration but from calculation. In this way the rising sun does not symbolize the sympathy of nature with human rapture, as Wagner reads it; its cold technical brilliance, which is not disguised by musical exaggeration, does not light a victory path for a people's liberator, but rather indicates the highroad to judgement and perdition for a demagogue and deceiver of the masses. That Meyerbeer's contemporaries, who wanted to see in Jean a new Masaniello or Rienzi, reacted to scenes like these with unease cannot be surprising. The time was not yet ripe for the understanding of musico-dramatic transpositions of those political and mass-psychological insights or intimations that stood opposed to the utopian ideals of the century.

It nonetheless has to be said that Jean's ambiguity is unsettling: he is a religious idealist, said to know the Bible by heart (Act 2), much in love with Berthe, with a hold over his troops whom he does lead successfully (Act 3), and whom he is loath to abandon (Act 5). He is strong yet weak, charismatic yet unable to curb the excesses of the movement he thinks he leads. His ambiguity is underscored by something highly original in his music. When Jean describes his recurring nightmare to the three Anabaptists ('Sous les vastes arceaux') (Under the vast arches) (Act 2), Meyerbeer gives us a *durchkomponiert* symphonic poem in miniature. The vocal line is sung in a monotone, as if the speaker were in a trance, while the scenic effects of his dramatic, apocalyptic descriptions are depicted in vivid detail by the orchestra. His messianic and psalmic rapture in the Act 3 finale, which is prayer/march/triumphal hymn all rolled into one, is given a special aura by its accompaniment of three timpani, two harps and the bass clarinet.

The transformation of historical realism into the phantasmagorical, which is alien to *Les Huguenots*, essentially determines the new tone of *Le Prophète*—and it does not need the direct apostrophizing of God and Satan in the Dream Narration to stir associations with *Robert le Diable*. *Le Prophète* actually reveals itself both dramaturgically and intellectually as a synthesis of both preceding works: historical opera as Romantic mystery play. Both instances depict sin as striving for power, in which the distinction between the spheres of magic and politics is actually secondary, because, both here as well as there, it concerns control—violence over people. And also in politics, so suggests *Le Prophète*, this control functions according to the working laws of magic. The realm of evil which, as *Robert* indicates, is not only a nocturnal matter but ever-present in shadowy form, is uncovered in *Le Prophète* simply as history itself. To carry the reconciling legendary conclusion of *Robert* across to the historical drama would indeed not only have worked against the norms of the genre, but would also have falsified the principle of the work.

The nuanced characterization of Jean does not, superficially at least, seem to find correspondence in the other characters. Jean's mother is indeed a role of similar dramaturgical significance, but is as much a personified idea as a rounded character—as her symbolic name suggests. Although all her words and actions are always in deeply human reaction to her son, she nevertheless is equally the hallowed representative of the divine law, obedience to which she demands, whose breach she condemns, and whose restoration she enforces. Her blessing of her son in Act 2 ('Ah! mon fils') (Ah! my son), aligns her with the divine dispensation. The F sharp minor-keyed strophe of her arioso is a type of dialogue between the voice and the orchestra. A cello motif rises, as from the depths of some ageless spiritual wisdom born of sorrow; her voice interjects, hypnotically, as if in response. The cool sacral flute continues the dialogue and provides the context for the blessing she is now empowered to impart (ex. 5.3b [a]). At the peroration, with the change into the major, the rapidly beating woodwind chords approximate the spiritual medium of the benediction, the emotion etched in the violin echoing her prayer (ex. 5.3b [b]).

Example 5.3b   *Le Prophète*: from Fidès's arioso (Act 2)

Fidès is a matriarch equal in nobility and pathos to the great father-figures of Verdi's operas. Her music is distinguished by its urgency and vitality, with melodic and harmonic material always the perfect expression of the continually changing passions found in Scribe's text. Conventional aria-cabaletta forms in her scene 'O prêtres de Baal' (O priests of Baal) (Act 5) are infused, by way of free-form, kaleidoscopic melody and variegated instrumentation (solo bass clarinet, combined woodwind timbres, then full chords on the harp), with an intense dramatic immediacy. Even her cadenzas transcend the bounds of mere vocal display and serve instead to intensify her intense outpourings of emotion.

Jean's denial and 'exorcism' of his own mother in the cathedral functions as the repudiation of the natural human bonds and also as rejection of the divine law, and finally puts the seal on the crimes of the Anabaptists for which he is partly responsible. Through this he tacitly subscribes to evil: is the power of his speech, seductive and slippery, that of the political manipulator raised triumphantly and realized in the deafening celebration of the bedazzled crowd? Is his prayer sincere, and are his motives genuine? Does he lead the people forward in some kind of mission, a social cleansing (as is eventually suggested by the fiery finale)? Only maternal love now remains as the bridge to salvation for the fallen creature, who, according to God's law, is now lost. Jean's renewed relations with his mother in the Dungeon Scene brings on the change: after Fidès has set the renunciation of power as the condition ('Renonce à ton pouvoir') (Renounce your power), she, as fully empowered mediatrix, bestows the absolution of divine mercy ('oui par lui... je te l'atteste, tous tes crimes s'effaceront') (yes, through him, I testify to you, all your crimes will be wiped away), until the mutual address ('mon fils—ma mère') (my son—my mother) confirms the forgiveness of the sinner and rehabilitation of Jean's repudiated bond. Through Jean's self-chosen expiatory death, the demise of the Anabaptist movement receives a metaphysical dimension. The flames, in which reactionaries and revolutionaries die together, is a kind of Parousia, signalling the end of history, functioning as a Sardanapalian Last Judgement.

Meyerbeer disposed his dark and expressive musico-dramatic vocabulary—so very different from that of *Les Huguenots*—to the service of his new conception with great stringency. A highly developed motif technique underscores the dramatic integration, and indeed secures for *Le Prophète* an important role in the development of the leitmotif. No fewer than eight motifs are here woven into a subtle semantic net of allusion. Three are related to the Anabaptists: their chorale, march and camp theme; three to Jean: his Pastorale, the Coronation March and the Chorus of Children; two to Fidès: her arioso and theme of rejected despair in the cathedral. The dark atmosphere of the subject (which Meyerbeer called *sombre et fanatique*) results in an intensive employment of covered sound colours, especially in the woodwind, in changing blends and contrasts, which capture the dramatic moments in all their varied hues. In the vocal parts, replacing more traditional periodic symmetry, and more than in the preceding works, a flexible *melos* makes its appearance, precisely reflecting the facets of expression. It is a structure that is not so much aria-like, but rather in the nature of a mosaic (like Berthe's cabaletta 'Dieu me guidera' [God will guide me] in the Act 4 duet with Fidès), or changing between a bound form and free declamation (like Jean's Dream Narration and Fidès's arioso, both in Act 2).

The complex nature even of these small-scale forms is one of the reasons why Meyerbeer was misunderstood by his contemporaries and criticized by some as having a poor melodic gift. Meyerbeer's French melodies are made up of numerous lyrical fragments welded together to form a complete musical thought. The invention of this mosaic style contributes to his music an ever-present sense of anticipation, of the unexpected, and writing of this kind authoritatively influenced the vocal style of both French and Italian opera in the middle of the century.

Luxurious *melos*, as always in such situations, infused with the breath of Italy, still fills the score with longing. The two female voices in their Act 4 duet of reunion combine in a melody spanning several octaves. Sensuousness is held in check, all the bitter-sweetness of the lost happiness considered by the two women reflected in the wide intervals of the line and its chromatic tincture, a sense of emptiness emphasized by the sparse accompaniment, with alternating strings and clarinets, the bass line reduced to minimal octave leaps for the horns and basses. The later manifestation of the pastoral in Act 5, under the tragic circumstances of delusion and imminent betrayal, is more powerfully evoked. The forcefulness, the full colouring, the dense harmonic textures, the Arcadian melting, reminiscent of a summer evening in the free open air, are all the while held in ironic tension by the enclosing vault and imminence of disaster, and add an additional distress to the shattering of this forlorn dream when Berthe discovers Jean's true identity, and sees no resolution to the problem other than suicide.

Even more purposefully than in the earlier operas, vocal virtuosity is put at the service of the drama. In its purest form, it is used to convey emotional retreat into an otherworldly idyll (as in the Italianate double cadenzas in the duets for Berthe and Fidès in Acts 2 and 4, the fioriture in Jean's Act 2 Pastorale 'Pour Berthe, moi je soupire' (I yearn for Berthe). It is used indirectly to sharpen the nature of a melodic phrase, adding, for example, a nervous allure to Jean's Drinking Song ('Versez! Que tout respire' [Pour out! Let everyone drink up] in Act 5). Otherwise it can convey religious ecstasy (as in Fidès's aria 'Comme un éclair' [like a lightning bolt] in the Act 5 Dungeon Scene), or at its most extreme function as a vector for a fraught state of mind, as in Berthe's anguish during the cabaletta of the Act 5 trio ('O spectre épouvantable') (O frightful spectre).

Structural and technical means are used to convey conceptual significance, as in the manneristic use of a neo-Baroque style, familiar from *Les Huguenots* (the Catholic Court in Act 2 and the Blessing of the Daggers in Act 4). This similarly conveys the profane/hypocritical, and even blasphemous nature of the Anabaptists, as in the Act 2 quartet ('Gémissant sous le loug et sous la tyrannie') (Groaning under the yoke of tyranny), the opening chorus of Act 3 ('Du sang! Que Judas succombe') (Blood! Let Judas die), and in Zacharie's warlike *couplets* ('Aussi nombreux que les étoiles') (As numerous as the stars) later in Act 3.

Illustration 5.3c *Le Prophète*: card depiction of the Act 5 trio (German, late nineteenth century)

The depiction of the three Anabaptists as an unholy trio is an ingenious musico-dramatic stroke. Jonas, Mathisen, and Zacharie fall midway in history between the Three Ladies of *Die Zauberflöte* and Ping, Pang and Pong of *Turandot*, an eerie triad capable of making solo utterances through three voices: the individuality of the figures is hardly allowed to show before their vocal merging into ensemble conveys a type of unity and lends to their invariably corporate appearances an aura of mystery, sometimes with a tinge of the farcical or macabre. The musical emblem of this unholy, even diabolical, trinity is the thematically recurring chorale 'Ad nos, ad salutarem undam' (To us, to the life-giving spring) which Meyerbeer himself wrote in the style of the sixteenth century. The composer used the opportunity of the expanded vocal possibilities offered by this sinister union to compose the extraordinary male quartet of Act 2 in which the trio induces Jean into assuming the 'sacred' leadership of their revolt. Because the three Anabaptists exist as a unit, having no dramatic individuality among themselves, there is a certain unearthly quality about them, noticeable when they first appear intoning their plainchant. Are they sanctimonious political rabble-rousers, or something more?

Meyerbeer's control of the orchestra assumes a new subtlety. *Le Prophète* is scored for piccolo, two flutes, two oboes, English horn, two clarinets, bass clarinet, four bassoons, four horns, three trombones, ophicleide (the bass brass instrument preceding the invention of the tuba), four trumpets (both natural and piston), timpani (three in the Act 3 finale), two harps, bass drum, cymbals, side drum, triangle, antique cymbals (played by the choirboys in the cathedral scene), organ, and enough strings to balance the winds. In addition there is a stage band in the *Marche du Sacre* consisting of 18 saxhorns of varying sizes (not to be confused with saxophones, also invented by Adolph Sax), two *cornets à cylindres*, two *trompettes à cylindres* and two side drums (*tambours militaires*).

As in *Les Huguenots*, tableaux conceived as historical panoramas have a prominent place. However, the very different working dramaturgy of *Le Prophète* means that these do not function as independent vectors of meaning (like the Pré aux clercs does in *Les Huguenots*). There is less dramaturgical weight put on the crowd scenes, which at the same time take on a sharpness in the presentation of the compromised, ambivalent nature of the masses themselves.

Thus in Act 1 the peasants, incited by the preaching of the Anabaptists, rise in revolt against Count Oberthal, but when he makes a sudden appearance, their resolution collapses immediately and they become abject underlings again. It is therefore interesting to see that the relation between solo and chorus operates here very differently from the similar dramatic idea developed in the Blessing of the Daggers. While there the ensemble structures are absorbed successively into choral movements, here the ensemble is simply superimposed on the cumulative arch of the piece, shaped, as it is, by the determining chorale and march forms. There is nevertheless unusual correspondence between inner creative impulses and outer political developments. The stretta to the Anabaptist sermon at the end of Act 1 emerged as an image of the revolutionary activities during the February Revolution of 1848 in Paris. March rhythms, Marseilles-type intonations, swirling peasants in military order relate to those things which Meyerbeer saw and heard on the streets in those days. Instead of peasants the workers were now marching. Meyerbeer needed to ensure that his work, which he had been carrying around with him since 1837, reflected the contemporary events, suddenly challenged by a highly remarkable actuality. The whole scene begins with the dark, creeping entry of the Anabaptists with their Reformation chorale, their incrementally inflammatory preaching illustrating the growing sense of unease and social unrest, the sustained pedal point suggesting the insidious infiltration of sedition, the tension growing until its bursts into a huge surge of defiant march-like energy, grandiose and triumphant in its forward progress and built-in power propulsion that then flows into the rising and falling walking ground-bass, a relentless dotted rhythm that moves progressively to the great unison outpouring of revolutionary fervour in the march (ex. 5.3c).

Example 5.3c   *Le Prophète*: from the Peasants' Insurrection in Act 1

In Act 3 the military campaign of the revolutionary movement is seen in action, in the dark, alienating sounds of the Anabaptist camp, the sinister timpani motifs and cold military signals, the frenzied chorus of bloodlust, jerky and broken, with its ironic interpolation of a medieval prayer of thanksgiving. The Anabaptists continue their identification with older, Baroque sounds and forms: Zacharie enters, swinging his battle axe, and sings his song of triumph over his enemies. The Handelian pastiche sounds disturbing like a hunting song, its dusky introduction with the solo horn triplets unmasking the murderous intention of the chase—only this time with human quarry.

    The undisputed focus of the tableau in *Le Prophète*, and the dramatic highpoint of the opera, is the Cathedral Scene. The contours are determined by the principle of contrast, designed with the big stage conceived as acoustic space, with a triple division into foreground, visible and invisible background, and a diagonal optical effect of recession. All this is realized in terms of the processing Coronation March with the stage band traversing the whole space, a cappella ensemble behind the scene, a chorus on stage for Fidès's curse, two mixed choruses with a children's choir and organ. By motival linking with the Dream Scene (in which Jean foresaw his later coronation in mythical imagery), the visible reality of the events now appears inverted in terms of the dream remembered (reflected back as unreal and magical reminiscence) ('Jean! tu règneras, ah!...c'est donc vrai') (John you will reign, ah!...so it is true). With the coup of the mother–son meeting, and the following exorcism of the mother by the son, the ambiguity of the levels of consciousness are broken open catastrophically and given musical expression in the shimmering strings that conjure up the vast space of the cathedral, and the convoluting solo cello and bass clarinet writing. They shape a theme where form alone provides the expression: the anguish of son and mother silently confronting each other, conveying a telepathy, a search for understanding too deep for words. All this is realized musically in a montage technique of many perspectives, with a realism of expression that engages even ugly and trivial dimensions of dramatic truth. The purely decorative elements of this tableau were much imitated (most individually by Verdi in the Auto-da-fé in *Don Carlos*, 1867), and thereafter became a feature of this type of representational scene. In the mingling of *spectacle* and *drame* in terms of the theatrical realization of a historical and philosophical idea, the scene remains unsurpassed.

Illustration 5.3d *Le Prophète*: contemporary painting by Ferdinand Keller of the Cathedral Scene, showing Pauline Viardot-Garcia and Gustave Roger

Illustration 5.3e *Le Prophète*: Gustave Roger in the Banquet Scene (contemporary
engraving by LD)

The premiere, which had been awaited by the musical world of Europe with
increasing expectation, proved to be a brilliant triumph, and consolidated
Meyerbeer's position, even in the opinion of his opponents, as 'le plus digne
représentant de la musique dramatique en Europe' (the most worthy representative
of dramatic music in Europe) (Paul Scudo, *Revue des Deux Mondes*, 22 April 1849).
With this model production, the Opéra reasserted its prime position among the
contemporary opera stages. Under the musical direction of Narcisse Girard, there
was a completely new ensemble: Viardot-Garcia as Fidès, Roger as Jean, Jeanne-
Anaïs Castellan as Berthe, Louis Gueymard as Jonas, Euzet as Mathisen and
Hippolyte Brémond as Oberthal. The only veteran of the old guard was Levasseur
as Zacharie. Viardot-Garcia's assumption of Fidès, vocally as well as dramatically,
created an overwhelming impression. With some reservations, this applied also to
Roger. Their realization of the confrontation of the two protagonists in the Cathedral
Scene was generally regarded as the interpretive highpoint of the performance. But
also for the majority of the public, for whom the novel musico-dramatic structure
of the work remained difficult, there was a theatrical experience of extraordinary
splendour. The stage designs were modelled on Old Netherlandish paintings (by
Charles-Antoine Cambon, Edouard-Désiré-Joseph Déspléchin, Charles-Polycarpe
Séchan and Joseph-François-Désiré Thierry). The suggestive realism of the *mise en
scène* had been perfected by Scribe, with sensational stage effects like falling snow,

the coronation procession, the palace fire and a sunrise realized for the first time by electric light. Not least was the appeal of the highly unusual ballet of the skaters (*Les Patineurs*) (with choreography by Auguste Mabille and Paolo Taglioni), which featured a new fashionable dance, the redowa, as the *pas de deux* (with Adeline Plunkett and Lucien Petipa). (See Pendle and Wilkins 1998: 198–206.)

After only a few years *Le Prophète* was in the repertories of all the bigger houses of Europe and overseas. Reception was occasionally controversial, especially in Germany where the resistance of the nationally inclined critics against the cosmopolitanism of *grand opéra* was ever more trenchantly articulated. On the whole, however, admiration for the work, regarded as the highpoint of modern music drama, prevailed. A determinative factor for the reception of the work was, from the beginning, the casting of the two principal roles. Jean could be seen as the development of an older role type; but with Fidès there emerged a completely new vocal *Fach*. In both cases the vocal demands are extraordinary. The part of Jean requires more strength and less flexibility than that of Raoul; casting the part for a *Heldentenor*, later the rule, was rather more justified, but led to a narrowing of the profile of the role, and meant that it could not be performed without cuts. on the other hand, the part of Fidès, shaped to the individuality of Viardot-Garcia, presented a synthesis of all the expressive possibilities of the female voice, something unique in the history of opera. An adequate casting, taking all the demands into account, could only be properly realized in exceptional cases.

Already in 1849 Covent Garden in London became the second stage to mount the work (in the Italian translation of Manfredo Maggioni, with Viardot-Garcia, Mario, and Michael Costa conducting). During 1850 the work appeared on many stages (often in the German translation of Ludwig Rellstab): among them Hamburg (with Johanna Wagner and Franz Ditt), Amsterdam, Dresden (Aloysia Krebs-Michalesi, Joseph Tichatschek, conducted by Karl Gottlieb Reissiger), Frankfurt-am-Main, Vienna (Anne-Caroline Lagrange and Alois Ander), Leipzig, Darmstadt, Berlin (with Viardot-Garcia, Louise Köster and Tichatschek), Munich (Antonia Viala-Mittermayr, Martin Härtinger, with Franz Lachner conducting), Prague (Auguste Knopp and Josef Reichel). First performances in other languages followed: in 1852 Stockholm (translated into Swedish by Carl Vilhelm August Strandberg, with Olof Strandberg as Jean) and Florence (with Giulia Sanchioli as Fidès). This performance consolidated this work as the centrepiece of the Italian reception of Meyerbeer. Sanchioli portrayed Fidès on further Italian stages, including Parma in 1853, Milan in 1855, Venice in 1855 and 1859, and Genoa in 1857. In St Petersburg a performance by a visiting Italian opera troupe in 1852 was followed by the first Russian production, and again in 1869 (translated into Russian by Piotr Kalashnikov) as *Ioann Leidenski* (Jelisaveta Lavrovskaya and Feodor Nikolski, with Eduard Napravnik conducting).

At the Opéra *Le Prophète* was on the performing roster almost continually for decades. As Fidès there were debuts by, among others, Marietta Alboni (1850), Palmyre Wertheimber (1854), Rosine Stoltz (1855), Adelaide Borghi-Mamo (1856), Désirée Artôt (1858); and as Jean, Gueymard (1850) and Alfred Chapuis (1851). In the Salle Garnier a new production was staged in 1876 with Rosine Bloch and Pierre-François Villaret, conducted by Edouard Deldevez. The work remained in the repertoire in various revivals until 1912. Other important interpreters of the principal roles on the big stages in those decades included: as Fidès—Guilia Grisi (London 1852), Rosa Csillag (Paris 1859, London 1860), Therese Tietjens (London 1869), Sofia Scalchi (London 1878, New York 1884), Marianne Brandt (New York 1884), Blanche Deschamps-Jehin (Paris 1892), Anna Elsbeth Stöbe-Hofmann (Prague 1891), Marie Delna (Paris 1898), Ernestine Schumann-Heink (New York 1900); as Jean—Enrico Tamberlik (London 1860), Albert Niemann (Berlin 1864), Julián Gayarre (London 1878), Roberto Stagno (New York 1884), Francesco Tamagno (Milan 1884, Rome 1888, London 1895), Jean de Reszke (Paris 1887, London 1890, New York 1892), Albert-Raymond Alvarez (Paris 1898, 1903, New York 1900), Charles Dalmorès (Brussels 1904).

In the 1900s there were productions in New York in 1900, Fiume in 1901 and Naples in 1910. An important revival of the work at a time of growing repudiation of the Meyerbeerian aesthetic took place in the Berlin Court Opera in 1910, admittedly under the repression of the concept of historical opera, in the production of Georg von Hülsen, with Marie Goetz as Fidès, Frieda Hempel as Berthe, Rudolf Berger as Jean, conducted by Leo Blech, an ensemble that allowed the musical qualities of the opera to shine.

In general, *Le Prophète* appeared in the following decades only when star singers could be found to interpret the roles: the Vienna Court Opera 1911 (with Margarete Matzenauer and Leo Slezak, conducted by Gustav Mahler) and 1931 (with Bella Paalen, Slezak, Maria Nemeth and Alfred Jerger); the Simin Opera, Moscow 1915 (with Vassili Damajev), the Maryinsky Theatre, St Petersburg 1916 (with Ivan Altschevski) and in Leningrad 1934; the Metropolitan Opera, New York 1918 (with Matzenauer and Caruso) and 1927 (with Matzenauer and Giovanni Martinelli); Hamburg 1922 (with Sabine Kalter and Wilhelm Wagner) and 1928 (with Lauritz Melchior); Brussels 1926; the Städtische Oper, Berlin 1927 (with Sigrid Onegin) and in 1930 (with Melchior); Monte Carlo 1932 (with Georges Thill).

After the Second World War only a few theatres could provide the kind of interpreters and elaborate production demanded by this work. Modest revivals took place in London (Steiner Theatre) in 1959 and in Siena 1974. More ambitious was Zurich in 1962, where Lotfi Mansouri produced a version with projected stage designs by Hainer Hill (featuring Sandra Warfield and James McCracken, conducted by Samuel Krachmalnick). McCracken also sang Jean at the Deutsche Oper Berlin in 1966 (with Warfield, conducted by Heinrich Hollreiser), and again at the Metropolitan, New York, 1977 (with Marilyn Horne, conducted by Henry Lewis); it was revived in 1979 (this time with Guy Chauvet as Jean and Charles Mackerras conducting). If Bohumil Herlischka's Berlin staging concept of the worn-out topos of the theatre-within-a theatre hardly captured the individuality of the work, John Dexter's parable-like production for New York allowed the structure of the work to shine through. This production was taken on tour to several American cities (New York 1975–77, Atlanta 1977, Dallas 1977, Minneapolis 1977, Detroit 1977). The New York version was notable for its largely intact musical context and stupendous interpretation by Marilyn Horne, captured on the CBS recording (1976). This was prepared for in a legendary concert performance by Radiotelevisione Italiana Turin in 1970, also conducted by Lewis; Nicolai Gedda, as Jean, embodied Meyerbeer's *ténor héroïque* to near perfection, and Margherita Rinaldi captured Berthe's vulnerability most touchingly.

John Dew's unbiasedly radical production for the Bielefeld Oper in 1986 (with Krystyna Michaelowska, Christine Weidinger, Stephen Algie, conducted by David de Villiers) provided an associative discourse with text and music, but inexplicably reversed the order of scenes in Act 4.

In the 1990s a critical edition of the score was tried out at Folkwang-Hochschule, Essen-Werden in 1997 (with Gloria Scalchi, Soto Papulkas, conducted by Franz Xaver Poncette), and a major revival followed in Vienna in 1998–99 (with Agnes Baltsa as Fidès, Victoria Loukianetz as Berthe, Plácido Domingo as Jean, conducted by Marcello Viotti); the significance and impact of this event were vitiated by the alienating and grotesque stage production of Hans Neuenfels. Far more successful was the musically reduced, but dramatically sensitive, realization in Stockholm in 1999 (with Ingrid Tobiasson, Christina Knochenhauer, Jean-Pierre Furlan, conducted by Gunner Staern).

The 2000s have seen a concert performance at Kiel in 2000 and a production in Münster in 2004 (with Suzanne McLeod, Carmen Acosta, Daniel Magdal, conducted by Bastian Heymel). The latter tried to serve the opera's dramatic and vocal demands faithfully, and used some of the pieces cut from the manuscript (especially in Jean's extended scene at the end of Act 3). (See Loewenberg 1970: 873–5: Wolff 1962: 177–9; Döhring 1991, 4: 150–1.)

5.4 L'Africaine (Vasco da Gama) [The African Woman]

Opéra en cinq actes [opera in five acts]
Text: Augustin-Eugène Scribe (with revisions, additions and translations by Charlotte Birch-Pfeiffer, Julius Duesberg and Giacomo Meyerbeer)
First performance: Opéra, Salle de la rue Le Peletier, Paris, 28 April 1865

Meyerbeer's first involvement with this work was at the beginning of 1837, in that fruitful period when, inspired by the success of *Les Huguenots* (1836), he considered a whole series of new plans and even began working at them. Without doubt the project *Les Anabaptistes*, from which *Le Prophète* (1849) would grow, was in the foreground. Dissatisfaction with the scenario, ready by the end of 1836, led Meyerbeer to decide to postpone this project in favour of another: an opera based on an exotic subject, with a leading female role for which he was considering Marie-Cornélie Falcon, the outstanding creator of Valentine in *Les Huguenots*. On 24 May 1837 Meyerbeer and Scribe signed a contract for the new *grand opéra L'Africaine*; the libretto was to be delivered in three months, the score in three years. Whether or not Meyerbeer actually began the composition at this time is not known, but in any case he turned away from the project in the summer of 1838, mainly because Falcon, afflicted with a vocal crisis, would not be available for the foreseeable future. He had further artistic reservations about the libretto, and turned back to *Le Prophète*. His doubts about *L'Africaine* can be derived from the libretto of 1837 (see extensive summaries of the action in Frese 1970: 219–26, and the libretto itself in

Roberts 1977: 89–92). The story was of the unhappy love of the African princess Gunima (in the scenario; in the libretto she is Sélica) for the Portuguese naval officer Fernand, whose affection is not returned and is eventually lost to his first love, the daughter of the governor Estrelle (the vice-regent's daughter Inès). She consequently breathes in the poisonous fragrance of the manzanilla (or manchineel or upas) tree. This story, after *Robert le Diable* and *Les Huguenots*, could have appeared only as a regression to the conventions of the older operas. Meyerbeer's glosses and proposed changes in the scenario show that he acknowledged these weaknesses, and obviously tried to invest the subject with historical features (like the opposition between Christians and Moors in Act 1), but the fundamental structure of the individual action remained untouched.

Scribe and Germain Delavigne produced a four-act libretto in 1838 with a contraction of the first two acts, but neither this nor a five-act version by Scribe alone in 1843 resulted in more than a half-hearted involvement in the project on Meyerbeer's part. In various private utterances the composer made it clear that he held the text and the music of *L'Africaine* in lower regard than that of *Le Prophète*, and that after such a long period of silence, he could not contemplate returning to the Opéra with this work. So he set aside this provisionally completed version of the work, which he called the *Vecchia Africana*, especially as his new duties as Generalmusikdirektor to the king of Prussia made heavy demands of him.

Only after the completion of *Le Prophète* could the issue of resuming the old project, on the basis of fundamental restructuring, be reconsidered. Certainly at the end of 1849 and beginning of 1850 the composer was reading Luís de Camões's epic *Os Lusiadas* (1572) and contemporary travel literature on India (the copper engravings of the Indian journey made by Prince Soltikoff) probably with the idea of using the Portuguese naval hero and explorer Vasco da Gama as a new protagonist for his old opera. In the autumn of 1850 Meyerbeer and Scribe resumed their discussion about the work, and in a letter of 27 October 1852 the composer reminded the librettist of his earlier promise 'to place the work on new foundations with an historical and noble background' (Becker and Gudrun Becker 1983: 196). Scribe delivered various scenarios and libretto drafts which Meyerbeer annotated with *remarques générales*. The extensive material allows a close look into the composer's working practice and shows yet again how much he initiated by way of scene and text. Partly descriptive, partly argumentatively, he proposed for the librettist the outline of the characters of Vasco, Sélika, and Yoriko (Nélusko), as well as general situations in the action (the Council Scene, the Adamastor Ballad). The new foundations were applied only in the first two acts of what now became known as *Vasco da Gama;* the dramaturgical structure of the other acts, on the other hand, remained unaltered in their basic features. In Acts 1 and 2 the scene of the action shifted from Cadiz or Seville to Lisbon; Acts 4 and 5 from a place near the source of the Niger in Central Africa (as the libretto the *Vecchia Africana* has it) to India; the setting of Act 3, on a ship's deck, was retained.

For a while the working contacts between Meyerbeer and Scribe were intensive, with a meeting in Berlin early in 1852, but in 1853 the project was again delayed. In the following year the composer's interest in the matter would flicker for a while, usually in connection with plans for the casting of the principal characters. But apart from a brief period near the end of 1857 when he completed the duet for Vasco and Sélika in Act 2 and two of Nélusko's arias, other projects took precedence: *L'Étoile du Nord*, *Le Pardon de Ploërmel*, the music for *La Jeunesse de Goethe*, some work on the three-act grand opera *Judith* (1854–58, text by Scribe, and uncompleted) as well as many other small occasional pieces.

The renewed work on *Vasco* in 1860 was soon interrupted by Scribe's death on 20 February 1861. As a result, Charlotte Birch-Pfeiffer was asked by Meyerbeer to provide alterations and extra verses at his direction; her German verses were then translated into French by Julius Duesberg. This collaboration continued until the preliminary completion of the score on 29 November 1863. Even at this stage important dramaturgical changes were made, such as the elimination of the slave market scene in Act 1, and, as a consequence of that, the insertion of the entry of Sélika and Nélusko into the Council Scene, as well as the new motivation for the love duet between Vasco and Sélika in Act 4 by means of a love potion. In September 1863 Meyerbeer decided to go to Paris to begin his deliberations about the casting. When he died suddenly just before the rehearsals began (2 May 1864), the score was complete apart from the ballet music. Since it was the composer's habit finally to establish the definitive shape of the work only during the rehearsal period as a result of insights gained from the process, this left open a number musical and dramaturgical problems.

After contractual clarification of complex questions of rights between the management of the Opéra and the widows of Meyerbeer and Scribe, the Belgian musicologist François-Joseph Fétis (assisted in textual matters by Camille Du Locle, Delavigne, Mélesville and Marie-Joseph-François Mahérault) was commissioned by Minna Meyerbeer to prepare a performing edition from the voluminous material of the score. He completed this very responsible task with competence and taste, and on the whole reached an acceptable compromise between the presumed artistic wishes of Meyerbeer and the practical necessities of performance (see the preface to the vocal score). For the obligatory ballet Fétis arranged two of the excluded numbers: a variant of Sélika's Lullaby (Act 2) and the sailors' *Ronde bachique* (Act 3). Perhaps his most daring contribution was simply to remove a duet movement for Sélika and Nélusko from the extended Act 3 finale and relocate it in Act 5, in order to give greater weight to Nélusko's presence at the end. He further implemented his proposal to change the title back to *L'Africaine*. Retaining the historical figure of Vasco, as well as the Hindu religion depicted in Act 4, led to almost irreparable absurdity in the action because of the locations given for Acts 4 and 5 on the printed libretto in the vocal score (an island on the east coast of Africa) and in the full score (an island in the Indian archipelago). At this time the name of Yoricko was also altered to Nélusko, the name of the high priest of Brahma (Zanguebar) cut, and the definitive spelling of Sélika fixed.

As with all Meyerbeer's later operas there is no direct textual source. The original scenario of 1837 had been drawn from an unidentified German tale and from a play by Antoine Lemierre (*La Veuve de Malabar*, 1770) treating of the love of a Hindu maiden for a Portuguese navigator. Further, several individual literary motifs can be identified, like the figure of the ocean giant Adamastor (in Nélusko's Act 3 ballad) from Camões's epic, and Sélika's love death under the manchineel tree (Act 5) from

Charles Millevoye's elegy *Le Mancenillier* (in *Elégies*, Paris 1812) and Alexandre Dumas's poem of the same name (1829).

Plot
Lisbon, on board a ship, and in India, 1497–98.

Act 1. The Council Chamber of the king of Portugal in Lisbon; in the background and on the sides there are doors; to the right on a podium the chair of the president, with benches of the councillors on either side. Inès, the daughter of the admiral Don Diégo, has been waiting with longing for two years for news of the expedition of Bartholomew Diaz to the Cape of Good Hope. Among his crew is the intrepid officer Vasco da Gama whom she loves. She recalls his song of farewell to the Tagus River. She is devastated to hear it is the king's wish that she should marry Don Pédro, and her sorrow is compounded by the news that Diaz's expedition has been shipwrecked with all his crew. The king's council gathers, led by the eight bishops of Portugal. They are startled by the unexpected entry of Vasco who has survived the disaster. He tells the Council of the marvels he has seen on the voyage, and asks for the means to lead a further expedition. To prove his report he brings in two slaves captured on the expedition, Sélika and Nélusko. The Council debate his proposal: those against led by Don Pédro, those for by Don Alvar. The vote goes against Vasco, who in fury denounces the Council as obscurantist. He is anathematized by the Grand Inquisitor and arrested.

Act 2. The prison of the Inquisition in Lisbon. On the left in the hinterground a bench, in the middle a pillar to which is attached a rough geographical map. Vasco has been imprisoned with his slaves. He is in a deep sleep, watched over by Sélika who loves him. Vasco mentions the name of his beloved Inès in a dream, to Sélika's grief. She soothes him with a lullaby. Her companion Nélusko sees her devotion and determines to kill Vasco. He pleads with Sélika to give up her love, revealing that she is a queen in their own country. He moves to stab Vasco, but is prevented by Sélika who rouses the sleeping explorer. Vasco tries to work out the mystery of the route to the east, and Sélika helps him to understand the proper way. In gratitude he embraces her, just as Don Pédro enters the prison with Inès. She draws the wrong conclusion about Vasco's feelings, and he feels her reserve as coldness. He presents the slaves to her as a sign of his devotion. Inès tells him that she has bought his freedom to her own cost: the condition is her marriage to Don Pédro who will now lead the expedition to the East, using Vasco's plans and maps. She bids him an anguished farewell.

Illustration 5.4a   *L'Africaine*: the first production at the Paris Opéra (the first panel,
            Act 1 Council Scene and Act 2 Dungeon Scene, of the triptych of
            engravings by Alphonse Neuville in *L'Illustration*, 1865)

Act 3. A ship on the ocean. The second deck is in two parts: on the one side Inès's cabin, on the other that of Don Pédro. Don Pédro's caravel is on the high seas. On board are the sailors, officers with the councillor Don Alvar, as well as Inès with followers, including the two slaves. Nélusko has offered his services as pilot. Inès's women companions sing as the ship travels through the night. With the break of dawn, the ritual of waking begins: the sailors' reveille, morning prayer and breakfast. Don Alvar conveys to Don Pédro his mistrust of Nélusko: under his guidance two ships have already been lost. The wind changes, and, at Nélusko's direction, the ship alters course for the north. Portentously, Nélusko now sings the Legend of Adamastor, the giant of the tempest, who brings death to mariners. The sailors are filled with dread. Vasco, who has fitted up his own expedition and has been pursuing them, now comes alongside and, boarding the caravel, also warns Don Pédro about Nélusko. Don Pédro accuses him of caring only for Inès, and a dispute ensues. He orders Vasco's arrest and execution. The women come running out at the uproar, and Sélika, snatching a weapon, threatens the life of Inès should Vasco die. Don Pédro gives in, but now orders Nélusko to kill Sélika. When he refuses, Pédro orders both slaves to be murdered. At this moment the tempest breaks upon the ship, which is grounded on the reef to which Nélusko has been steering it. Indians clamber on board and begin slaughtering the Europeans. They are welcomed by Nélusko who presents Sélika to them as their queen.

Act 4. A tropical paradise. On the left is an Indian temple, on the right a palace, in the background beautiful monuments. Sélika is welcomed back to her country with rituals of celebration. She swears to uphold the laws of her land which demands the death of all strangers. All the Portuguese men have been massacred, and only the women and prisoners found on the ship are left. The women are led off by the sacrificing priests to die under the manchineel trees which exude a poisonous vapour. All go into the temple. Vasco, who was held prisoner, has escaped the fate of the crew. He emerges, enraptured with the beauty of this wonderful country. The priests enter and demand his death, but Sélika saves him by pretending that he is her husband, and obliges Nélusko to perjure himself by witnessing to this. To contradict Sélika would mean her death. Vasco's life is saved, and now, according to the laws, the marriage must be celebrated with Hindi rituals. Invoking the Hindu Trinity, the High Priest of Brahma proffers Sélika and Vasco a sacred drink which induces a narcotic rapture. As the drug takes effect, Sélika points to Vasco's ship which waits for him just off the coast. But as his senses are gradually intoxicated, he does not wish to flee but thinks only of Sélika. He declares himself her husband, and they are lost in voluptuous bliss. The High Priest blesses the couple, and they retire into a gauzy tent, fêted by dancing. From the distance can be heard the voices of Inès and the Portuguese women singing the farewell song to the Tagus.

Act 5. Scene 1. The queen's garden, with tropical trees, flowers and fruit; on the left, the entry to the palace. Inès alone has escaped the poisonous fragrance of the manchineel trees. She marvels at the beauty of her surroundings. Vasco enters and they are happily reunited. Sélika disturbs them, and in anguish has Vasco taken away. Full of jealousy, she confronts Inès who tells the queen that she will respect the vow, as will Vasco. But Sélika, realizing that she can never have his love, decides to forgive Inès and let Vasco go. She orders Nélusko to lead Vasco and Inès to the

Portuguese ship, and then to meet her on the great cape overlooking the sea. Nélusko warns her that this is the place where the feared manchineel tree grows.

Scene 2. A promontory with a view of the ocean; in the middle grows a large tree full of beautiful flowers. Sélika approaches the tree and looks across the sea. She greets the tree as a temple, and inhales deeply of its flowers. She is intoxicated by the fragrance and, in her increasing delirium, feels herself transported to paradise where she is reunited with Vasco. A cannon shot announces the departure of the ship bearing away Vasco and Inès. Nélusko enters with the news to find her dying. She bids farewell and dies as the people enter but do not dare approach the tree. Nélusko kneels motionless before Sélika as an unseen chorus proclaims the liberation she will find in the kingdom of the spirit.

The original *Africaine* was conventional from a generic point of view, but integral in itself. Meyerbeer's desire that the new version should present a historical and noble background demanded a radical departure from the model, and really required a completely new work. Both composer and librettist did not seem to understand this consequence, perhaps because of their intention to rescue as much text and music as possible from the first version. The result was a compromise in which the introduction of Vasco da Gama's world historical perspectives are neglected, or seem to diminish, in the course of the action. With Acts 4 and 5 Vasco moves in the steps of Fernand, his predecessor in the original version. Other than in *Le Prophète*, public historical/political/social and private individual action would not seem to engage in a productive tension, which, in the conflict between history and individual, generally determines the dramaturgy of the historical opera. In *L'Africaine*, rather, the historical action seems to resolve itself almost casually in private. The difference is that individuals in the latter opera have assumed dimensions of significance almost allegorical in their wider implications.

If one wonders what could have induced Meyerbeer to have tackled another such 'historical opera' after *Le Prophète*, the answer lies above all in the material. The story from the early days of colonialism unfolds novel political and social antagonisms whose musico-dramatic treatment were a challenge to the composer. As always, he avoided casting the historical parties in a superficially effective black and white opposition by simply idealizing the alien as the 'noble savage'. Portugal and also India are depicted as totalitarian political states in which the respective guardians of religion, the Grand Inquisitor and the High Priest of Brahma, uphold their rigid sway, disposed against everything new. Even the alien queen and her weird servant are faceted characters, as Meyerbeer had already asked of Scribe in his *remarques générales*: he saw Sélika as affected by 'l'impétuosité et la jalousie que le climat brûlant inspire aux passions' (impetuosity and jealousy inspired by the scorching climate), and Nélusko as 'un mélange de haîne, de méchanceté et d'ironie contre tout chrétien' (a mixture of hate, malice and irony towards all Christians). Sélika's later magnanimity in sacrificing her life is not because she particularly represents the *nouveau monde*, but is rather a mark of her universal humanity. Even if the variants of the closing scene leave open the possibility of several interpretations, Sélika's Love Death under the manchineel tree (a symbolic expression of world renunciation in the original *Africaine*) should certainly be retained as the finale of the later opera—which is more than just a historical work.

And if at the beginning of the opera the Council Scene in Lisbon (as an event of imperial politics) and at the end the intimate Act 5 finale (as an act of mystical self-offering) remain in rather abrupt dramaturgical relationship to each other, it indicates a new expression of Meyerbeer's historical pessimism. This comes to the fore not in historical discourse (as in *Les Huguenots* and *Le Prophète*), but as a poetic scenario that has both a historical and a spiritual hermeneutic.

The Council Scene of Act 1 nevertheless shows that Meyerbeer adhered to the high standards of his earlier operas in the musico-dramatic shaping of this work, and demonstrateshis concerns with the forces of history and historical motivation. The defenders of Vasco, like the hero himself, are all in the higher registers—soloists (Don Alvar) and chorus; his opponents are in the basses (Don Pédro, the Grand Inquisitor, the eight bishops). In the course of the fervent debate and confrontation, the tenors weaken, eventually all moving over to the opposing side, when Vasco goes too far in insulting both state and religious authorities. The vocal divisions, and their dispositions in the course of the scene, are dictated not by musical considerations but by dramatic ones. When compared with the original first finale of the *Vecchia Africana*, dominated by personal motivation, in which the chorus stands about as an undivided, uncommitted monolithic entity, Meyerbeer's later conception represents the last victory of the historical opera. The national and philosophical conflicts are made comprehensible for the audience of 1865 in the person of Vasco, with his new ideas and bold demeanour, and his challenge to the status quo. At the same time, the fundamental dramatic constellation has been proposed for the rest of the work, whether this is worked out in terms of Vasco in relation to Don Pédro (and all he represents about the Old World), or in relation to Nélusko (and all he signifies for the New World) (Frese 1970: 237–8).

After the premiere many critics felt that Meyerbeer's last opera revealed a rupture in the coherence of its dramaturgy, partly because of apparent absurdities in the action, particularly in relation to the figure of Vasco da Gama. These are not always firmly founded, however. Thus even Eduard Hanslick's criticism cannot be taken seriously because it is based on a textual misunderstanding: Vasco is 'less caught between two world spheres than between two women, and is always in love with the one he finds himself alone with' (1875: 146). Actually the text and stage directions leave not the slightest doubt that Vasco loves Inès exclusively, and that his expressions of dedication and passion for Sélika are actually the result of overwhelming thanks (Act 2) and the consequence of a rapture induced by the love potion (Act 4). The problem is that the theatrical situation for considering both meetings between Vasco and Sélika as love scenes is strengthened by the musical style. It is therefore understandable that Hanslick and others were unable to appreciate their latent ambiguity, especially since Vasco's devotion to Inès is not given much tangible expression.

The problem relates more deeply to the very dramatic conception of this opera and its appeal to various layers of reality. Careful reading, and attention to both the literary and musical language of the text, reveals a modal mix of elements, a complex and sustained musico-dramatic conception in which verisimilitude, after the crucial semiotic shift of theme in the ocean crossing of Act 3, is systematically eroded away and merges into a legendary realm. The cold light of history is slowly refracted into an iridescent patina of epic, romance and myth. This has always been an aspect of interpreting this explorer's historical legacy (see Subrahmanyam 1997: 2, 5, 7, 8, 21). Throughout the opera, reflection on the conflict between two worlds, cultures and religions means that characters exist on both a surface reality and on a deeper allegorical level. Vasco comes to represent the spirit of bold Western enterprise and Sélika the exotic Eastern world of novelties and ancient wisdom. Failure to appreciate this modal mix means a limited understanding of the dramaturgical dynamic. This also relates to the religious subtext explored as in the other three major French operas. The circle of spiritual exploration closes with *L'Africaine*. The imagery, returning to the frames or reference found in *Robert le Diable*, is more mythological. Sélika becomes the ultimate mediatrix, a disciple of love and reconciliation, who has a vision of true values, who sacrifices herself and essays the life of the spirit. The manchineel tree in the final scene of *L'Africaine* is of huge symbolic significance in this respect. Sélika, having granted Vasco and Inès their freedom, sheds herself of the earthly vanities of power expressed in patriotism and imperialism, and the beautiful but invariably vain and tragic bonds of love. She is free to seek death under the great tree on a promontory overlooking the vast empty ocean which is carrying away the Portuguese ship. She attains her own liberty in a mystical love-death induced by the poisonous flowers of the legendary tree. This tree becomes the dominant image of the opera, an Edenic symbol of paradise lost (the Tree of the Knowledge of Good and Evil) and an apocalyptic one of paradise regained (the Tree of Life). It captures the mystique of the new, beautiful but dangerous world of the East, and becomes the vector of all transition and change in this story, where the boundaries and categories of old and new, history and myth, life and death become blurred in the attainment of a spiritual insight born of self-sacrifice.

Without perception of this modal mix, the nature of the rupture experienced by Hanslick makes it very difficult to achieve a definitive dramatic profiling of the principal character in terms of psychological mimesis alone. Vasco, the visionary politician and explorer, the intrepid opponent of intolerance and obscurantism (as depicted in Acts 1–3), changes in Acts 4–5 into someone dependent on an alien woman, entangled in illusions of feeling, concerned only for the life of his beloved. Statements by Meyerbeer during the preparations for the rehearsals reveal that he was aware of the problem and was considering a solution. In the working libretto there are texts for alternative conclusions 'pour réhabiliter le caractère de Vasco' (to rehabilitate Vasco's character), among them a version in which Vasco returns to the dying Sélika to establish her death as a necessary, if tragic, sacrifice for his political mission: 'Le Portugal dans l'Inde va régner' (For Portugal to reign in India). That Meyerbeer could have found such a convincing conventional solution to Vasco's departure, and that either this or some similar version could have worked, must be doubtful because the (apparently faulty) delineation of Vasco's character in terms of dramatic verisimilitude cannot be removed simply by adding a scene—resting, as it does, on the collision of irreconcilable conceptions in the redrafting of a private tragedy (*Vecchia Africana*) into a historical drama with symbolic overtones (*Vasco da Gama*). However, from the tempest in Act 3 onwards, Vasco is in fact caught up in an inevitable, but symbolically purposeful, process of fragmentation that is reflected in his characterization—both dramatic and musical.

Illustration 5.4b *L'Africaine*: the first production at the Paris Opéra (the central panel, Act 3 Shipwreck, of the triptych of engravings by Alphonse Neuville in *L'Illustration*, 1865). Marie-Constance Sass, Jean-Baptiste Faure and Emilio Naudin appear in the lunettes

The musical characterization further reveals Meyerbeer's close relationship to the material and its ideas. The dramatic use of motif, so important for *Le Prophète*, focuses here on the theme of farewell—the elegiac lament of Inès's song of parting which dominates the overture and the Act 2 finale (ex. 5.4a [a]), and the fourfold quotation of the opening of Inès's Act 1 romance ('Adieu mon doux rivage') (Goodbye, my gentle shore)—which indeed initiates the whole opera and occurs at the end of Act 4 to shatter Vasco's reverie of love (ex. 5.4a [b]). These themes personify her as the representative of the traditional Western values of ancient Portugal, and, as melodic emblems of the faraway, introduce that intimate and melancholic tone which characterizes the whole work.

Each character moreover discloses a musical gesture corresponding to their moral and dramaturgical disposition. This is by no means to be identified with an unchanging leitmotif, but relates more to Mozart's technique of characterization. Many of Vasco's motifs begin with a rising fourth or sixth, followed by a falling secondary figure that lingers on suspended notes. This melodic pattern defines the character as impulsive, heroic, aggressively disturbing, and throughout the opera imparts to it an unmistakable profile. This is reinforced by a recurrent tendency to enrich the soaring vocal part at moments of high emotion with woodwind and strings, either doubling it or thickening it in harmoniously spacious octaves. The crisp sprung dotted rhythms of Vasco's balletic entries in Acts 1 and 3 develop the image of the young explorer with attractively forceful energy, an impression sustained in heroic tessitura of the role and its consistent gravitation upwards to high A. His aim is a personal quest for the immortality of fame and ultimately entails a tacit disregard of the conventions of romantic love. Inès, his beloved, becomes an embodiment of the muse of his high calling to heroic quest for Portugal. His concealed plans of conquest are never more apparent than in the famous greeting to the Eden of the new world of his discoveries: in the midst of his enraptured apostrophe, almost hidden brassy fanfares reveal the concealed acquisitive intention ('A nous des campagnes merveilles') (Ours will be these luxuriant fields) (ex. 5.4b [a]). Even in the moment of death from the menacing priests, Vasco's plea is to be spared for his own immortal reputation. To give way to this new world is be subjugated by it (as he is by the narcotic of the wedding potion). This is the siren call of the unconscious, the impulse to oblivion. The only modus operandi et vivendi is to overcome it. So even though he owes his life to Sélika, his professed love is a drugged delusion and he is able to leave her without gratitude or regret. The analogies of Aeneas leaving Dido by fateful compulsion in *Les Troyens* are evident. Vasco is not criticized, blamed or spoiled; he simply fades away, dramaturgically speaking.

Indeed, no character or position is denounced in this musico-dramatic conception: both the would-be explorer/conqueror and life-affirming, self-sacrificing queen are held in consistent thematic and musical tension throughout. She too, like Vasco, has her own explicit musical gestures (her recurring cries of sorrow in Acts 2 and 4, with their distinctive falling fifths) and grows in stature until she is central to the action (ex. 5.4b [b–c]). If Vasco dominates Act 1 where Sélika is largely silent, the reverse is the case in Act 5 where the hero fades away ignominiously, and the stage is devoted to the queen's oblation of herself for the sake of love. There can be no doubt where the real sympathy of the work is vested (see Letellier, 2005: 215–18).

Example 5.4a   *L'Africaine* (*Vasco da Gama*): a) Inès's theme from the overture,
b) the Ballad of the Tagus (Act 1)

When it comes to comparing this work with the preceding operas, the lyrical character of the subject, especially in the last two acts, stimulated the composer to embark on new paths that occasionally appear to turn from earlier principles. Apart from the Council Scene, with its explosion of political and private actions that again reflects the grandiose flair of the historical opera, the *tableau* has forfeited its dramaturgical importance and serves to establish the framework for genre pictures (the Sea Scene in Act 3, the Oriental rituals of coronation and marriage in Act 4). So Meyerbeer developed a flowing *melos* of external simplicity that traces the nuances of text and scene with sublime effect (as with Hoël's romance 'Ah! Mon remords te venge' [Ah, may my remorse avenge you] in Act 3 of *Le Pardon de Ploërmel*). Nélusko's cavatina 'L'avoir tant adorée' (To have loved her so much) (Act 4), as well as the two duets for Vasco and Sélika, 'Combien tu m'es chère' (How dear you are to me) (Act 2) and 'O transport, ô douce extase' (O transport, O gentle ecstasy) (Act 4), give cogent examples of a melodic type whose medium, even by Meyerbeer's standards, shows unusual homogeneity of composition and instrumentation. Often an Italianate tone comes to the fore, not oriented towards Rossini as in the early works, but in the manner of the contemporary Italians, especially Giuseppe Verdi, whose artistic development Meyerbeer followed closely from the late 1840s. Later *L'Africaine* would, in its turn, have an influence on Verdi, especially in *Aïda* (1871).

This enrichment of his musical idiom was used by Meyerbeer to intensify lyrical–contemplative situations. At the dramatic highpoints, and also in the psychologically distanced moments of the action, such as Sélika's ambivalent feelings (in her lullaby 'Sur mes genoux' [On my knees], Act 2) and Nélusko's range of emotions (in his extended scena 'Fille des rois' [Daughter of kings], Act 2), Meyerbeer spanned the spectrum of vocal expression, having developed this to perfection in his earlier works. Here, as in Nélusko's exotic, bizarre and demonic ballad ('Adamastor, roi des vagues profondes' [Adamastor, king of the trackless depths], Act 3) (ex. 5.4b [d]), vocal virtuosity is used in limited measure: while it facets the vocal line if need be, it is largely lacking.

Vasco's fervent greeting of the *nouveau monde* (the aria 'Pays merveilleux' [Wondrous land], Act 4), in the perfection of the freely ranging melodic line, almost forgets the strong declamatory style, and therewith the French heritage. The dramatic summary of the work is vested in Sélika's closing monologue, which, in its novel disposition, bursts antecedent bounds, revealing only remotely its origins in the generic traditions of the finale and mad scene. For the full potential of the scene to be realized there must be a return to the original form in the sources, something which has never happened yet. This would mean the limiting of Nélusko's entry to the minimum and therefore the elimination of the interpolated duet passage for Sélika and Nélusko lifted from Act 3. It would also mean opening the cuts made by Fétis. The episode 'O douce extase' (O gentle ecstasy) prior to the onset of the vision widens the musical spectrum, restoring the otherwise missing Allegro and the part 'O moment enchanteur' (O enchanted moment), the slow sinking into a deathly sleep that brings in the morendo conclusion of the monologue, indispensable to the situation, before the chorus of the spheres (Döhring 1991, 4: 164).

Example 5.4b   *L'Africaine* (*Vasco da Gama*): a) from Vasco's Grand Air (Act 4),
                b–c) the motif of Sélika's sorrow in Acts 2 and 4, d) Nélusko's
                Ballad (Act 3)

a.

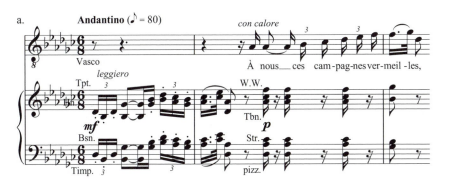

b.

c.

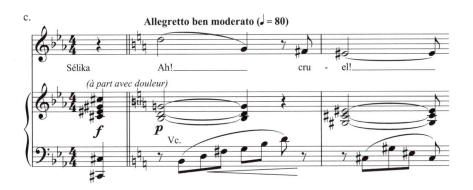

Example 5.4b   continued

d.   **Allegro ben moderato** (♩ = 60) *(avec une énergie sauvage)*

Nélusko A - da - mas - tor, roi__ des__ va - gues__ pro - fon - des,

Fl.
Ob. **fp** *léger*

Bsn. & Vc.

At a time when the great powers of Europe were pursuing the colonialization of whole continents, Scribe and Meyerbeer wrote an opera about the sacrificial courage of a single person belonging to a subject race regarded as morally inferior. In the person of Sélika all the problems that Meyerbeer tried to examine in his heroines are combined. She represents a female figure standing outside society who at the same time has the insight and ability to integrate and heal. No matter how respectfully the achievements of the composer were received and his music appreciated, a Europe of growing nationalism, aggressive and global, did not respond to them in an ideological sense. Even the earlier works fitted awkwardly into the prevailing world views. And this was one of the principal reasons for their progressive silencing after the First World War. It is significant that 'Meyerbeer societies' and similar ideology-shaping institutions were never formed. *L'Africaine*, in particular, was the profession of universal humanity mediated through music, and, in its own way, stood as a countersign to the burgeoning imperialism of the age (Zimmermann 1991: 422).

When the opera, already a legend from the expectation of decades, eventually appeared on the stage, the event from both artistic and social points of view was sensational. The participation of the musical public, stimulated by innumerable reports in the international press, reached unprecedented heights, and provided Second Empire society with its most exalted self-presentation in terms of an opera premiere. The first night, in the presence of Emperor Napoleon III and the Empress Eugénie, became a posthumous triumph for the composer: his newly sculpted bust by Jean-Pierre Dantan was unveiled on stage at the conclusion of the opera. The most modern techniques were placed at the disposal of the event: during the performance hourly telegraphic reports on the reception of the work were sent out to the European capitals. Apart from a few exceptions, the critics celebrated *L'Africaine* as Meyerbeer's *chef d'oeuvre*, and there was almost unanimous praise for the brilliant production (conducted by Georges-François Hainl, produced by Alexis Colleuille), whereby the Opéra once more justified its reputation as the leading opera house of Europe.

Illustration 5.4c *L'Africaine*: the first production at the Paris Opéra (the third panel, Act 4 the Hindu Temple and Act 5 the Manchineel Tree, of the triptych of engravings by Alphonse Neuville in *L'Illustration*, 1865)

Among the ensemble of singers, the greatest impression was made by Marie-Constance Sass as Sélika, who was regarded as a great *tragédienne* and worthy successor to Falcon; and by Jean-Baptiste Faure for his realization of Nélusko, which was magisterial both vocally and dramatically. Marie Battu was convincing as Inès, but Emilio Naudin as Vasco received criticism, as well as praise, because of his Italianate style of singing. The interpreters of the demanding secondary roles were acknowledged, and demonstrated the experienced resources of the house: Victor-Alexandre-Joseph Warot (Don Alvar), Louis-Henri Obin (The High Priest of Brahma), Belval (Don Pédro) and Armand Castelmary (Don Diégo). The stage designs were created by Auguste-Alfred Rubé, Philippe Chaperon, Charles-Antoine Cambon, Joseph-François-Désiré Thierry, Jean-Baptiste Lavastre and Edouard-Désiré-Joseph Déspléchin, the last with the manchineel tree attracted particular attention because of its originality. Perhaps because of the exaggerated expectations, the stage effects of Act 3 (the change of ship direction and the shipwreck), effected by large numbers of stagehands, made a rather disappointing impression according to the press. Nevertheless, Arthur Pougin later reckoned this scene the highpoint of the *mise en scène* at the Opéra (1885, 523). The opulent costumes were created by Paul Lormier and Alfred Albert; the choreography, much less important this time, was devised by Arthur Saint-Léon. During the following years this production was one of the Opéra's great attractions. After the move to the Palais Garnier in 1877 there was a new version (with Gabrielle Krauss as Sélika, Marius Salomon as Vasco, Jean-Louis Lassalle as Nélusko, conducted by Charles Lamoureux), and another in 1902 (with Auguste Affre as Vasco and Jean Noté as Nélusko).

Stages everywhere hurried to produce the new success story. As was so often the case, Covent Garden in London was the first (1865): a production in Italian (translated by J. Nicodemo), with Pauline Lucca as Sélika (Meyerbeer had long before proposed her as his favourite singer for this role), Theodor Wächtel as Vasco, Francesco Graziani as Nélusko, and Michael Costa conducting. In the same year there were also performances in English (translated by Charles Lamb Kennedy) by the Pyne-Harrison Company (with Louisa Pyne as Sélika). The opera further appeared in 1865 in Madrid (in the Italian translation by Marco Marcelliano Marcello), in Bologna (with Graziani as Nélusko), Berlin (in the German version by Ferdinand Gumbert, with Lucca as Sélika), Antwerp, Brussels (with Jean Morère as Vasco), New York, Parma (with Giuseppe Capponi as Vasco) and The Hague. In 1866 it appeared in Vienna (with Karoline Bettelheim as Sélika and Johann Nepomuk Beck as Nélusko) and in Milan (with Antonietta Fricci as Sélika, Xaver Ferenc Steger as Vasco and Leone Giraldoni as Nélusko). The first Swedish performance in Stockholm in 1867 (translated into Swedish by Ernst Wallmark, with Louise Michaeli as Sélika, Fritz Arlberg as Nélusko, directed by Ludvig Josephson, with scene designer Fritz Ahlgrensson) made theatre history because of the spectacular staging of the shipwreck in Act 3, which in general was considered as fine as the original Paris production.

As with other Meyerbeer operas, Covent Garden became the most important stage for *L'Africaine* in the late nineteenth century. It was Pauline Lucca's presentation of Sélika that, more than anything, became an institution for two decades. Others who made outstanding debuts with her were Naudin (1866) and Pietro Mongini (1871) as

Vasco and Antonio Cotogni (1867) and Victor Maurel (1874) as Nélusko. The highpoint and conclusion of this performing tradition came in 1888, with Lillian Nordica as Sélika, Lassalle as Nélusko, and the brothers Jean and Edouard de Reszke as Vasco and Don Pédro, conducted by Luigi Mancinelli. The opera appeared in New York in 1892 at the Metropolitan Opera with the same cast, and again in 1907 with Olive Fremstad as Sélika, Enrico Caruso as Vasco and Riccardo Stracciari as Nélusko—an ensemble that united the very best of contemporary Meyerbeer singing.

In comparison with the composer's other *grands opéras*, the roles in this work make fewer virtuoso demands, and this increased their vocal attractiveness at a time when strength and beauty of tone determined new vocal ideals. This modern profile of the roles contributed to *L'Africaine* being regarded as a new type of singers' opera, maintaining a favoured place in the international repertoire, and in the twentieth century becoming Meyerbeer's most performed work. Whenever it was possible to propose outstanding dramatic sopranos, tenors and baritones in brilliant roles, then *L'Africaine* was on the shortlist (or rather *L'Africana*, because on the internationally oriented stages the work was mostly given in Italian).

As perhaps the most important presenter of Sélika at the turn of the century, Félia Litvinne, who vocally still belonged to the Falcon type, triumphed in this role on many stages of the world, among them Brussels in 1886, Paris in 1889, New York in 1897, Monte Carlo in 1905 and Paris (Gaité-Lyrique) in 1910. After her came Lucienne Bréval (Paris, 1902), Ester Mazzoleni (Naples and Milan, 1910), and Rosa Raisa (Buenos Aires 1915). Apart from Amelita Galli-Curci as Inès and Bernardo De Muro as Vasco, Raisa's partner as Nélusko in this performance was the phenomenal Titta Ruffo, who knew how to bring out the heroic aspects of the part in his impressive interpretation. He also sang this role in Naples in 1908 (with Salomea Krusceniski as Sélika and Francisco Viñas as Vasco) and in Madrid in 1912. Other remarkable exponents of Nélusko were Antonio Aramburo between 1875 and 1892 (Moscow, Seville, Bilbao, Madrid, Prague, Valencia, Montevideo, Warsaw and Odessa) and the so-called *rè dei baritoni*, 'king of baritones', Mattia Battistini, between 1880 and 1902 (Ravenna, Florence, Buenos Aires, Rio da Janeiro, São Paulo, Madrid, Milan, Bilbao, Cadiz, Warsaw, St Petersburg and Vienna, 1912 and 1924).

Rosa Ponselle also provided an important interpretation of Sélika which she sang at the Metropolitan for over a decade (1923–34, first with Beniamino Gigli as Vasco in 1923, later with Giovanni Martinelli). The opera enjoyed 58 performances in 23 seasons in New York and was last performed there on 24 February 1934 (with Elisabeth Rethberg as Sélika, Queena Mario as Inès, Martinelli as Vasco, Armando Borgioli as Nélusko, Virgilio Lazzari as Don Pédro and Ezio Pinza as both the Grand Inquisitor and the High Priest of Brahma).

Gigli, Caruso's heir to role of Vasco at the Metropolitan, became the most important interpreter of the role in the 1920s and 1930s, singing it at the Verona Arena in 1932 (with Lina Bruna Rasa as Sélika and Armando Borgioli as Nélusko), as well as in Rome in 1937 (with Maria Caniglia as Sélika and Mario Basiola as Nélusko). Jussi Björling sang Vasco in the last of 153 performances of the opera at the Royal Opera House in Stockholm on 26 December 1938 (with his brother Sigurd as Nélusko).

The special popularity that *L'Africaine* enjoyed internationally in these years was not least because of its position on the German-speaking stages. There was again a spectacular production by Leo Blech at the Berlin Hofoper in 1916 with Barbara Kemp as Sélika, Hermann Jadlowker as Vasco and Joseph Schwarz as Nélusko, which set standards for a long time. In the following years there were other productions in Vienna (Hofoper) in 1924 under Clemens Krauss, Hamburg in 1928 (with Sabine Kalter as Sélika and Hans Reinmar as Nélusko), Frankfurt-am-Main in 1930 (with Beatrice Sutter-Kottlar as Sélika and John Gläser as Vasco), and again at the Vienna Hofoper in 1935 and 1937 (with Anny Konetzni as Sélika and Alfred Piccaver as Vasco). Other productions were in Florence (1931), Genoa (1933) and Brussels (1938–39).

After a break of 20 years, a period which saw the Nazi ban on performing Meyerbeer's operas, in 1950 the Opera in Cassel undertook the first German production of the work after the Second World War, and in the translation and arrangement by Julius Kapp (with Hildegard Jonas as Sélika, Karl Ostertag as Vasco, conducted by Karl Elmendorff). Other isolated performances followed, always in Kapp's version: the Städtische Oper Berlin in 1951 (with Elfriede Wasserthal as Sélika, Hans Beirer as Vasco, Josef Metternich as Nélusko, conducted by Leopold Ludwig, produced by Kapp); Aachen in 1960 (with Gloria Davy as Sélika, Rudolf Lustig as Vasco, conducted by Wilhelm Pitz), and Munich in 1962 (with Ingrid Bjöner as Sélika, Jess Thomas as Vasco and Heinrich Bender as Nélusko). All these proved, as was verified by the press reports, that the old aesthetic prejudices were extremely tenacious and prevented an unbiased reception in Germany (see Reininghaus 1988: 4–10).

Significant concert performances were given in Frankfurt in 1952 (with Aga Joestén as Sélika, Heinrich Bensing as Vasco, Carl Kronenberg as Nélusko, conducted by Paul Schmitz), Vienna in 1956, and London BBC in 1963 (in English, with Josephine Veasey as Sélika, Robert Thomas as Vasco, and Raimund Herincx as Nélusko).

The 1960s saw more productions, like Naples in 1963 (with Antonietta Stella as Sélika). But it was reserved for Belgian and French stages to reconnect with the performing tradition of the 1930s. The production of 1955 in Marseilles (revived in 1964) was followed in 1956 by one in Ghent, prepared with great care, where Huberte Vécray as Sélika and Jean Lafont as Nélusko proved to be interpreters who tried to retain the correct singing style for Meyerbeer, as did Geri Brunincx as Sélika and Guy Fouché as Vasco in the revival of 1961. The productions in Bordeaux in 1962 (with Martina Arroyo as Sélika and Gustave Botiaux as Vasco) Toulouse in 1963 (with Brunincx and Botiaux) and Rouen in 1965 also concentrated on the singing aspects. Unlike the recent new productions of *Les Huguenots* and *Le Prophète*, where the historical and philosophical implications of the works provided an additional dimension, the latest productions of *L'Africaine* are thanks to the splendid singing roles. There was a dignified production in Graz in 1971 (with Roberta Knie as Sélika), and in the same year, more significantly, another in the context of the Maggio Musicale Fiorentino conducted by Riccardo Muti (with the brilliant Jessye Norman as Sélika and Veriano Luchetti as Vasco, with Franco Enriquez as producer, and costumes by Fiorella Mariani, after the original designs).

This initiated a rich series of productions in the 1970s and 1980s. The Florentine production was taken to Covent Garden in 1978 (with Grace Bumbry as Sélika,

Plácido Domingo as Vasco, Silvano Carroli as Nélusko, conducted by Peter Maag), and revived in 1981 (with Bumbry, Franco Bonisolli and David Atherton conducting). Domingo whose richly coloured and powerful tenor is eminently suited to the part of Vasco, performed in the opera in San Francisco in 1972 (with Shirley Verrett as Sélika) and again in 1988 (with Verrett, as well as Ruth Ann Swenson as Inès and Justino Diaz as Nélusko). He also sang in it in Barcelona in 1977 (with Monserrat Caballé, Christine Weidinger and Guillermo Sarabia). There was a concert performance in New York in 1972 (which preserved the sterling interpretation of Richard Tucker's Vasco) and a performance in Caracas 1981. All these productions presented the work with severe, often disfiguring, cuts. A singular exception was the concert performance by the Bavarian State Radio in 1977, conducted by Gerd Albrecht in a stylistically sure and musical way and with a bare minimum of omissions (with Martina Arroyo as Sélika, Evelyn Brunner as Inès, Giorgio Casellato Lamberti as Vasco and Sherrill Milnes as Nélusko).

A return to some exploration of the historical and philosophical implications of the opera emerged in the revivals of the 1990s: at Bielefeld in 1991 (with Susan Maclean, Zachos Terzakis, Michael Vier, and Rainer Koch conducting) and in Berlin (Staatsoper) in 1992 (with Jane Henschel, George Gray, Michael Lewis, and Wolfgang Rennert conducting). The French vocal tradition was recalled at Marseille in 1992, while an attempt at more thoughtful production and beautiful singing marked the production in Strasbourg in 2004 (with Sylvie Brunet, Bojidar Nikolov, Peter Sidhom, and Edward Gardner conducting). (See Loewenberg 1970: 971–3; Wolff 1962: 25–6; Döhring 1991: 4:164–6.)

Chapter Six

French Operas: *Opéra Comique*

Only one day after Emile Perrin, the director of the Opéra Comique, expressed his wish that Meyerbeer should write a work for his house, on 29 January 1849 the composer, who had long cherished the idea of writing an *opéra comique* since his visit to Paris in 1815, discussed the matter with his librettist, notwithstanding the pressures of the many preparations for the first performance of *Le Prophète* at the Opéra. He noted a 'Conference with Scribe concerning the *prophète* and the *Feldlager*' (*BT*, 4:471), which suggests the spontaneous interest generated by the proposal. He always had it in mind to reuse material from *Ein Feldlager in Schlesien* (1844), the *Singspiel* composed expressly for the reopening of the Berlin Opera House. An earlier attempt to free this interesting work from its overtly Prussian associations, with a fresh adaptation of the text by Rellstab and a newly composed Act 3, for presentation in Vienna with Lind as Vielka (1847), had only limited success. The solution was to write a different work with no nationalistic overtones, making use of some earlier material. Another entry in his pocket diary on 3 June 1849, two and a half months after the *prophète* premiere, reveals that the new libretto was ready.

6.1 *L'Étoile du Nord [The Star of the North]*

Opéra comique en trois actes [comic opera in three acts]
Text: Augustin-Eugène Scribe
First performance: Opéra Comique, Salle Favart, Paris, 16 February 1854

Meyerbeer began composition of the new work in the late summer of 1849. The title changed from *La Vivandière*, to *La Cantinière*, and finally to *L'Étoile du Nord*. Composition was spread intermittently over several years, not least because less music from the *Feldlager* was used than anticipated: eventually there were only six numbers, all of them from Act 2, including the extensive finale.

   Scribe's libretto followed a typical pattern in which four traditions about Tsar Peter the Great were interwoven, despite spatial and temporal differences: his sojourns incognito as a shipwright in Saardam and Deptford (1697–98), the rebellion of the Strelitzy (1698), his courting and marriage to the Lithuanian peasant girl Catherine (1712), who later became the Empress Catherine I (1725). Two of these connections had already been made in Jean-Nicolas Bouilly's libretto for Grétry's *Pierre le Grand* (1790) which placed the action in a Livonian village. Grétry's opera provided the point of departure for a series of separate but mutually influential adaptations for both spoken and musical theatre in France, Germany and Italy, especially by Vaccai (*Pietro il Grande*, 1824), Donizetti (*Il borgomastro di Saardam*, 1827), and

Lortzing (*Zar und Zimmermann*, 1837), works that presented Scribe and Meyerbeer with a reservoir of various materials and motives. Contemporary sources reported that Scribe had found ideas for the intrigue in Mlle Raucourt's drama *Henriette* (Paris, 1782).

Plot

In Finland and Russia (1698 conflated with 1712 and 1725).

Act 1. A village in Viborg. On the left a peasant house; on the right the entrance to the village church; in the background rocks and a view of the Gulf of Finland. Tsar Peter the Great is working incognito as a carpenter in the shipyard, under the name of Peter [Péters] Michaeloff. He is angered by his co-workers who are sympathetic to Sweden and toast King Charles XII. Things nearly come to blows when the Russian confectioner Danilowitz refuses to join in toasting the opponent of the tsar, and is taken under Peter's protection. Peter has fallen in love with the canteen girl Catherine. In order to be close to her, he is having flute lessons from her brother George. Peter's courting of Catherine is received with reserved sympathy. She thinks of the prophecy of her late mother, that her destiny is linked to a Star of the North, and that she will have a high-born and heroic man for her husband. She hopes that Peter, whose masterful character both fascinates and repels her, will become just such a man in the future. She herself shows wisdom and courage when the village is overrun by a group of Cossack soldiers commanded by Gritzenko: disguised as a Gypsy, she tells their fortunes and successfully sees them off. The soldiers have conscripted the young men of the village for the Russian army, including George, even though he is preparing for his marriage with Prascovia. Catherine decides to disguise herself as a man and go in her brother's place. Amidst the bustle of the wedding celebrations she leaves the village, embarking on a ship with the other recruits, and praying for her mother's protection.

SCENE FROM MEYERBEER'S NEW OPERA, "L'ETOILE DU NORD," AT DRURY-LANE THEATRE.—(SEE NEXT PAGE.)

Illustration 6.1a *L'Étoile du Nord*: design for Act 1 (Louis Palianti, *Mise en scène 'L'Étoile du Nord'*, Paris 1854); Act 2 at Drury Lane, London (engraving from the *Illustrated London News*, 1855)

Act 2. The camp of the Russian army. In the background is a tent. Ismailoff, a cavalry officer, and Gritzenko, now a corporal in the infantry, sing the praises of their regiments, as the new recruits march past. Catherine is not recognized by either Gritzenko or Danilowitz. The latter has become a confidant of the tsar, who still remains incognito, calling himself a captain. By chance Catherine overhears a conspiracy to revolt against the Tsar's despotic command and harsh discipline. The signal for the uprising and handing over of the camp to the Swedes will be the playing of the tsar's Marche sacré. Gritzenko posts Catherine on sentry duty outside Peter's tent, and she witnesses his profligate behaviour with Danilowitz, as he drinks and wenches with some of the camp followers, Ekimona and Nathalie. She peers into the tent and is accused by Gritzenko of spying. Out of jealousy and anger she slaps him, and Gritzenko complains to the tsar. Peter, in his drunkenness, orders her to be shot. She calls out to him as she is dragged off, and her voice stirs something through his befuddlement. She has left a message warning of the conspiracy so that when the danger approaches, the tsar is able to deal with the situation. Ismailoff announces that the tsar is in the camp, and urges them to rise up and kill him. Peter prays for guidance, Danilowitz for the tsar, and the others for vengeance. When the Marche sacré sounds, Peter is able to confront the assembled troops. He accuses them of treason, and asks them to follow him against the enemy; then he will deliver the Tsar to them. When they swear, he reveals his identity as their ruler, and by the power of his personality is able to exact their obedience. As the tsar's Marche resounds, all promise loyalty while his regiments of Grenadiers and Tartars enter the camp.

Act 3. An apartment in the tsar's palace. in the background a window with gold frames; to the left a door into a garden. The tsar bemoans the loss of Catherine and the happy days of their love. Danilowitz brings in Gritzenko who reveals that the sentry who had been sentenced to death has in fact escaped. Prascovia and George arrive from Finland at the tsar's behest. Danilowitz has been able to find Catherine who has been wandering about the countryside in a demented state, having lost her reason after her terrible experiences. The tsar has her brought to the palace where he has recreated an illusion of her home village, peopled by her friends and relations who have been summoned from Finland. The evoked memories of earlier times and happiness enable the clouds to lift from Catherine's mind. When she hears the sound of George's and Peter's flutes, her cure is completed, and her reason restored. She falls into the arms of her beloved, and the court hails her as the new empress. The prophecy of her mother has been fulfilled.

Illustration 6.1b *L'Étoile du Nord*: Palianti's costume designs for Catherine (Act 1), Peter (Act 1), Catherine (Act 2) and Prascovia (Act 1)

The treatment of historical themes within the limits of mixed genres had a tradition at the Opéra Comique, as demonstrated by Hérold's *Le Pré aux clercs* (Paris 1832; text by Planard) and Halévy's *Les Mousquetaires de la reine* (Paris 1846; text by Jules-Henri Vernoy de Saint-Georges). It is not on account of the subject that *L'Étoile du Nord* bursts the boundaries of genre, but rather because of the external musical and scenic apparatus which causes the work to appear as a grand opera with dialogue, particularly in Act 2. Rather differently from the other plays and operas about Peter, the tsar here is not the popular regent and sentimental lover, but an ambivalent character, presented with thoroughly repellent characteristics, something that offered the composer the opportunity for a musical portrait full of glittering, expressive facets. The violent–choleric dimension of Peter's character is especially emphasized with a frequently recurring, exclusively personal semitonal motif, which in its instrumental colour (bassoons and deep strings) and technical structure (chromatically discordant melodic scales) offers the typical Meyerbeerian topoi for presentation of the demonic.

Other characters are also associated with a specific sound or style that is maintained throughout the opera: Catherine's entries are coloured by flute accompaniments and vivacious coloratura; Prascovia has a more sentimental sound profile, with serene melodies, more restrained and flightier decoration, a breathless ingenuousness. Even the smaller figures have their own tonal characteristics: Gritzenko has a blustering coarse delivery with a hint of Cossack cadence and harmony, while Danilowitz is lighter and more sentimental, with folksy patter alternating with suave cantilena.

There is considerable wit in the buffo numbers, where humour is constructed either on the surface of the music by use of alliterative and imitative effects (the Act 2 sextet and the Act 3 duet for Prascovia and George), or emanates from within the melody and the rhythm itself (as in the women's duet in Act 1). A kaleidoscope of changing moods and modes is reflected in correspondingly quicksilver generic adaptation of style (as in the heroic Act 1 duet for Péters and Catherine, or the constantly shifting movements of the Act 3 buffo trio for Péters, Danilowitz and Gritzenko).

The expositional dramaturgy, very much in the manner already developed to perfection by the composer, is again evident in the Introduction where the private action is unfolded in the context of the historical and local determinants. The 'militaristic Rococo' of Act 2 (Hanslick 1875: 155), embodied in the opening genre numbers (ex. 6.1 [a]), is enriched with new compositions of a musical prettiness and mannerist charm, which integrate the Catherine–Peter action into the existing context: especially the quartet for Nathalie, Ekimona, Danilowitz and Péters ('Sous les remparts du vieux Kremlin') (Beneath the ramparts of the old Kremlin) in which realistic tone painting (dice rolls, sabre thrusts) is converted through repetition, imitation and *hoquet*-like compositional technique into vocal and instrumental structures of filigree virtuosity.

Act 3 is characterized by the restored pastoral, announced immediately in the charming, gracious prelude, and Péters' nostalgic evocation of childhood and lost happiness ('O jours hereux') (O happy days). Quite singular, and independent of antecedent generic types is the likewise newly composed Mad Scene for Catherine. It is conceived as a greatly expanded free rondo that binds together the musical and scenic reminiscences from the first two acts, turning the recalled fragments into a collage of citations. The conclusion of the scene uses the aria with two obbligato flutes taken from the *Feldlager*. Through the triple echo figurations (a cypher for pastoral blessedness), the musical reprise is understood—from the point of view of action and psychology—as restitution of the former idyll, both as psychotherapy and objective correlative of healing. The opening of the final section captures a mood of contained rapture and ecstatic perception (ex. 6.1 [b]).

Example 6.1 *L'Étoile du Nord*: a) the Chanson de Cavalerie (Act 2), b) from Catherine's Mad Scene (the healing) (Act 3)

Ovations at the premiere and for the larger part of the following reprises were not only for the performances by the brilliant cast: with Caroline Duprez as Catherine, Charles Battaille as Péters, Constance-Caroline Lefebre as Prascovia, Ernest Mocker as Danilowitz, Pierre-Victor Jourdan as George, Hermann-Léon as Gritzenko and Mlle

Lemercier as Nathalie. The work itself attracted the admiration of the public as well as of the connoisseurs. Within a year 100 performances had been staged, and the World Exhibition of 1855 further prompted a rise in public interest. In the meantime there were several changes in the cast: with Delphine Ugalde (Catherine), Charles-Marie-Auguste Ponchard (Danilowitz), and particularly Jean-Baptiste Faure (Péters) for whose baritone voice Meyerbeer especially adjusted the role. The following two new productions of the work at the Opéra Comique were also in the context of world exhibitions: in 1867 (with Marie Cabel as Catherine and Battaille as Péters), and 1878 (with Cécile Ritter-Ciampi, and, later Adèle Isaac). The final revival was in 1885 (with Isaac and Victor Maurel), the work ultimately attaining 406 performances by 1887.

The opera reached many stages in an extremely short time: later in 1854 Brussels (with Anna Lemaire) and Stuttgart (translated into German by Ludwig Rellstab, with Mathilde Marlow). On the occasion of the German-language production in Dresden in 1855, Meyerbeer added two tenor arias to expand the role of Danilowitz for Joseph Tichatschek: the Act 1 polonaise 'Wenn Mut und Vertrau'n im Herzen wohnen' (If courage and trust live in one's heart) and the Act 3 arioso 'Ach, wie matt, schmachtend und bleich'(Ah, how wan, languid and pale). Both numbers were included in the second version with recitatives Meyerbeer composed to an Italian text by Manfredo Maggioni as *La stella del nord* for Covent Garden in London (19 July 1855), another great triumph (with Angiolina Bosio as Catherine, Karl Johann Formes as Péters, Italo Gardoni as Danilowitz, Luigi Lablache as Gritzenko, conducted by Michael Costa).

The work enjoyed a special popularity in Sweden later in the century (as *Nordens Stjärna*). The premiere (2 December 1881) at the Royal Opera (with S. Ek as Catherine, D. Niehoff as Prascovia, A. Willman as Péters, G. Henrikson as Georges, R. Sellman as Danilowitz and P. Janzon as Gritzenko) initiated a run of 34 performances until 1908.

By the end of the century, this work, once praised by Berlioz for its originality of ideas and the refined combinations of its finish, was reduced by radical cuts to something unrecognizable, a vehicle for great coloratura sopranos: Mathilde Wildauer, Caroline Carvalho, Adelina Patti, Zina Dalti, Marcella Sembrich, Emma Albani, Betty Frank. The Flute Aria retained its aura as one of the peaks of nineteenth-century vocal virtuosity, even into the era of the gramophone (with Amelita Galli-Curci and Luisa Tetrazzini). Some of the melodies were kept in musical currency by Constant Lambert who used four pieces (as well as the ballet from *Le Prophète*) in the suite arranged for Frederick Ashton's ballet *Les Patineurs* (16 February 1937). (See Loewenberg 1970: 911–12; Döhring 1991: 4:154.)

The first revival of the complete work took place at the Camden Festival, London, on 25 February 1975 (with Janet Price as Catherine, Malcolm King as Péters, Deborah Cook as Prascovia, Alexander Oliver as Danilowitz, Bonaventura Bottone as George, conducted by Roderick Brydon). The second occurred at the Wexford Festival in October 1996 (with Elizabeth Futral as Catherine, Vladimir Ognev as Péters, Darina Takova as Prascovia, Aled Hall as Danilowitz, Juan Diego Flórez as George, conducted by Vladimir Jurowski).

No sooner had Meyerbeer completed and successfully produced his first *opéra comique* than he turned his thoughts to the second, as though the two together represent complementary halves of experiences enshrined in the traditions of this very French genre.

6.2 *Le Pardon de Ploërmel (Dinorah) [The Pardon of Ploërmel]*

Opéra comique en trois actes [comic opera in three acts]
Text: Jules-Paul Barbier and Michel-Florentin Carré (with additional words and translations by Charlotte Birch-Pfeiffer, Georges-Frédéric Burguis and Giacomo Meyerbeer)
First performance: Opéra Comique, Salle Favart, Paris, 4 April 1859

The first proposal by Jules-Paul Barbier (13 May 1854) was for a one-act piece in the lighter genre, which, by its intimate and unusual colour, immediately appealed to Meyerbeer. When he later decided to expand the work, this was not only because of the pressure brought to bear by the director of the Opéra Comique, Emile Perrin, who hoped for a more substantial work for his house from the famous composer. While working on the score, Meyerbeer himself was convinced of the further dramatic and symbolic potential of the material. In any case, now began a period of several years when the work was newly conceived—an expansion and reworking in which Meyerbeer not only encouraged his librettists, but also actively shaped the text himself.

The sources of the libretto can be traced to two Breton tales by Emile Souvestre, 'La Chasse aux trésors' and 'Le Kacouss de l'amour'—both published in the *Révue de deux mondes*, 5 (1 January 1850) and 7 (15 August 1850) in the series *Les Récits de la muse populaire*. The first tells of a cursed treasure and two male characters, Claude and Jean-Marie, who try to manoeuvre each other into the deadly position of touching the treasure first. Eventually Claude persuades Jean-Marie to use his idiot sister Marthe for the purpose, and the tale ends with her tragic death as the result of a fall. In the second a Breton girl called Dinorah is prevented from eloping with Beuzec, who is discovered to be an arsonist and a thief. The tale ends with Dinorah looking on at the captured felon as she takes part in a religious procession. Only the basic situations and the *couleur locale* of the material were adopted; the characters and the motivation of the action, as well as the closure of the story, were decisively changed. Various motifs and the names of some of the characters were taken by the authors from another of Souvestre's works, the collection *Le Foyer breton, Traditions populaires* (1845), but not the idea of bringing a live goat on to the stage. The motifs of madness and the pet goat have been traced to episodes in the novels of Laurence Sterne (see Law 1989). In *Tristram Shandy* (1759–67) the hero comes across a poor country girl Maria who has lost her reason because of the intrigue of a village curate who prevented the publication of her wedding banns. She sits on bank playing her pipes with her little goat beside her. In *A Sentimental Journey through France and Italy* (1768) Maria's pathos is increased because the goat has deserted her. A more contemporary influence came more from the example of Esmeralda's goat Djali in Victor Hugo's novel *Notre Dame de Paris. 1482* (1831), especially in the popular balletic version by Jules Perrot, with music by Cesare Pugni (*La Esmeralda*, 1844). Both Fanny Cerrito and Fanny Elssler had been able to elicit moving reactions from their appearances on stage with a trained goat.

For the virtuoso role of Dinorah, Meyerbeer originally had Caroline Carvalho in mind, but contractual obligations had made her engagement by the Opéra Comique impossible at that time. So he accepted Marie Cabel for the part. As with all his new operas, the premiere was preceded by lengthy rehearsals during which important changes to the work took place.

Plot
Rural nineteenth-century Brittany.

Prehistory, as depicted in the extended overture in the form of a tone poem. Every year the inhabitants of Ploërmel stage a procession to the nearby shrine of the Blessed Virgin. On one such particular day the goatherd Hoël and his bride Dinorah, daughter of the farmer Herbier, join the procession in order to be married in the chapel. A thunderstorm breaks over them, scattering the procession and demolishing the farmstead. Hoël, full of despair at the future prospect of his bride reduced to poverty, remembers the whisperings of the old wizard Tonic who spoke of a secret treasure guarded by the elfin folk, the korrigans. In order to win this treasure, Hoël must spend a year of testing in complete solitude, without ever explaining his intentions. The first to touch the treasure, however, will die. Hoël undertakes this mission, and Dinorah, thinking herself abandoned, seeks refuge in madness, and wanders about the forest accompanied by her goat, Bellah. Tonic dies before the termination of the period of trial, without revealing the hiding place of the treasure. On the eve of the pilgrimage Hoël returns to Ploërmel.

Act 1. The evening. A wild, hilly landscape, with a thatched cottage in the foreround. The sun is setting as the peasants and shepherds return homewards. Dinorah appears on the hill and sings a lullaby to her goat. Corentin, a bagpiper, returns to his cottage, filled with superstitious dread of the fairyfolk. He falls asleep but is disturbed by Dinorah who bursts in, and forces him to dance with her. They both fall asleep, exhausted, but are interrupted by the knocking of another stranger, whereupon Dinorah jumps out of the window. Hoël enters, on his search to find someone to accompany him on his mission. The possession of the treasure is dependent on a secret condition: the first one to touch the treasure will die within a year. Hoël thinks that in Corentin he has found the perfect dupe and victim, and promises him half the treasure if he will help him find it that very night. A goat will direct their way, and with the help of a magic formula, they will dispel the evil spirits. Corentin is blinded by the prospect of wealth, and agrees. As a storm begins to gather, they hear the sound of a goat's bell (Dinorah's), which they take as the signal to begin.

Act 2. The night.
Scene 1. A beechwood. Moonshine. On the way home from Yvon's inn, the woodcutters pass through the wood with their wives. When they have gone, Dinorah

appears. She is full of sadness, and bemoans her misfortune in love—something a wise man once prophesied to her. Her mood changes with the emergence of the moon, and in exalted spirits she dances in the moonshine with her shadow. The approaching storm awakens her memory of the pilgrimage with Hoël.

Scene 2. Dark night. The edge of a rocky glen. In the background a watercourse with a fallen tree trunk forming a bridge across the gully. Hoël and Corentin, following the sound of the goat's bell, reach the dark glen. While Hoël goes to investigate the lie of the land, Corentin, alone, tries to keep up his spirits. Dinorah emerges from the darkness, on a height. Corentin's talk about treasure stirs her memories, and she sings of an old legend with its warning that whoever touches the treasure will die within the year. Dinorah withdraws into the darkness. Corentin now grasps Hoël's intentions, and when Hoël reappears, the bagpiper refuses to be the first to descend into the glen. Dinorah emerges again, and Corentin has the idea of using her for the deadly mission. With enticing descriptions, he tries to induce her come down, but she remains loftily indifferent. The approaching storm with its thunderclaps raises the excitement, and on hearing its bell, Dinorah sees the goat on the tree trunk bridge, crossing the ravine. As the storm worsens, she rushes after the goat, just as a bolt of lightning shivers the trunk, sending Dinorah down into the torrent. The horrified Hoël springs in after her.

Act 3. The morning. A rural landscape at sunrise.

Scene 1. This is a pastoral intermezzo (vilanelle). The storm has passed, and with the break of the serene day, the various denizens of the countryside pursue their occupations: a hunter, two goatherds, three reapers. They all pray the Our Father together before moving on.

Scene 2. Hoël enters carrying the unconscious Dinorah in his arms. He has rescued her from the stream, and places her exactly where the storm interrupted the procession the previous year. He is overcome with remorse at having abandoned her to pursue a chimera of wealth. Dinorah opens her eyes: the shock of the events have restored her sanity and blotted out the memories of the past year. She believes it is her wedding day and that she has woken up in the arms of her bridegroom after a frightening dream. Snippets of memory disturb her thoughts, and he tries to reassure her. The Marian hymn of the approaching procession of the Pardon is heard, and while Dinorah prays, Hoël asks the pilgrims not to shatter her temporal illusion. The couple join in the hymn of thanksgiving, and move with the procession to the chapel where their wedding will finally take place. For Hoël, Dinorah's love is the real treasure found.

Illustration 6.2a   *Le Pardon de Ploërmel*: the original playbill depicting Corentin, Dinorah and Hoël

Le Pardon de Ploërmel realizes the original attempt to renew the old pastoral genre in terms of the advanced medium of contemporary operatic dramaturgy, as it had been developed by Meyerbeer himself, and thereby to reflect on the genre itself. In alienating play with the traditional topoi, the classical light of the idyll is transformed into the Romantic darkness of the nightpiece. The natural phenomenon of the day–night antithesis receives a religious and metaphysical dimension that continues, and indeed comments on, the subtexts of faith unfolded in the *grands opéras*. In these four operas it is apparent that Meyerbeer expresses a belief in the power of faith to bring about redemption, but has significant reservations about what would be termed today 'organized religion'. This does not necessarily suggest an entirely individualistic notion of religion, but it certainly does indicate a desire for a somewhat Romantic notion of a unified faith untainted by internal conflict. This theme seems to be drawn together in this slighter *opéra comique Dinorah*. Here both hero and heroine are saved through an active selfless decision by the hero. This act of faith is not, however, sufficient for Meyerbeer, as their salvation is confirmed only after an immersion and apparent death in turbulent waters, which signify the sacramental power of baptism and a continuing role for the Church in salvation, this being confirmed in the final Procession of the Pardon. The issues are reflected in the confrontation between the Marian cult and demonic superstition. In the tempest that breaks over the procession and destroys Dinorah's bourgeois milieu, and in the later nocturnal storm in the *Val maudit* that threatens Dinorah's life, evil spirits seem to release their destructive power. Only the sunrise on the next morning and the new appearance of the Procession is able to banish the ghosts and restore order in nature and society. Day and night actually function as physical metaphors. The shock unleashed by the original tempest propels Dinorah into spiritual darkness from which she awakes healed in the light of psychological reminiscence. Healing is depicted as the restitution of the emotional equanimity, of spiritual energy through the purging displacement of the horrible in the realm of dreams. It nonetheless impresses on the happy end the traces of enduring unease.

Both spheres are vested in the unconscious creature symbolized by the goat. Within the plans of the demonic powers, a mysterious goat will show the way to the treasure; in reality this turns out to be Bellah, Dinorah's tame companion, which leads Hoël to his real treasure—not the buried rubies and gold, but Dinorah herself. If magic is cast ambiguously, it is by no means demythologized. Play with the set pieces of Romantic opera means their recreation in the medium of irony. So in the comic foil of the superstitious Corentin, the fantastic is not abolished but rather shifted inwards. If the demons have withdrawn from the real world, they work even more powerfully in dreams, hallucinations and hysterical imagination.

Ambivalence is characteristic of all Meyerbeer's operas, and here he packages his Enlightenment intentions in softly subtle musical mode. At one moment the orchestra is let loose in tremendous evocation of tempest, at another it is chained in a series of reduced, chamber-like harmonic sequences. The score of this opera is Meyerbeer's most virtuosic instrumental achievement. In the Act 1 Berceuse, for example, the orchestral atmosphere is sustained by the transparency of the scoring, setting the bass free of its normal harmonic dominance, with the cellos carrying a variant of the melody in the depths, the high strings weaving a gossamer web, with the woodwinds (especially the cor anglais) adding treble fragments of motif and imparting brushstrokes of colour (ex. 6.2a [a]). Such writing is characteristic of this score. Corentin's anxiety is conveyed in the smallest shifts from major to minor tonalities. The composer's usual search for the perfect combination and exploration of solo voice and instrument is here used to recreate Dinorah's deluded lunar fantasies. Hoël's Treasure Aria in Act 1 ('O puissante magie') (O powerful magic) depicts a demonic possession, whose expressive ambivalence the composer realizes in sounds that look forward to the savage music of Nélusko in *L'Africaine*, and which was to be of influence on Offenbach in drawing his villains in *Les Contes d'Hoffmann* (1881) (ex. 6.2a [b]). Hoël's dark fears sustained in his Conjuration are based on the same deep thirds used by Weber to express Max's sense of entrapment by evil powers in *Der Freischutz*.

Example 6.2a   *Le Pardon de Ploërmel* (*Dinorah*): from a) Dinorah's Berceuse, b) Hoël's Treasure Aria (Act 1)

b.   **Allegro con spirito (♩ = 88)** *(avec énergie)*

The rhythms of the dance infuse a great proportion of the pieces in Acts 1 and 2, with the dizzy highpoint reached in Dinorah's famous Shadow Song. This, and its carefully realized context, adds something new and original to the mad scene. The charge of a certain musical heaviness in this score is counteracted by the permeation of galop, tarantella, bolero and waltz forms, the predictability and regularity of the of the dances elegantly varied, the symmetry of phrase lengths transformed by the subtle insertion of extra bars working against any rhythmic monotony. The fluency of style is an indication of the sophistication, fantasy and complete mastery that the composer reveals in this work. Even such techniques as the medieval hocket (*hoquet*), with its insertion of rests into vocal parts, is casually introduced to intensify the grotesque element in the Act 2 duet for the male characters, to demonstrate the naïveté and slavish dependence of Corentin on Hoël's every word (ex. 6.2b [a]).

In stylistic opposition to the dancing rhythms is the Marche religieuse that dominates the middle of the overture and recurs in the finale as the prelude to the Pardon. This brings together all that Meyerbeer understood by way of a noble melody, with careful attention to the construction of the whole idea (ex. 6.2b [b]). The 1840s and 1850s saw the emergence of several of these thematic types in his work: the Motif of Peace in *Ein Feldlager in Schlesien* (1844), a melody from the *Festhymnus* written for Friedrich Wilhelm IV (and later used for Inès in *L'Africaine*) (1848), and the Marche religieuse in *Dinorah* (1859). In these forms an Italian heritage is evident in the melodic arch and the very French compression of rhythm at the phrase end, both characteristics typical of Meyerbeer's style at this period (Zimmermann 1991: 390).

Example 6.2b   *Le Pardon de Ploërmel* (*Dinorah*): from a) the Duo Bouffe (Act 1),
b) the overture (*marcia religiosa*), c) Dinorah's Légende (Act 2)

The concept of the libretto, which relates authoritatively back to the composer, reveals the artificial tendencies of Meyerbeer's late style. As an example of Neo-Mannerism, the work demonstrated the high- and endpoints of a development which was not continued in *L'Africaine* (1865), but only partially revisited. The dramatic centre of the opera is Dinorah's big scene in Act 2. This is made up of three or four contrasting numbers, textually and musically closely related to each other: a melancholy, picturesque romance ('Le vieux sorcier') (The old sorcerer), an exultant virtuoso rondo ('Ombre légère') (Fleeting shadow)—the so-called Shadow Song—a melodrama constituted as a montage of motifs ('Mais voici Hoël! Donne ton bras et partons!') (Here is Hoël! Give me your arm and let's set out) which is not only bound to the other numbers by a thematic mode of recollection, but serves dramaturgically as a kind of dream protocol bridging the two catastrophes. This is reinforced when Corentin is left for a moment by himself, and Dinorah emerges from the shadow of

Die Wallfahrt nach Ploërmel: Dinorah stürzt in den Strom (Act II, letzte Scene).

Illustration 6.2b *Le Pardon de Ploërmel*: Mühldorfer's design for Act 2 (from
Pracht-Album für Theater und Musik, Leipzig and Dresden, n.d.)

the rocks and trees to sing her Légende of the fated treasure ('Sombre destinée! Ame
condamnée!') (Dark destiny! Condemned soul!) (ex. 6.2b [c]). These dark, entranced
strophes, with rustling strings and ominous horn calls, as simple as a folksong, are
in the remote key of E flat minor that shifts to the tonic E flat major only in the last
bars by a magical sequence of three notes (E flat–F–G).

Corentin's couplets, through their bizarre rhythmic, harmonic and instrumental
effects, sustain a background of ironic comedy: 'Dieu nous donne à chacun en
partage' (God gives each of us as our lot) in Act 1, 'Ah! Que j'ai froid' (Ah! I'm
so cold) in Act 2. Ensembles that illustrate compositional mastery are the Act 1
Terzettino de la clochette ('Ce tintement que l'on entende') (This tinkling sound one
hears), in which the simultaneity of rolls of thunder and the notes of the goat-bell
presents an example of extreme bitonal instrumentation.

At a time when *opéra comique*, like *grand opéra*, began opening itself to the
emotional cult of the *drame-lyrique*, the cool intellectualism of this '*Freischütz* à
l'aquerelle' (Arthur Heulhard, *Revue musicale*, 27 August 1874) must have had
an astonishing effect. Comparable in its time to Offenbach's witty *causerie*, *Le
Pardon de Ploërmel* shares much in common with Ravel's ironic and alienating
reconstruction of the idyll *L'Enfant et les sortilèges* (1925) (Döhring 1991, 4:158).

This last opera produced by Meyerbeer again brought him a great and enduring success, but on the whole winning for him a restrained admiration rather than spontaneous acclamation. The principal singers were, however, enthusiastically praised: Marie Cabel for her vertiginous–virtuoso interpretation of Dinorah; Sainte-Foy for his overwhelmingly convincing characterization of Corentin, lyrically as well as dramatically; Jean-Baptiste Faure for his fascinating stage presence as Hoël, Meyerbeer's first big baritone role. In the appealing subsidiary roles, each provided with a characterful solo number, Barreille proved most effective as a hunter, as was Victor-Alexandre-Joseph Warot as a reaper. A sensational element was provided in the stage designs by Edouard-Désiré-Joseph Despléchin and Jules Chérets (Acts 1 and 3), with the complicated technical challenges of the Act 2 finale (with running water) entrusted to Joseph and Karl Wilhelm Mühldorfer.

The critics expressed admiration for the originality of the magisterial score, but the libretto, with the unsuspected co-authorship of Meyerbeer himself, met with a corresponding lack of comprehension, if not ridicule. During the first run of 87 performances until 1860 there were cast changes, with Mme Monrose as Dinorah and the contralto Palmyre Wertheimber taking on Hoël. There were revivals at the Opéra Comique in 1874 (Zina Dalti, Paul Lhérie and Jacques Bouhy), 1881 (with Marie van Zandt as Dinorah), 1886 (Cécile Merguiller), 1896 (Jane Marignan), and finally 1912 (Marianne Nicot-Vauchelet, Maurice Capitaine, Henri Albers).

The reception of the opera (as *Dinorah*) was even more positive in Covent Garden, London, where Carvalho interpreted the title role (with Italo Gardoni as Corentin and Francesco Graziani and, later, Faure as Hoël). Already as with *L'Étoile du Nord*, Meyerbeer replaced the spoken dialogue with recitative, and also provided the role of the Goatherd (Constance Nantier-Didieé) with a technically demanding aria at the opening of Act 2 ('Dites-moi, dites vite') (Tell me quickly). Shortly afterwards, Covent Garden saw another production, this time in English (translated by Henry Chorley) given by the Pyne-Harrison Opera Company (with Louisa Pyne and Euphrosyne Parepa as Dinorah, and Charles Santley as Hoël). In 1862 the young Adelina Patti appeared as Dinorah in London and set new standards by her vocal perfection. During the next two decades she appeared constantly in this role in London, with changing partners, mostly with Sofia Scalchi, Alessandro Bettini and Santley. Apart from Patti, others who sang Dinorah were Ilma di Murska, Marcella Sembrich and Ella Russell, while portrayers of Hoël included Victor Maurel, Jean-Louis Lassalle, Antonio Cotogni and Francisco d'Andrade.

Outside the French-speaking areas, and not only in London, the opera was almost exclusively performed in the second version with recitatives. Around 1900 it became the favourite piece of the great singers of the soprano lirico-leggiero type, such as: Angela Peralta (Venice 1875), Betty Frank (Prague 1891), Luisa Tetrazzini (Madrid 1896, Manhattan Opera New York 1908), Regina Pinkert (Naples 1900, Buenos Aires 1904, with Giuseppe De Luca as Hoël and Arturo Toscanini conducting) and María Barrientos (Milan 1904). After 1900 the performing tradition broke off rather abruptly, with the opera valued only as a concession to the virtuosity of the prima donna. There were productions for Amelita Galli-Curci in Chicago 1917 and in 1923 (with Giacomo Rimini as Hoël) and in New York in 1925 (with De Luca); as well as for Clara Clairbert in Brussels in 1932 (with André D'Arkor as Corentin and Emile Colonne as Hoël).

After the Second World War there was a production in Brussels 1953 (with Giulia Bardi, Francis Bartel, Gilbert Dubuc, conducted by Marcel Bastin). The signal for the recovery of the work was given by the studio recording (Opera Rara in London 1979), a textually complete and precise performance of the whole opera in the second version (with Deborah Cook, Alexander Oliver, Christian du Plessis, conducted by James Judd). This was followed by a musically commendable production in Trieste in 1983 (with Luciana Serra, Max René Cosotti, Angelo Romero/Brian Kemp, conducted by Baldo Podic). The direction of Alberto Maria Fassini and the designs by William Orlandi, influenced by the original staging, created a historical context. (See Loewenberg 1970: 941–2; Döhring 1991, 4:158.)

Subsequent revivals have seen a split between alienating postmodern production, as in Dortmund 2000 (with Marisol Montalvo/Eun-Joo Park, Frederic Hellgren, Thomas De Vries, conducted by Axel Kober) with the opera set in a hospital ward, and imaginative, but more traditional and symbolically atmospheric, realizations: as at the Teatro Regio Parma in 2000 (with Eva Mei, Jörg Schneider, Fabio Previati, conducted by Mats Liljefors) and the Théâtre Impérial de Compiègne in 2002 and 2004 (with Isabelle Philippe, Frédéric Mazzotta, Armand Arapian, conducted by Olivier Opdebeeck).

PART 3
Plays

Chapter Seven

Plays (Masque/Incidental Music)

By 1838 Scribe had provided Meyerbeer with two new scenarios (*Le Prophète* and *L'Africaine*), but these were not to be completed for many years. The most decisive event was of great social significance for the composer: in 1842 Meyerbeer assumed his new, prestigious role of Generalmusikdirektor to the king of Prussia. His duties included not only the overseeing of the important court concerts, but also the musical direction of the Royal Opera House in Berlin, where among others he brought out performances of Gluck, Grétry, Rossini, Auber, Adam, Halévy, Weber, Spohr and Marschner.

7.1 *Das Hoffest von Ferrara [The Court Festival at Ferrara]*

Maskenspiel in lebendigen Bildern [masque in *tableaux vivants*]
Text: Ernst Raupach, after Torquato Tasso
First performance: Royal Palace, Berlin, 28 February 1843

Among his routine courtly duties people naturally expected bigger works from the new Generalmusikdirektor. On 28 February 1843, at the Berliner Schloss, Meyerbeer prepared an occasional piece, a masque for a ball at court for some 3000 guests. Called *Das Hoffest von Ferrara*, the text was by the poet Ernst Raupach, a successful stage writer who produced some 117 pieces, mostly for the court stages. His work covered most genres: sentimental comedies in the manner of Kotzebue, like *Der Müller und sein Kind* (1835), and other more historically-oriented pieces with some social content, like the series *Die Hohenstaufen* (1837, in five volumes) which gave an overview of historical events with a glorification of German history from the Prussian perspective. The masque was a paraphrase of elements taken from Torquato Tasso's *Gerusalemme liberata* (1581), a Renaissance epic celebrating the First Crusade. Members of the Royal Family appeared in costume as guests from the House of D'Este of Ferrara, forming part of a series of *tableaux vivants* presenting scenes from the famous epic:

A. The Entrance of the Court and the Guests
B. The Procession of Masks
    1. The Christian Army
    2. Magicians and Fairies
    3. The Adventurers
C. The *Tableaux vivants*
    1. The Angel Gabriel appears to Duke Geoffrey of Bouillon
    2. The Crusaders look on Jerusalem for the first time
    3. Armida is presented for the first time to Geoffrey of Bouillon by his brother Eustace
    4. Herminia, in Clorinda's armour, with the shepherds
    5. The dying Clorinda, having fallen in battle, is baptized by Tancred
    6. Herminia and Vafrin find the unconscious Tancred

Illustration 7.1   *Das Hoffest von Ferrara*: costume designs for the Court masque (contemporary lithograph, from the collection of the late Heinz Becker)

Tableaux vivants were a popular social pastime and entertainment in the nineteenth century, before the invention of the staged revue. A historical or mythological event was stylized into a theatrical scene which the producer would arrange into a tableau with the appropriate costumes and scenery.

Meyerbeer composed music for all the scenes, some for soloists, some for chorus. Most is known from contemporary newspaper reports, because the score is lost. Herminia's Romance was the only piece to be published; the processional march has survived in manuscript. Meyerbeer's diary of 28 June 1848 reveals that the opening chorus of peasants in *Le Prophète* was lifted directly from the *Hoffest* (C. No. 4) (ex. 7.1 [a]).

The masque is interesting beacuse it focuses on particular and recurrent features of Meyerbeer's style—the pastoral topos, exemplified in the Chorus of Shepherds, and the military mode in the *Festmarsch* for the entry of the guests (ex. 7.1 [b]). This 'military' overtone is so often identifiable, characterized by strutting dotted rhythms and relentless propulsion. On 25 August 1842 Meyerbeer completed the first of his four *Fackeltänze*, the ceremonial polonaises written for the special torchlit rituals attendant on the public betrothal of a member of the Prussian Royal Family. The fervent first themes are interspersed with slower inner movements, often declamatory orchestral recitatives, or stately waltzes full of echo effects, syncopations and chordal punctuation. The slow middle section of the Blessing of the Daggers in Act 4 of *Les Huguenots* is kindred to the striding, pointed rhythms of the *Fackeltänze* (ex. 7.1 [c]). Indeed, the original opening scene of Act 3 of the 1836 opera uses just this heavy dotted mode, and was later appropriated for the overture to *Ein Feldlager in Schlesien* and then *L'Étoile du Nord*. It is an inescapable feature of the nineteenth-century sound-world, born of the universal military movements of the Napoleonic Wars and the culture of military pomp and circumstance that established itself in the courts, ballrooms and popular culture of the age. The pacific Meyerbeer, basically uneasy with Prussian militarism, was haunted by the rhythm, which entered operatic vocabulary forcefully through Spontini's heroic minuets.

Example 7.1 *Das Hoffest von Ferrara*: a) the Pastoral Chorus, b) the Entry of the Guests, c) from *Les Huguenots*, the Blessing of the Daggers (Act 4)

7.2 *Struensee*

Trauerspiel in fünf Aufzügen mit Musik [tragedy in five acts with music]
Text: Michael Beer
First performance: Schauspielhaus, Berlin, 19 September 1846

Michael Beer's idealistic tragedy *Struensee* concerns the German-born physician Johann Friedrich Struensee (1737–72) who gained ascendancy over the degenerate Danish king Christian VII and implemented an enlightened despotism, carrying out sweeping reforms in the realm—of the legal system, serfdom, censorship, and the administration of Norway. His hasty methods, personal arrogance and illicit relations with the young Queen Caroline Matilda (1751–75) led to a conspiracy by the nobles and his mortal downfall.

The play was first performed on 27 March 1828 at the Königliche Theater, Munich, rather than in Beer's home city of Berlin, where it was banned for 19 years. The sanction had been imposed in 1827 despite the attempts of Count Brühl, the director of the Royal Theatres. Because the play took place in the Danish Court involving social and political intrigue of the highest order, the seizure of power by the Royal Physician, his love affair with the queen, the execution of the former and the banishment of the latter, the material was regarded as too explosive for comfort. It was further feared that offence would be taken by the Danish Royal Family, who were in any case related to the Prussian dynasty. Twenty years later, in 1846, the ban on the performance of *Struensee* was lifted. With a changing political circumstance, and under the friendly disposition of Friedrich Wilhelm IV, Amalie Beer secured permission from the king for a production of her youngest son's tragedy, with incidental music especially composed by her eldest son.

Illustration 7.2   *Struensee*: Johann Friedrich Struensee and Queen Caroline Matilda
(engravings by M. Mohan after contemporary portraiture)

Plot
Various locations in and around Copenhagen, 1772.

Act 1. Struensee, the son of a German pastor, has become the physician to the king of Denmark, Christian VII. Because of great skills and political acumen, he has been raised to the position of prime minister. He is planning the regeneration of the Danish people by reducing the power of the proud and tyrannical nobility. One of his major acts in this respect is the licensing of the Norwegian Guard, where all the officers are nobles. This licensing comes into effect at the commencement of the drama, in 1772, at the royal castle of Christiansborg. Count Rantzau, Struensee's predecessor as prime minister, tries to turn Struensee away from his reform projects, reproaching him, as a stranger, for his attachment to the queen, Mathilda of England, another stranger, in order to profit from the weakness of the king, and for upsetting the status quo in the kingdom. They part without reaching agreement, and Struensee, left alone, trembles in recalling that his face must have betrayed his emotion on hearing the queen's name mentioned, since he secretly loves her (No.2 Melodrama). His father, the Pastor Struensee, enters at that moment, and vainly begs his son to renounce his dangerous power and return with him to his retreat.

(No.3 First Entr'acte)

Act 2. The news of the revolt of the Norwegian Guard is brought to Struensee and Queen Mathilda. Struensee had at first decided to resist their demands, but, out of devotion to the queen, and in order to avoid greater sorrow, he submits to them. He comes to announce to the queen that in accordance with her desire, he has given way to the current and has rescinded the order. A joyful march resounds as the soldiers depart into the distance (No. 4 March and Chorus). Struensee now feels his work has been in vain, and wants to resign. The queen begs him to stay on, and he agrees readily. He has let slip his love for the queen, and after his departure she seeks to control her weakness and envisages the future with horror (No. 5 Melodrama). She leaves and the queen dowager, Julie, enters. As mother of the king, she is the enemy of Mathilda and of Struensee, and is busy plotting their downfall with her ally Rantzau. It is agreed that Struensee must be arrested that very night at one o'clock during a masked ball (No. 6 Melodrama).

(No. 7 Second Entr'acte)

Act 3. The masked ball. Various incidents take place at the ball. Struensee ignores advice to be on his guard against treachery. Count Rantzau, himself one of the conspirators, comes to warn him of the dangers which threaten him. Rantzau is masked, and Struensee, not recognizing him, refuses to listen to his counsel. Struensee returns home. Soon after, he is arrested, while Rantzau and some officers go to the queen's apartments to arrest her.

(No. 8 Third Entr'acte)

Act 4. Some drunken peasants gathered in an inn and discuss the recent events. They inform Pastor Struensee, who arrives by chance at the inn and hurries away at the news of his son's arrest. In order to complete the ruin of the prime minister, and to send him to the scaffold for high treason, Queen Mathilda is tricked into handing over Struensee's written declaration of love, having been persuaded that the king would not want to strike those who have the queen as their accomplice.

(No. 9 Fourth Entr'acte)

Act 5. Struensee, imprisoned in the Citadel, slumbers restlessly, frequently uttering the name of Mathilda (No. 10 Struensee's Dream). Rantzau comes to offer him the means of escape, on condition that he leaves Denmark. Struensee refuses when he realizes that his friends are involved in his disgrace, and that the divorce and banishment of the queen have been announced. He is shown his death warrant. His father comes to help him in this solemn moment, before a cortège of soldiers and magistrates advance to conduct him to the place of execution (No. 11 Death March). The pastor blesses his son, and Struensee is led off to death (No. 12 Benediction). A moment later a lugubrious roll of drums announces Struensee's end. His father kneels in prayer for his son (No. 13 The Last Moment).

The proposed premiere of *Struensee* had to overcome various difficulties. Heinrich Laube had recently completed a play with same title (produced in Mannheim 1844, published in 1847), which he had also submitted for consideration, but which was set aside in favour of the older project (Laube's play would come to the stage in Berlin in 1848). These unedifying developments provided occasion for scurrilous attacks in the press, as in the *Leipziger Illustrierten Theaterzeitung* (October 1846):

> The Beer family has not erred in asserting their wealth, in propelling the brother Michael (whom Laube had beaten) on to the boards, and with the brother Meyer composing thirteen pieces of music for it. The family should be careful! One just doesn't know how much the public is prepared to take, and whether in this badly-behaved situation the soother with the glockenspiel is a help or not...Laube ought to find himself a brother who can also make good music, and then we would see if he would weather the competition. Poor German stage of today! What you have to put up with!

Meyerbeer's new incidental music to his brother's play is made up of an overture and 13 pieces—some of them short, others more extensive. In the Melodrama composed for Act 1 Scene 12 where the father of the protagonist, the country parson Struensee, is introduced, Meyerbeer used the first theme of the overture, taken from his unused music for the opera *Noëma, ou Le Répentir* (by Augustin-Eugène Scribe and Henri-Vernoy de Saint Georges 1846) where it was to represent a vision of heaven. In the play it is likewise associated with a religious ideal, with a righteous view of the world, with a series of family values that ultimately relate to the pastoral heredity (ex.7.2a [a]). It is opposed by the dark, weaving theme of sexual and political intrigue, the first subject of the formal exposition (ex.7.2a [b]), and this in turn is counterposed to an aspiring, emotional melody that represents the illicit but heroic love between Struensee and the queen. Struensee, her doctor, regardless of social status, becomes her favourite and gains the highest power in the Danish state. Something of the innately doomed nature of this love is captured in the tenuous, downward pull of the melodic contour (descending by degrees from the tonic to the dominant), its fragile and melancholic colouring that essentially captures the personality of the queen—generous, ardent, noble, a conscience calm and serene. Its brief measure speaks of sentiment both profound and discrete (ex. 7.2a [c]).

Example 7.2a   *Struensee*: a) Pastor Struensee's Benediction (the Ideal), b) the
              Theme of Political Intrigue, c) the Love Theme

No. 2 Melodrama for Act 1 Scene 12 shows Struensee thinking of the queen, his
heart pounding at the mention of her name. The love theme fixes the association, and
is immediately challenged by the unexpected entry of his father, the Pastor Struensee,
his tranquil and portentous theme confirming the symbolic juxtapositioning. The
entr'acte to Act 2, No. 3 (Der Aufruhr), represents the revolt of the Norwegian
Guards, an event that marks the beginning of Struensee's fall from power. It is
dominated by the love theme which passes through thunderous timpani rolls into
a quiet stately melody that is fraught with tragic intimation (ex.7.2b [a]). This dies
away and moves into the Danish folksong 'König Christian stand am Mast' (King
Christian stood at the mast), which is given in several variant forms, both choral and
instrumental, and in varying degrees of power, before trailing away into nothing.
The Danish anthem was included at the special request of King Friedrich Wilhelm,

who had hoped that Meyerbeer would paraphrase it in the overture—an idea that the composer did not take up.

There is a fanfare behind the scenes for three trumpets and military drum, for Act 2 Scene 11; No. 4 is for Scene 12 (Marsch und Chor), a triumphant repeat of 'König Christian' representing the onward rush of Struensee's crisis as he is obliged to withdraw his orders. No. 5 is for Scene 15 (Königin Mathilde), depicting the queen's involvement in her dangerous liaison. As she leaves the stage, a deep sinuous theme, ruminating in the bass, induces a sense of unease and menace, indicating the danger of the situation (ex. 7.2b [b]). The music rises and falls in eerie reflection, and soon the danger materializes as the queen mother Julie and the privy counsellor Count Rantzau enter, walking in deep conversation. They represent Struensee's nemesis personified. The theme is resumed in No. 6 (Melodram zur letzten Szene II. Akts) which shows the finalization of the conspiracy against Struensee initiated by the queen mother and Rantzau. They have agreed to arrest Struensee at one in the morning, during the court ball. The serpentine musings die away pianissimo.

Act 3 opens with the second entr'acte, No. 7 (Der Ball), a brilliant polonaise that conjures up the masked festivities at the palace during which Struensee, at the apogee of his influence, is arrested and imprisoned. The events off-stage are vividly depicted in the music, as the stately, sumptuous progress of the dance is dramatically interrupted and broken.

Act 4 begins with No. 8 (Die Dorfschenke), the third entr'acte, a country dance with Nordic overtones, a musette with peasant drone—a pastorale in fact. The great events of state are discussed in a little country inn far away from the tumults of Copenhagen. The introduction to Act 5, the fourth entr'acte No. 9, depicts Struensee's imprisonment with the return of the solemn theme associated with his father and the idealistic values he represents (the compressed theme and variations that open the overture), dying away into sad reflection. No. 10 is for Scene 3, where the psychological state of Struensee is further developed (Der Traum Struensees), depicting his dream of the love shared with Caroline Mathilda whom he has now lost (a gentle, remote variant on the love music) enclosed by the theme of conspiracy, as Rantzau enters. It passes into the theme of benediction as Rantzau contemplates the sleeping prisoner before awakening him to harsh reality, and the love theme flits by. No. 11 (Trauermarsch) is for Scene 7, the death march that accompanies Struensee to his execution, very simple and fraught, remarkably Mahlerian in feel (ex. 7.2b [c]). No. 12 Melodram zur gleichen Szene (Die Segnung) follows on immediately. A solo violoncello (con espressione doloroso) marks the entry of Struensee's father. Three cellos accompany the blessing of the son by the father, as Struensee kneels in front of the pastor. The theme of benediction marks their final embrace. The last scene No. 13 (Der letzte Augenblick) sees the resumption of the funeral march as Struensee is led off to his execution, which happens off-stage. The drums roll, the old man kneels in silence, and the play ends with bright radiant harmonies as the curtain falls.

Example 7.2b   *Struensee*: a) the Revolt, b) the Conspiracy, c) the Death March

The overture, which musically depicts the rise of the ambitious upstart from his parental home to the highest office in the land, and then his fall, uses the themes of intrigue and love from the individual scenes of the incidental music and concludes with a victorious apotheosis, as the solemn theme associated with Pastor Struensee and the noble, religious ideal, transformed in metre, rhythm, harmony and key, proclaims the enduring legacy of Struensee's vision, in spite of his personal weakness and tragedy. 'Le péroraison est resplendissante, évocatrice; on le dirait, d'une victoire d'âme', (The peroration is splendid, evocative; one could call it a victory of the soul) (Dauriac 1913: 134).

Performances of both play and music followed: ten in Berlin in 1846, 13 in 1847, two each in 1851 and 1853, and another in 1858. In 1847 there were productions in Frankfurt, Dresden and Weimar; in 1849 in Hamburg, Frankfurt, Dresden, Magdeburg, Königsberg, Breslau, Bremen and London, Prague; in 1849 in Klagenfurt and Munich; in 1851 in Königsberg; in 1852 in Wiesbaden, Rostock, Hamburg and Rotterdam; in 1853 in Leipzig, Freiburg-in-Breisgau and Schwerin; in 1854 in Darmstadt and Danzig; in 1856 in Magdeburg and Munich; in 1858 in Vienna; in 1867 in Mannheim; in 1881 in Vienna (27 cities in all).

Soon after its first performance the overture made the rounds of the European concert halls: in 1847 alone it was performed by the Gewandhaus Orchestra in Leipzig, the Dresden Hofkapelle, and in Magdeburg, Bremen, Vienna, Pressburg (Brno), Prague, St Petersburg, Liège and Milan—always to great applause. It was played regularly in Berlin (1847, 1850, 1851, 1852, 1853, 1858, 1860), Brussels (1846, 1850, 1852, 1852), London (1848, 1853, 1859, 1862) and Paris (1857, 1860, 1864). All the incidental music featured in concerts in London (16 July 1853) and Paris (8 February 1860). On many occasions Meyerbeer investigated the possibility of having a special linking text prepared so that the music could be played as a dramatic entity apart from the whole play. Discussions were held with Rellstab (1846), Dr Frankl (1847), Théophile Gautier who wrote a preface (1848, 1852, 1854), Sternau (1852), Gabriel Seidl (1854) Gassmann (1858) and Duesberg (1864), but nothing seems to have resulted from any of these negotiations. An Italian translation of the play by Martellini appeared in 1856 and a French version by Guillaume in 1860.

The music for *Struensee* was the last big work written while Meyerbeer was Prussian Generalmusikdirektor. The fine recording made by the NDR Chor and Radio-Philharmonie Hannover des Norddeutscher Rundfunk conducted by Michail Jurowski (1998) reveals the power and poetry of Meyerbeer's musical response to his brother's work, and constitutes a worthy companion to other such Romantic incidental music—Beethoven's *Egmont* (1810), Schubert's *Rosamunde* (1823) and Mendelssohn's *A Midsummer Night's Dream* (1826/1842).

7.3 *La Jeunesse de Goethe, ou L'étudiant de Strasbourg [Goethe's Youth, or The Student of Strasbourg]*

Mélodrame en trois actes [melodrama in three acts]
Text: Henri Blaze de Bury
Unperformed. The manuscript is lost.

In 1859 the French poet Henri Blaze de Bury proposed a project to Meyerbeer for future production in one of the big Parisian playhouses. It was called *La Jeunesse de Goethe* and concerned the great German poet's *Sturm und Drang* youth in Strasbourg and its environs like Sesenheim (1770–71). Several of Goethe's most popular poems were to be interpolated. Meyerbeer reacted enthusiastically, especially when the director of the Odéon, La Rounat, suggested that the third act be set as a melodrama. An agreement was reached on 31 August 1860, and Meyerbeer began composing right away. The record from his diary gives a listing of the pieces and provides some idea of the plan and extent of his contribution to the project. He completed Mignon's song ('Kennst du das Land?') (Do you know the land?) on 31 September, Marguerite's ballad ('Le Roi de Thules') on 15 October, the Scene of the Fates from *Iphigénie* on 31 October, the *Faust* scene on 20 November, the Chorus of Angels from the finale of *Faust II* on 10 December, the *Erlkönig* melodrama on 13 December, and an instrumental passage on 19 December. The score was then set aside for nearly two years because of the uncertainties besetting the project. In the meantime the composition of *L'Africaine* consumed Meyerbeer's creative attention and energies. A revision of the material and its orchestration was undertaken during August 1862, and completed on 9 September 1862. Thereafter the work is not mentioned again by the composer. It appears to have been lost with many others of his manuscripts during the upheavals of the Second World War when parts of the archives of the State Library were taken from Berlin to Silesia and Poland for safekeeping. Only some of this material has so far been recovered.

In the light of the tantalizing and incomplete nature of the history of this project, and the unknown whereabouts of the finished score, it is best to hear the story from the memoirs of Blaze de Bury himself, as recounted in translation and explained by Joseph Bennett (1884–8: 38–42):

> It has often been remarked that Meyerbeer had no very exalted notions of an operatic subject; preferring bustling, blatant, and sometimes vulgar historic scenes, more or less travestied by Scribe, to those of a refined and classic nature. In this respect some injustice has been done to the composer. As a matter of fact, he was always prospecting for a truly noble subject. 'Hero and Leander' at one time attracted him; so did the 'Orestes' of Aeschylus; while of 'Faust' he thought seriously, having been designated by Goethe as the musician of that great drama. But all this coquetting came to nothing. The case was somewhat different with another work, the history of which has been told by M. Blaze de Bury at great length. M. de Bury had written a drama for the Odéon, entitled *La Jeunesse de Goethe*—a fantastic affair, apparently, in which the poet was represented as 'vivant ses oeuvres', however that may be. While engaged in distributing the parts and so forth, the manager, Rounat, called M. de Bury's attention to a night scene in the third act, where he thought a *mélodrame*, or orchestral symphony, would be effective. ...

Eventually Meyerbeer undertook the work, but on his own plan and conditions, expressed in remarkable words. The master said:

> 'I have thought much about your piece, about the part that music ought to take in it, and the manner in which, to succeed, it should intervene. Perhaps we are on the track of a discovery. *The old forms are used up; operas in five acts are no longer possible.* Let us seek in the conditions of modern art the alliance of music and drama which the ancients appear to have established. That tempts me, I vow; I even say that I have long dreamed of it, and reckon to prove it, if we have a success, by making further proposals to you. Meanwhile, I shall intervene in your work without mixing myself up with it.'

Meyerbeer went on to explain that not even a violin should be heard till the time for the *intermezzo* arrived. Then he would 'let loose' all his forces, beginning with .a grand overture. De Bury was charmed with Meyerbeer's idea, but nothing came of it till four years later (September 1861), when the dramatist and composer met at Ems. M. de Bury writes:

> One morning, as we were breakfasting in his room, he cried, "Ah! that 'Jeunesse de Goethe'; now is the time to speak of it. Would you like to see the score ?" He opened his

desk and took out a voluminous packet, which he put upon the piano. I turned over the leaves hungrily. It was complete! The "Erl-king", the Hymn of the Fates in "Iphigenia", the scene of *Margaret* in the church, the immense seraphic Hosanna of the second Faust. I saw it; I touched it. Meyerbeer, all the while, looked at me, happy in my joy, and satisfied with himself. "Another time", he said, "you shall hear it, for today it is enough that you have seen. You can now say to our good friends that Meyerbeer keeps his word." Then, taking the volume, seven times sealed, he placed it in the desk and locked it up.

According to the evidence of M. Blaze de Bury, there was undoubtedly an intention on the part of Meyerbeer to produce his 'Jeunesse de Goethe' at the Odéon, but, unfortunately, the time which suited the composer did not fit in with the manager's arrangements. The matter is referred to at some length in a letter written by Meyerbeer to his literary colleague on 28 January 1861:

'You tell me that as regards the month of April, when it would be convenient to me to give my work, M. de la Rounat has an engagement with Madame Ristori, and that, consequently, he proposes to bring out the piece in the Spring of 1862. At that time I shall certainly be free, musically speaking, and I see no difficulty so far; nevertheless, my dear friend, to take a definite engagement for a time so distant, and that will not be reached for fourteen months, is what, in my position, I cannot see my way to do. A head of a family, living out of France, and under the circumstances of these times—who knows, as regards a future so distant, what may happen to keep me at home? If we wait till October next to sign an engagement for April, 1862, the date which M. de la Rounat proposes, he will be sure to have the work seven months in advance, while, on our side, the future will not be hampered to such a length of time. Now, let us talk a little about our piece. The scene for which I had most fear (that of the cathedral in "Faust") is that which comes out best of all, and I hope you will not be dissatisfied with it. As regards the rest, I shall not ask you to make any further change. Musically speaking, only one number disquiets me, and about it I hesitate, and scarcely know what to do, I mean the "Erl-King". Schubert's music to that ballad has become so popular throughout the entire world that it seems to me impossible to make the public accept any other to the same words, while, for myself, am so much under *its* influence that I do not see my way to compose anything which would give me satisfaction. I have an idea, therefore, to preserve Schubert's melodies, putting them underneath the choruses for the "Erl-King's daughters", and at the same time, as I need not say, scoring for orchestra what Schubert has written for the pianoforte only. However, there are two courses before me. One is to make the father and son speak in *melodrame*, accompanied by Schubert's melodies in the orchestra, and allow only the *Erl-King* and his daughters to sing. The other is to make the parts of father and son singing parts. Be good enough to let me know which of these two plans you prefer. From a purely musical point of view it is advisable that all three should sing, but I will act according to your decision. Send me also, and at once, the "Chorus of Students", for I should better like to write it just now, when the impression of the rest of the music is warm in my imagination, than later , when other work has driven the matter from my mind.'

Unhappily, *La Jeunesse de Goethe* was never produced, and M. Blaze de Bury tells us why. He says:

Kept at Berlin as much by his court duties as by the state of his health, Meyerbeer seemed to the public as though he had forgotten the road to Paris. Nevertheless, the desire to possess the masterpiece increased in proportion to the obstacles. ...Each year a place was kept for it—the best that could be secured in the arrangements of the repertory. At length, in the autumn of 1863, Meyerbeer arrived in Paris, settled down there, and deliberations were immediately resumed. This time the affair was complicated by the question of the "Africaine", which, just then on the cards, had possession of the public mind. Hence the production of the work "La Jeunesse de Goethe" that winter could not be thought of, and another year's delay took place. ...Meyerbeer's score exists complete, finished, authentic, and others beside myself have had it in their hands.

A natural question is: What has become of *La Jeunesse de Goethe*? We can find no trace of it in musical record since the composer's death, and are bound to infer that it still remains in manuscript, kept thus from a world which would be very glad to receive it.

Illustration 7.3   *La Jeunesse de Goethe*: the young Goethe (from a portrait by J. H. Lips)

Conclusion

Giacomo Meyerbeer, once regarded as a luminary of the musical firmament, and whose works were performed on all the operatic stages of the world with a fame like that of Mozart's, has been under a cloud for too long. The violent swing in his fortunes, and the extreme nature of reaction to him—the Wagnerian critique, the turn away from bel canto, historicism and the heroic during the first part of the twentieth century—has been one of the most extraordinary in the history of music. It is now time to see him and his work in the context of his brilliant career and his very significant contribution to the heritage of dramatic music. The variety of his compositions, his constant responses to dramatic impulses in the various lands of his travels and adoption, the huge impact of his operas all over the world and their enduring influence can now increasingly be assessed afresh, and begin to take their proper place in the public consciousness. The variety of his dramatic activity in so many genres, the sensitivity of his reactions to existing traditions and types, and his capacity to take these and reshape them according to his particular concerns and artistic understanding is worthy of study and respect. The issues of his life—his sense of exclusion as a Jew, his ambiguous attitude to his Prussian homeland and the demands of nationalism, his strong, enduring religious sensibilities and compassion—give his works a underlying unity of theme and a topicality pertinent to his life, personal concerns and the historical realities of intolerance in the past century. Faith, exile and integration, partisanship and universality, hatred and sacrificial love are ever-recurrent issues informing his choices of subject and text. His considerable musical education and talent, his vital dramatic responses—with all the gifts of rare melody, inventive harmony, gorgeous orchestral colouring, rhetorical force, consistency of musical treatment, a gift for characterization, the accentuation of individual types and symbolism—give his work a vibrancy and freshness that can still surprise and delight.

Far from being the facile products of a populist showman, Meyerbeer's dramatic *oeuvre* shows musical consistency and high seriousness, and provides an invitation to reflect on the processes of history and some of the most moving issues of human experience. Why, at a time of a great secular impulse in France, did he focus his French operas almost exclusively on essentially religious–spiritual themes? In fact he pursued an argument based on disillusionment with established faith and attempts to reform religion by political radicalism. Meyerbeer sought an aspiring faith, reflected in the ideals of personal spirituality, morality and the essential nobility of humanity. In this, secularism is rejected and a unified Church seen as preferable to anarchy and total individualism. The subtexts of his operas reveal an almost prophetic recognition of the dangers lying ahead amongst the secular paths that were eventually followed in continental Europe. *Robert le Diable* posits a unified faith and a Romantic concept of the power of intercession; *Les Huguenots* presents a critique of a failing religious ideal whilst individual nobility wins through; *Le Prophète* and *Struensee* warn of the dangers of political excess and the blandishments of personalism in attempts to reform faith and transform society, and again elevate the role of the individual in intercession, mediation and repentance/atonement; *Dinorah* illustrates the power of individual faith, goodness and love over superstition and fear; *L'Africaine* depicts the ultimate goal of personal love and self-sacrifice in a context of an expanding global politics of power and control.

Meyerbeer's work deserves attention for its meticulous research, its integration of music, text and design, its dramatic pacing, brilliant vocal writing and highly original scoring. His operas reveal him as one of music's great dramatists, and so long as intensity of passion and the power of lyricism are regarded as indispensable characteristics of dramatic music, there will be a place for his art, and it will continue to survive and find new life. It has much to offer—indeed, it constitutes an enduringly enriching experience.

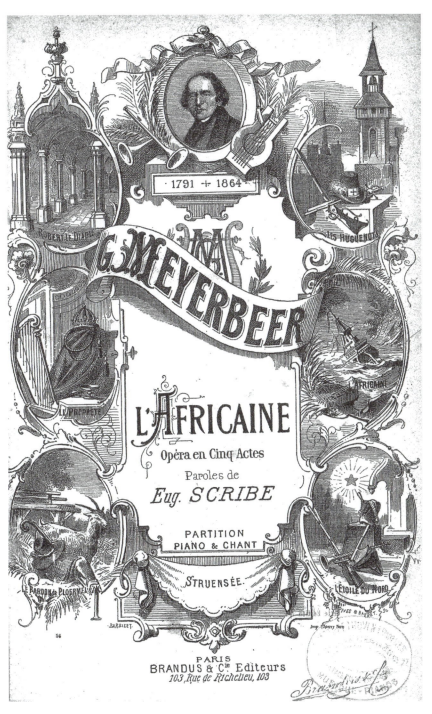

Endpiece: *Meyerbeer's Works*: title-page of the Brandus vocal score of *L'Africaine* with iconographic insets of composer's principal works (Paris, 1865)

Appendix

The Meyerbeer Librettists

Jules Barbier (b. Paris, 8 Mar. 1825; d. Paris, 16 Jan. 1901) and **Michel Carré** (b. Paris, 1819; d. Argenteuil, 27 June 1872). They collaborated on many libretti, specializing in texts derived from several authors, including Goethe, Shakespeare, Dante and E.T.A. Hoffmann, regularly transforming the subjects in a conventionalized, often sentimentalized, version of the original, a formula that was extremely effective in terms of contemporary French opera. They wrote for Gounod (*Faust, Roméo et Juliette*); 'Meyerbeer (*Dinorah*); Thomas (*Hamlet, Mignon, Françoise de Rimini*); Offenbach (*Les Contes d'Hoffmann*), and Massé (*Les Noces de Jeannette*).

Michael Beer (b. Berlin 19 Aug. 1800; d. Munich, 22 Mar. 1833), the third and youngest brother of Giacomo Meyerbeer. His precocious dramatic gift, in many ways anticipating the psychological art of Hebbel, found expression in the tragedy of racial and religious exclusion, *Der Paria* (1823, in one act), and the historico-political chronicle of personal hubris and betrayed idealism, *Struensee* (1829). He spent the last years of his life working in Munich in close association with his friend, Eduard Schenk.

Charlotte Birch-Pfeiffer (b. Stuttgart, 23 Jun. 1800; d. Berlin, 25 Aug. 1868) was a noted actress and popular dramatist. She made her debut in Munich and played principal leads from 1818. She married C.A. Birch in 1825. For six years (1837–43) she was in charge of the Zurich theatre, before returning to acting in Berlin in 1844. Her 74 plays are mainly adaptations of novels, executed with a keen eye for theatrical effect, and predominantly sentimental in tone. They include *Der Glöckner von Notre-Dame* (1839, after Victor Hugo), *Dorf und Stadt* (1847, after Auerbach's *Die Frau Professorin*), *Die Waise von Lowood* (1856, based on Charlotte Brontë's *Jane Eyre*), and *Die Grille* (1856, after George Sand's *La Petite Fadette*). She helped Meyerbeer with advice in the transformation of *Ein Feldlager in Schlesien* into *Vielka* for Vienna, and with fresh ideas and new German words for both *Le Pardon de Ploërmel* and *L'Africaine*.

Ange-Henri Blaze de Bury (1813–88), son of the critic Castil-Blaze, was first a diplomatic attaché before turning to journalism, particularly as a music critic for the *Revue de deux mondes* and *Le Ménestral*. He wrote books on composers (Mozart, Beethoven, Meyerbeer) and literary figures (Goethe, Alexandre Dumas *père*, Merimée).

Emile Deschamps (Deschamps de Saint-Armand) (b. Bourges, 20 Feb. 1791; d. Versailles, 23 April 1871) was a minor poet of the Romantic Movement, one of the founders of *La Muse française* (1823), a good friend to younger authors, notably Vigny and Hugo. His writings, mainly translations and imitations, stimulated interest in German, Spanish, and English literature, and included *Études françaises et étrangères* (1828), poems prefaced by an essay on Romantic doctrines, and also translations of plays like *Romeo and Juliet* (1839), *Macbeth* (1844), and libretti.

Julius (Heinrich Joseph Maria) Duesberg (b. Münster, 20 Sept. 1793; d. Paris, 6 Jul. 1864). He was a historian, journalist, music critic and *littérateur* living in Paris, where he made translations for Maurice Schlesinger's *Revue et Gazette musicale*, including articles by Richard Wagner (1840–42). He also prepared the German version of Berlioz's *Roméo et Juliette* (1839). Meyerbeer employed him to translate the German additions and alterations to *Dinorah* and *L'Africaine* into French.

Conte Lodovico Piossasco Feys (1773–1848), a Piedmontese nobleman, was active as magistrate, politician and amateur *littérateur* in Turin where he provided libretto adaptions for Mayr, Mercadante and Meyerbeer.

Theodor Goltdammer (Goldtammer) (1799–1972) was a prominent Berlin professional—lawyer, poet, author and book editor. He wrote the occasional verses for Meyerbeer's *Maria und ihr Genius*.

Johann Christoph Grünbaum (b. Haslau bei Eger, 18 Oct. 1785; d. Berlin, 10 Jan. 1870). He won fame as a tenor, singing in Prague (1807–11) and then at the Court Opera in Vienna until 1832, before moving to Berlin where he was active as a singing teacher and translator. For Meyerbeer, he provided the German versions of *Dinorah* and several of his songs.

Etienne Lauchery (b. Lyons, Sept. 1732; d. Berlin, 5 Jan. 1820). French dancer, choreographer and ballet master who worked in Mannheim from 1746, where he became court dance master in 1756, then ballet master in Cassel (1764–72). The *Recueil de Ballets* (1768) lists 37 of his works. He later worked in Munich and Berlin (1788–1813). He was the father of the dancer and teacher Albert Lauchery (1779–1853).

Ludwig I, King of Bavaria [House of Wittelsbach] (1786–1868, reg. 1825–48). Inheriting the most liberal constitution in Germany from Maximilian I, Ludwig became a great patron of the arts. He rebuilt Munich as a classical city, but his reactionary political measures, and relationship with the dancer-adventuress Lola Montez, alienated his subjects, and he was obliged to abdicate. Meyerbeer set his patriotic verses for the *Bayerischer Schützenmarsch*.

Pietro Metastasio (b. Rome, 3 Jan. 1698; d. Vienna, 12 Apr. 1782). He was given a classical education, entered into theatrical life in Naples, rising to fame with his libretto *Didone abbandonata* (for Domenico Sarro, 1724). He returned to Rome, and in 1729 was invited to Vienna as *poeta cesareo* to Emperor Charles VI. His work was the clearest expression of the new ideals of the *opera seria*. During his years in Vienna he became the most famous Italian poet of his day and the most frequently set librettist of all time. His mobile, elegant verse dominated the Italian lyric theatre. A great poet and dramatic structuralist, he realized the principle common to all opera: the librettist must always hold his lyricism in check in order to allow the music sufficient scope for its own proper expression.

Ernst Raupach (1784–1852) was the author of many historical dramas (including a series of 16 on the Hohenstaufens), published in a collected edition of eight volumes (1837–43). *Genoveva* and *Der Nibelungenhort* (both 1828) were popular, but the sentimental melodrama *Der Müller und sein Kind* (1835) was especially so. He was the subject of witty attacks by Platen, Immermann and Heine.

Ludwig Rellstab (b. Berlin 1799; d. Berlin, 1860). He was first an artillery officer, and then became an author and journalist. He wrote poems, some of which were famously set to music by Franz Schubert, the first seven songs of *Schwanengesang*. His poems appeared in *Griechenlands Morgenröte* (1822), *Gedichte* (1827) and *Erzählungen, Skizzen und Gedichte* (1833). He provided the libretto for an opera by Berhard Klein (*Dido*, 1823) and wrote the tragedies *Karl der Kühen* (1824) and *Eugen Aram* (1839). He also wrote two novels: the historical *1812* (4 vols, 1834), his most successful work, and *Der Wildschütz* (1835). His musical journalism, mostly for the *Vossische Zeitung*, was collected as *Musikalische Beurteilungen* (1848) and an anthology of stories as *Sommerfrüchte* (1852). His autobiography, *Aus meinem Leben* (2 vols), appeared posthumously (1861); his *Gesammelte Schriften* (20 vols) was first publishedin 1843–48, and posthumously (24 vols) in 1860–61.

Felice Romani (b. Genoa, 31 Jan. 1788; d. Moneglia, 28 Jan. 1865). His first libretti were written in Milan for Mayr. He moved to Turin to take up an editorship, and developed skills which made him the most sought-after librettist of his day, with over 100 composers setting his texts. He collaborated with Rossini (*Il turco in Italia*), Meyerbeer (*Margherita d'Anjou, L'esule di Granata*), and Verdi (*Un giorno di regno*), but his most significant work was done with Donizetti and Bellini. His classical training gave him an overriding sense of balance, so that he used Romantic ideas rather than being overtaken by them. His dramatic instinct and elegant verse was supremely suited to the musical sensibilities of Donizetti and Bellini. The number of his commissions meant that much of the work was done in haste, was not always profound and not free of clichés. His best books are among the most enduring of the early nineteenth century; they include the pastoral idylls *La sonnambula* and *L'elisir d'amore*, and the tragic dramas *Anna Bolena* and *Norma*.

Gaetano Rossi (b. Verona, 18 May 1774; d. Verona, 25 Jan. 1855). He worked in Venice and Verona, writing some 120 libretti for many composers, including Carafa, Coccia, Donizetti, Mayr, Mercadante, Meyerbeer, Nicolai, Pacini and Rossini. While having no great literary ambitions, and tending to prolixity, his work nonetheless tapped an extensive range of sources, and injected many of the themes of Romanticism into operatic currency, with plots derived from classical and historical drama, and also fashionable Spanish, Nordic and British subjects. His literary techniques did much to loosen the set forms characteristic of the reforms of early nineteenth-century opera. Neither his verse nor choice of subject showed the same sensitivity and aesthetic judgement as his greatest rival, Romani.

Alois Wilhelm Schreiber (b. Kappel unter Wiedeck in Baden, 10 Oct. 1761; d. Baden Baden, 21 Oct. 1841) was successively a schoolmaster in Baden, a dramatic critic in Mainz and Frankfurt and professor of aesthetics at Heidelberg University. A prolific writer, he produced novels, stories and plays (*Scenen aus Fausts Leben*, 1792), also publishing historical writings, topographical essays and guidebooks (*Heidelberg und seine Umgebung*, 1811; *Handbuch für Reisende am Rhein*, 1816). Most important was his textbook on aesthetics and several opera libretti and lieder texts.

Augustin-Eugène Scribe (b. Paris, 14 Dec. 1791; d. Paris, 20 Feb. 1861). He began his theatrical career as a writer of comedies, but by appreciation of the theatrical condition in Paris and of the sensibility of his audience, he gave *opéra comique* a new strength (*Le Maçon* and *La Dame blanche*, 1825) and animated the genre of French *grand opéra* (*La Muette de Portici*, 1828). His keen historical awareness was inherited from Jouy's work for Spontini, and he fully utilized the opportunities for staging on an elaborate scale at the Paris Opéra. His plots draw on historical sources that are reworked rather than adapted. He often dealt with the clash of religious, national and political issues, and the lives of both famous and ordinary people caught up in crisis, capturing an epic sense of the movement of peoples and giving the chorus a more dramatically functional role. He regularly used collaborators to write verse for his strong stage situations. The effectiveness of his 76 libretti resulted in great success, his brilliant sense of the stage confirmed by the number of composers who turned to him, pre-eminently Auber (38), Boieldieu (4), Cherubini (1), Cilea (1), Donizetti (5), Gounod (1), Halévy (6), Hérold (2), Meyerbeer (6), Offenbach (2), Rossini (2), and Verdi (2).

Johann Emanuel Veith (1788–1876), a veterinary surgeon, writer and chorus master in Vienna, was the librettist of Adalbert Gyrowetz's successful opera *Der Augenarzt* (1811). Gyrowetz may well have recommended him to Meyerbeer for the text of the occasional *Singspiel, Das Brandenberger Tor* (1814).

Johann Gottfried Wohlbrück (1770–1822) was an actor at the Court Theatre in Munich and appeared as guest artist in Darmstadt where Meyerbeer certainly made his acquaintance. He provided the young musician with the libretto of *Wirt und Gast*, also wrote the text for Weber's cantata *Kampf und Sieg* and was the father of W.A. Wohlbrück (who wrote the libretti *Der Vampyr* and *Der Templer und die Jüdin* for Heinrich Marschner, his brother-in-law).

Select Bibliography

Letellier, Robert Ignatius and Pellegrini, Marco Clemente. *Giacomo Meyerbeer: A Guide to Research*. Newcastle: Cambridge Scholars Publishing, 2007.

1. BIOGRAPHICAL AND GENERAL STUDIES

Diaries and Letters

Meyerbeer, Giacomo. *Briefwechsel und Tagebücher*. Eds Heinz and Gudrun Becker, Sabine Henze-Döhring. 7 vols. Berlin: De Gruyter, 1960, 1970, 1975, 1985, 1998, 2002, 2006.
Meyerbeer, Giacomo. *The Diaries of Giacomo Meyerbeer*. Translated, edited and annotated by Robert Ignatius Letellier. 4 vols. Madison, Teaneck: Fairleigh Dickinson University Press; London: Associated University Presses, 1999–2004.
Becker, Heinz and Becker, Gudrun. *Giacomo Meyerbeer: Ein Leben in Briefen* (Taschenbücher zur Musikwissenschaft, 85). Wilhelmshaven: Heinrichshofen, 1983. Rpt. Leipzig: Reclam, 1987. [Trans. Mark Violette. *Giacomo Meyerbeer: A Life in Letters*. London: Helm; Portland, OR: Amadeus Press, 1989.]

Selected Biographical and General Studies

Becker, Heinz. 'Giacomo Meyerbeer: On the Occasion of the Centenary of His Death'. In *Year Book IX of the Leo Baeck Institute*. London, 1964; pp. 178–201.
——*Giacomo Meyerbeer in Selbstzeugnissen und Bilddokumenten* (Rowohlt-Monographien, 228). Reinbek: Rowohlt, 1980. [Trans. Czech, Prague 1996.]
Bennett, Joseph. *Giacomo Meyerbeer*. (Novello's Primers of Musical Biography.) 5 vols. London: Novello & Co. [1884–85] [47 pp.]
Charlton, David (ed.). *The Cambridge Companion to French Grand Opera*. Cambridge: Cambridge University Press, 2003. [Contains 20 chapters, grouped as Part I: The Resourcing of Grand Opera; Revaluation and the Twenty-First Century; II: Grand Operas for Paris; III: Transformations of Grand Opera.]
Cohen, H. Robert (ed.). *The Original Staging Manuals for Ten Parisian Operas 1824–1843/Dix livrets de mise en scène lyrique datant des créations parisiennes 1824–1843* (La Vie musicale en France en XIXe siècle, 6). Stuyvesant, NY: Pendragon, 1998. [Incl. the production book of *Les Huguenots*.]
Cohen, H. Robert and Gigou, Marie-Odile (eds). *The Original Staging Manuals for Twelve Parisian Operas/Douze livrets de mise en scène lyrique datant des créations parisiennes* (La Vie musicale en France en XIXe siècle, 3). Stuyvesant, NY: Pendragon, 1991. [Incl. the production books for *Robert le Diable*, *Le Prophète*.]

Coudroy, Marie-Hélène. *La critique parisienne des grands-opéras de Meyerbeer: Robert le Diable, Les Huguenots, Le Prophète, L'Africaine* (Etudes sur l'Opéra français du xixe siècle, 2). 2 vols. Saarbrücken: Musik-Edition Lucie Galland, 1988.

Crosten, William L. *French Grand Opera: An Art and a Business*. New York: King's Crown Press, 1948. Rpt. New York: Da Capo Press, 1972.

Curzon, Emmanuel Henri de. *Meyerbeer: biographie critique*. (Les Musiciens célèbres). Paris: H. Laurens, 1910.

——'Meyerbeer et l'opéra comique'. In 'L'Opéra comique aux XIXe siècle', *La Revue musicale*, 140 (November 1933): 244–320.

Dauriac, Lionel. *Meyerbeer*. (Les Maîtres de la Musique). Paris: Felix Alcan, 1913. 2nd ed., 1930.

Döhring, Sieghart. 'Die Autographen der vier Hauptopern Meyerbeers: Ein erster Quellenbericht'. *Archiv für Musikwissenschaft* 39:1 (1982): 32–63.

——'Giacomo Meyerbeer: Grand Opéra als Ideendrama'. *Lendemains* 31/32:8 1983: 11–12.

——'Meyerbeer, Giacomo'. In *Pipers Enzyklopädie des Musiktheaters*. Eds Carl Dahlhaus and Sieghart Döhring. 6 vols. Munich and Zurich: Piper, 1986–97; 4 (1991): 111–66.

——and Henze-Döhring, Sabine. 'Meyerbeers Grand Opéra: Historische Oper als Ideendrama'. In *Oper und Musikdrama im 19. Jahrhundert* (Handbuch der musikalischen Gattungen, 13). Ed. S. Mauser. Laaber: Laaber, 1997.

——and Jacobshagen, Arnold (eds). *Meyerbeer und das europäische Musiktheater* (Thurnauer Schriften zum Musiktheater, 16). Laaber: Laaber, 1998. [27 contributions from the Thurnau Symposium of 1991.]

——and Schläder, Jürgen (eds). *Giacomo Meyerbeer – Musik als Welterfahrung: Heinz Becker zum 70. Geburtstag*. Munich: Ricordi, 1995. [Articles on libretti, reception, *Les Huguenots*, *Gli amori di Teolinda*, *Robert le Diable*, the edition of the *Briefwechsel*, unpublished letters, Meyerbeer and the Berlin *salons*, Meyerbeer and Verdi, Meyerbeer and Mendelssohn, the Heine songs.]

Dole, Nathan Haskell. 'Meyerbeer'. In *The Lives of the Musicians* (also as *Famous Composers*). 2 vols. London: Methuen & Co., 1903; pp. 327–46. [Rev. and enlarged in one vol. London: George Harrap & CP, Ltd, 1929.]

Everist, Mark. *Giacomo Meyerbeer and Music Drama in Nineteenth-Century Paris*. (Variorum Collected Studies Series). Aldershot: Ashgate, 2005.

Eymieu, Henri. *L'Oeuvre de Meyerbeer*. Paris: Fischbacher, 1910.

Fétis, François-Joseph. *Biographie universelle des musiciens et bibliographie générale de la Musique*. Brussels, 1833–44; 2nd ed. 8 vols. Paris: Firman Didot Frères, 1860–65; VI: 118–29. Two supplementary volumes by A. Pougin. Paris, 1870–75. Rpt. Brussels: Culture et Civilisation, 1963.

Frese, Christhard. *Dramaturgie der grossen Opern Giacomo Meyerbeers*. Berlin: Robert Linau, 1970.

Fulcher, Jane. 'Meyerbeer and the Music of Society'. *The Music Quarterly*, 67 (1981): 213–29.

——*The Nation's Image: French Grand Opera as Politicized Art*. Cambridge: Cambridge University Press, 1987.

Gautier, Théophile. *Histoire de l'art dramatique en France depuis vingt-cinq ans*. Paris: Magnin Blanchard, 1858–9.

Gerhard, Anselm. *Die Verstädterung der Oper: Paris und das Musiktheater des 19. Jahrhunderts*. Stuttgart and Weimar: Metzler, 1992. [In Eng. as *The Urbanization of Opera: Music Theater in Paris in the Nineteenth Century*. Trans. Mary Whittall. Chicago and London: The University of Chicago Press, 1998.]

Hanslick, Eduard. 'Meyerbeer: Mit besonderer Berücksichtigung seiner drei letzten Opern'. In *Die moderne Oper: Kritiken und Studien*. Berlin, 1875; 3/1911: 138–73.

Heine, Heinrich. *Sämtliche Schriften*. Ed. Klaus Briegleb. 5 vols. Munich: Hanser, 1976.

Hervey, Arthur. *Meyerbeer and His Music* (Masterpieces of Music). London and Edinburgh: T.C. & E.C. Jack, 1913. Rpt. Temecula: Reprint Services Corp.

Huebner, Stephen. 'Italianate Duets in Meyerbeer's *Grands Opéras*'. *Journal for Musicological Research* 8:3–4 (1989): 203–58.

——'Meyerbeer [Beer], Giacomo [Jakob Liebmann Meyer]'. In *The New Grove Dictionary of Opera*. Ed. Stanley Sadie. 4 vols. London: Macmillan, 1992; III: 366–71.

Jacobshagen, Arnold and Pospísil, Milan (eds). *Meyerbeer und die Opéra comique um die Mitte des 19. Jahrhunderts* (Thurnauer Schriften zum Musiktheater, 19). Laaber: Laaber, 2000. [17 essays.]

Kapp, Julius. *Giacomo Meyerbeer*. Berlin: Schuster & Loeffler, 1920. Rev. ed. 1930, 8/1932. Rpt. Schaan-Liechtenstein: Sändig-Reprint-Verlag, 1982.

Le Bon, Gustave. *La Psychologie des foules* [1895]. (The crowd; a study of the popular mind.) New York: Viking Press, 1960.

Letellier, Robert Ignatius. 'Music's Great Enigma: Giacomo Meyerbeer: Neglected Master of Grand Opéra' [1976]. See below in *Meyerbeer Studies*, pp. 19–39.

——'The nexus of religion, politics and love in the operas of Giacomo Meyerbeer' [1991]. See below in *Meyerbeer Studies*, pp. 64–95.

——*Meyerbeer Studies. A Series of Lectures, Essays, and Articles on the Life and Work of Giacomo Meyerbeer*. Madison, Teaneck: Fairleigh Dickinson University Press; Associated University Presses, 2005. [10 essays.]

Loewenberg, Alfred. *Annals of Opera 1597–1940* [London, 1943]. Second edition revised and corrected with an introduction by Edward J. Dent. New York: Rowman & Littlefield, 1970.

Marx, Adolf Bernhard. *Erinnerungen aus meinem Leben*. 2 vols. Berlin, 1865.

Niecks, Friedrich. 'The Chief Musical Forces of the 19th Century'. *The Etude Magazine*, August 1914: 1–4.

Pendle, Karin. *Eugène Scribe and French Opera of the Nineteenth Century* (Studies in Musicology, 6). Ann Arbor: UMI Research Press, 1979.

Pougin, Arthur. *Dictionnaire historique et pittoresque du théâtre*. Paris, 1885.

Reininghaus, Frieder. 'Tot oder wiedererweckt? Meyerbeers Opern auf den deutschen Bühnen nach 1945'. *Neue Zeitschrift für Musik* 149:6 (1988): 4–10.

Riemann, Hugo. 'Meyerbeer'. In *Musik-Lexicon* [1882]. Rev. and rewritten periodically. 9th–11th ed. Alfred Einstein. 11th ed. Berlin: M. Hesse, 1929.

Wagner, Richard. *Prose Works*. 8 vols. Trans. William Ashton Ellis. London: Kegan Paul, Trench, Trubner, 1892–1912. Leipzig: Breitkpof & Härtel, 1907.
——*Sämtliche Briefe*. Eds Gertrud Strobel and Werner Wolf. Leipzig: Deutsche Verlag für Musik, 1967–70.
Wild, Nicole, and Charlton, David. *Théâtre de l'Opéra Comique, Paris: Répertoire 1762–1971*. Sperimont, Belgium: Pierre Margaga, 2005.
Wolff, Stéphanie. *L'Opéra au Palais Garnier, 1875–1962*. Paris: L'Entr'acte, 1962.
Zimmermann, Reiner. *Meyerbeer: Eine Biographie nach Dokumenten*. Berlin: Henschel Verlag, 1991. Rev. ed. 1998.

2. DRAMATIC WORKS

Libretti

Meyerbeer, Giacomo: *The Complete Libretti in Five Volumes. In the Original and English Translation by Richard Arsenty with an Introduction by Robert Letellier*. London: Cambridge Scholars Press, 2004.

Modern Anthologies

Kaiser, Peter (ed.). *Giacomo Meyerbeer: Opern-Arien*. 4 vols. Cassel: Bärenreiter, 1995–98.
——*Opern-Arien (Tenor)* (1995) (20 arias).
——*Opern-Arien (Bass/Bariton)* (1995) (15 arias).
——*Opern-Arien (Alt/Mezzo-Sopran)* (1996) (15 arias).
——*Opern-Arien (Sopran)* (1998) (10 arias).

Sources (Editions and Bibliographies)

'Meyerbeer, Giacomo'. In *Pipers Enzyklopädie des Musiktheaters*. Eds Carl Dahlhaus and Sieghart Döhring. 4 vols. Munich and Zurich, 1986–91; 4: 111–66.

Individual Works

1) Ballet

Der Fischer und das Milchmädchen
Becker, Heinz. 'Meyerbeers erstes Bühnenwerk: *Der Fischer und das Milchmädchen*'. *Kleine Schriften der Gesellschaft für Theatergeschichte* 16 (1958): 26–36.

2) Cantata (Oratorio/Dramatic Monologue/Duodrama)

Gott und die Natur

Score:
Meyerbeer, Giacomo. *Gott und die Natur*. Ed. Peter Kaiser. Munich: Ricordi, 1999.
Bibliography:
Istel, Edgar. 'Meyerbeer's Way to Mastership: Employment of the Leading-Motive before Wagner's Birth'. *The Musical Quarterly* 12 (January 1926): 81–83.

Gli amori di Teolinda

Becker, Heinz. 'Doppelporträt in Tönen: Meyerbeers Kantate *Gli amori di Teolinda*'. In *Ludwigsburger Schlossfestspiel 1981, Almanach*. Eds Wolfgang Gönnenwein and Matthias Strasser. Ludwigsburg, 1981.
Engelhardt, Markus. 'Sujetkantate und Opéra imaginaire: Meyerbeers *Gli amori di Teolinda*'. In Sieghart Döhring and Jürgen Schläder (eds). *Giacomo Meyerbeer: Musik als Welterfahrung: Heinz Becker zum 70. Geburtstag*. Munich: Ricordi, 1995; pp. 63–88.

Das Bayerische Schützen-Marsch

Anon. 'Meyerbeers *Baierischer Schützenmarsch*'. *Neue Berliner Musikzeitung* 24 (1870): 165.

Maria und ihr Genius

Score:
Meyerbeer, Giacomo. *Maria und ihr Genius*. Kantate zur Feier der silberen Hochzeit Ihrer Königliche Hoheheiten, des Prinzen und der Prinzessin Karl von Preussen, für Sopran und Tenor Soli mit Chor und Orchester. *Componiert von G. Meyerbeer*. Berlin: Schlesinger, 1852.

3. OPERA

1) German Operas: *Singspiel*

Jephthas Gelübde

Score:
Meyerbeer, Giacomo. *Jephthas Gelübde: A Manuscript Facsimile*. Intro. and ed. Robert Letellier. Newcastle: Cambridge Scholars Publishing, 2008.

Bibliography:
Heidelberger, Frank. '*Jephthas Gelübde* – Charakteristische Form und musikalische Gestalt in Meyerbeers Frühwerk' (Thurnau Symposium 1991). See Sieghart Döhring and Arnold Jacobshagen (eds). *Meyerbeer und das europäische Musiktheater*. (Thurnauer Schriften zum Musiktheater, 16). Laaber: Laaber, 1998: 1–26.

Istel, Edgar. 'Meyerbeer's Way to Mastership: Employment of the Leading-Motive before Wagner's Birth'. *The Musical Quarterly* 12 (January 1926): 83–102.

Wirt und Gast

Score:

Meyerbeer, Giacomo. *Wirt und Gast: A Manuscript Facsimile*. Introduced and edited by Robert Letellier. Newcastle: Cambridge Scholars Publishing, 2008.

Bibliography:

Istel, Edgar. 'Meyerbeer's Way to Mastership: Employment of the Leading-Motive before Wagner's Birth'. *The Musical Quarterly* 12 (January 1926): 102–108.

Das Brandenburger Tor

Score:

Meyerbeer, Giacomo. (1814) and Zimmermann, Reiner. *Das Brandenburger Tor*. Full score arranged for the Berlin performance of September 1991 from the manuscript (Mus. M 9.14417) held at the Staatsbibliothek, Berlin. Berlin, 1991.

Bibliography:

Anon. '"Wohl mir, dass ich ein Preusse bin"': Giacomo Meyerbeer und das Brandenburger Tor'. *Programm Berliner Festspiele* (September 1991): 35.

Kruse, Georg Richard. '*Das Brandenburger Tor*'. *Berliner Tageblatt* (3 May 1914).

Zimmermann, Reiner. 'Dem Staate die Person veruntreut: Giacomo Meyerbeer und Preussen'. *Ein Branderburger Thor-Concert: Soirée zum 200. Geburtstag von Giacomo Meyerbeer (5. September 1791)*. In *41. Berliner Festwoche 91*. Berlin: Berliner Festspiele, 1991. [5 pp.]

Ein Feldlager in Schlesien/Vielka

Score:

Meyerbeer, Giacomo. *Ein Feldlager in Schlesien: A Manuscript Facsimile*. Introduced and edited by Robert Letellier. Newcastle: Cambridge Scholars Publishing, 2008.

Bibliography:

Becker, Heinz. '"Es ist ein ernstes Lebensgeschäft für mich"': zur Genese von Meyerbeers Preussenoper *Ein Feldlager in Schlesien*'. In *Traditionen – Neuansätze: Für Anna Amalie Abert (1906–1996)*. Ed. Klaus Hortschansky. Tutzing: Hans Schneider, 1997; pp. 41–63.

2) Italian Operas: *Opera Seria/Semiseria*

Everett, Andrew. 'Bewitched in a Magic Garden: Giacomo Meyerbeer in Italy'. *The Donizetti Society Journal* 6 (1988): 163–92.

Gossett, Philip. *Giacomo Meyerbeer: Excerpts from the Early Italian Operas (1817–1822)*. New York and London: Garland Publishing, Inc., 1991; pp. [i–xiii].

Schuster, Armin. *Die italienischen Opern Giacomo Meyerbeers*. Vol. 1: *Il crociato in Egitto*; Vol. 2: *Von 'Romilda e Costanza' bis 'L'esule di Granata'*. Marburg: Tectum Verlag, 2003.

Romilda e Costanza

Score:

Manuscripts scores are held in Berlin (Staatsbibliothek), Bologna (Civio Museo Bibliografico Musicale), Florence (Conservatorio di Musica Luigi Cherubini) and Milan (Archivio Storico Ricordi).

Bibliography:

Commons, Jeremy and White, Don. *Romilda e Costanza*. In the introductory booklet to *A Hundred Years of Italian Opera, 1810–1820*. London: Opera Rara, 1988; pp. 152–64.

Gossett, Philip. *Romilda e Costanza*. In *Giacomo Meyerbeer: Excerpts from the Early Italian Operas (1817–1822)*. New York and London: Garland Publishing, Inc., 1991; pp. [ii–iii].

Schuster, Armin. '*Romilda e Costanza* (1817)'. In *Die italienischen Opern Giacomo Meyerbeers*. Marburg: Tectum Verlag, 2003, 2: 28–59.

Semiramide [riconosciuta]

Score:

Meyerbeer, Giacomo (1819). *Semiramide. Edizione critica di Marco Beghelli and Stefano Piana*. Università di Bologna. Versione provvisoria ad uso del Festival 'Rossini in Wildbad', 2005.

Bibliography:

Beghelli, Marco, Piana, Stefano, Reinke, Stephan and Schönleber, Jochen. *Semiramide*. Bad Wildbad: Kurhaus Bad Wildbad, 2005.

Commons, Jeremy and White, Don. *Semiramide riconosciuta*. In *A Hundred Years of Italian Opera, 1810–1820*. London: Opera Rara, 1988; pp. 195–202.

Gossett, Philip. *Semiramide riconosciuta*. In *Giacomo Meyerbeer: Excerpts from the Early Italian Operas (1817–1822)*. New York and London: Garland Publishing, Inc., 1991; pp. [iv–v].

Schuster, Armin. '*Semiramide (riconosiuta)* (1819)'. In *Die italienischen Opern Giacomo Meyerbeers*. Marburg: Tectum Verlag, 2003, 2:60–103.

Emma di Resburgo

Score:

Meyerbeer, Giacomo and Schmidt, Johann Philipp (1820). *Emma von Roxburgh. Grosse Oper in zwei Aufzügen .Vollständiger Klavier-Auszug mit deutschem und italienischem Text von J.P. Schmidt*. Berlin, 1820.

Bibliography:

Commons, Jeremy and White, Don. *Emma di Resburgo.* In *A Hundred Years of Italian Opera, 1810–1820,* London: Opera Rara, 1988, pp. 202–12.

Gossett, Philip. *Emma di Resburgo.* In *Giacomo Meyerbeer: Excerpts from the Early Italian Operas (1817–1822).* New York and London: Garland Publishing, Inc., 1991, pp. [v–vii].

Schuster, Armin. *Emma di Resburgo* (1819). In *Die italienischen Opern Giacomo Meyerbeers.* Marburg: Tectum Verlag, 2003, 2: 104–60.

Margherita d'Anjou

Score:

Meyerbeer, Giacomo. (1827). *Margherita d'Anjou. Opera semiseria in due atti. Composto e ridotto per il cembalo da G. Meyerbeer.* [Vocal score.] Paris: Chez Maurice Schlesinger, 1827.

Bibliography:

Commons, Jeremy and White, Don. *Margherita d'Anjou.* In the introductory booklet to *A Hundred Years of Italian Opera, 1820–1830.* London: Opera Rara, 1994; pp. 5–16.

Everist, Mark. 'Giacomo Meyerbeer, the Théâtre Royal de l'Odéon, and Music Drama in Restoration Paris'. *Nineteenth-Century Music* 17:2 (Fall 1993): 124–48.

——Introduction to the libretto for the recording. London: Opera Rara, 2004; pp. 10–43.

Gossett, Philip. *Margherita d'Anjou.* In *Giacomo Meyerbeer: Excerpts from the Early Italian Operas (1817–1822).* New York and London: Garland Publishing, Inc., 1991; pp. [viii–ix].

Schuster, Armin. '*Margherita d'Anjou* (1820)'. In *Die italienischen Opern Giacomo Meyerbeers.* Marburg: Tectum Verlag, 2003, 2: 161–230.

L'esule di Granata

Score:

Meyerbeer, Giacomo. *L'esule di Granata.* London: Opera Rara, 2004.

Bibliography:

Commons, Jeremy and White, Don. *L'Esule di Granata.* In *A Hundred Years of Italian Opera, 1820–1830.* London: Opera Rara, 1994; pp. 54–66.

Gossett, Philip. *L'Esule di Granata.* In *Giacomo Meyerbeer: Excerpts from the Early Italian Operas (1817–1822).* New York and London: Garland Publishing, Inc., 1991; pp. [ix–xi].

Loomis, George. '*L'esule di Granata*'. Introduction to the libretto for the recording. London: Opera Rara, 2005; pp. 8–36.

Schuster, Armin. '*L'esule di Granata* (1822)'. In *Die italienischen Opern Giacomo Meyerbeers,* 2: 231–55.

Il crociato in Egitto

Score:

Gossett, Philip (ed.). *Il Crociato in Egitto: A facsimile Edition of a Manuscript of the Original Version Edited with an Introduction by Philip Gossett* (Early Romantic Opera, 18). New York and London: Garland Publishing, Inc., 1972. 2 vols; I: [i–v].

Schmid, Patric (ed.). *Il Crociato in Egitto. Opera in Two Acts by Giacomo Meyerbeer. The original version as first given December 26, 1824 in Venice, Reassembled and edited for Opera Rara by Patric Schmid*. London: Josef Weinberger, 1990.

Bibliography:

Claudon, François. 'Meyerbeer: *Il Crociato*: le grand opéra avant le grand opéra'. In *L'Opéra tra Venezia e Parigi*. (Studi di musica veneta 14). Ed. Maria Teresa Muraro. Florence: Olschki, 1988; pp. 119–31.

Everist, Mark. 'Meyerbeer's *Il Crociato in Egitto*: *Mélodrame*, Opera, Orientalism'. *Cambridge Opera Journal* 8:3 (1997): 215–50.

Porter, Andrew. 'Crusaders'. In *Music of Three More Seasons 1977–1980*. New York: Alfred A. Knopf, 1981; pp. 337–44.

Schuster, Armin. *Die italienischen Opern Giacomo Meyerbeers*. Vol. 1: *Il crociato in Egitto*. Marburg: Tectum Verlag, 2003.

White, Don. 'Meyerbeer in Italy'. Introduction to the libretto for the recording of *Il Crociato in Egitto* by Opera Rara for the bicentenary of the composer's birth. London: Opera Rara, 1992; pp. 13–70.

3) French Operas: *Grand Opéra*

Robert le Diable

References and Score:

Giuliani, Elisabeth (bibliography). *Meyerbeer: 'Robert le Diable'*. (*L'Avant-Scène Opéra*, 76). Ed. Alain Duault. Cabourg, Jean and Voisin, Georges (discography); (June 1985). Paris: ABexpress, 1985; pp. 98, 108–13.

Meyerbeer, Giacomo. *Robert le Diable: The Manuscript Facsimile*. Intro. and ed. Robert Letellier. With a preface 'Some General Remarks on the Meyerbeer Papers'; pp. vii–ix. Newcastle: Cambridge Scholars Press, 2005; pp. xiv + 636.

Gossett, Philip and Rosen, Charles (eds). *Robert le Diable: Facsimile of the Schlesinger Full Score (1832)*. (Early Romantic Opera, 19). 2 vols. New York and London: Garland Publishing, Inc., 1980.

Bibliography:

Berlioz, Hector. 'De l'instrumentation de *Robert le Diable*'. *Gazette musicale de Paris* 2 (1835): 229–32. Quoted in *Robert le Diable* (*L'Avant-Scène Opéra*, 76): 73–6.

Charlton, David. 'Meyerbeer's *Robert le Diable*'. In *The New Oxford History of Music*, IX: 93–7.

Donnington, Robert. 'The Operatic Tradition'. In *The Heritage of Music. The Romantic Era*. Oxford: Oxford University Press, 1989: 211–17.

Dreyer, Claus and Moeller, Hans (eds). *Giacomo Meyerbeer: 'Robert le Diable'. Materialien für ein Seminar an der FH Lippe, Abt. Detmold, im Sommer Semester 1989*. Detmold: Horst Rügge, 1989. [Historischer Kontext – Individuum vs. Gesellschaft – Das Drama der Familie – Natur vs. Zivilation – Romantik vs. Revolution.]

Everist, Mark. 'The Name of the Rose: Meyerbeer's *opéra comique, Robert le Diable*'. *Revue de Musicologie* 80:2 (1994): 211–50.

Fournier, Edouard (ed.). *Le Mystère de Robert le Diable, mis en 2 parties avec transcription en vers modernes, en regard du texte du XIVe siècle*. Paris: E. Dentu [1879].

Guest, Ivor. *The Romantic Ballet in Paris*. London: Sir Isaac Pitman & Sons Ltd, 1966; pp. 109–12.

Join-Dieterle, Catherine. '*Robert le Diable*: le premier opéra romantique'. *Romantisme: Revue de la Société des Etudes Romantiques* 28–9 (1980): 147–66.

Jullien, Adolphe. '*Robert le Diable*, le *Mystère*: l'opèra-comique avant l'opéra'. *Revue et Gazette Musicale de Paris* 46:48 (30 Nov. 1879): 386–88; 46:49 (7 Dec. 1879): 395–6; 46:50 (14 Dec. 1879): 403–404.

Jürgensen, Knud Arne and Hutchinson Guest, Ann. *Robert le Diable: The Ballet of the Nun*. (Language of Dance Series, 7). Amsterdam: Gordon & Breach Publishers, 1997.

Keller, W. 'Von Meyerbeers *Robert der Teufel* zum zweiten Aufzug *Parsifal*'. *Tribschener Blätter* 30 (Dec. 1971): 6–12. Rpt. 'Von *Robert der Teufel* zu *Parsifal*'. In *Parsifal Variationen: 15 Aufsätze über Richard Wagner*. Ed. W. Keller. Tutzing: Hans Schneider, 1979; pp. 81–89. [English: 'From Meyerbeer's *Robert le Diable* to Act 2 of Wagner's *Parsifal*'. *Great Britain* 13:2 (May 1992): 83–9.]

Liszt, Franz. 'Scribe und Meyerbeers *Robert der Teufel*' [1854]. In *Gesammelte Schriften von Franz Liszt*. Ed. L. Ramann. 10 vols. Leipzig: Breitkopf & Härtel, 1881; III: 48–67.

McDonald, Hugh. '*Robert le Diable*'. In *Music in Paris in the Eighteen-Thirties* (La Vie musicale en France au XIXe siècle, 4). Ed. Peter Bloom. Stuyversant, NY: Pendragon, 1987; pp. 357–69.

Möller, Hans and Berg, Eberhard. 'Regiekonzeption zu *Robert le Diable*', Detmold 1989, Ms.

Pendle, Karin. 'The Transformation of a Genre: Meyerbeer's *Robert le Diable*'. In *Eugène Scribe and the French Opera of the Nineteenth Century* (Studies in Musicology, 6). Ann Arbor: UMI Research Press, 1979; pp. 427–55.

Pleasants, Henry. *The Great Tenor Tragedy: The Last Days of Adolphe Nourrit As Told (Mostly) by Himself*. Edited, annotated, and with an Introduction and Epilogue. Portland, OR: Amadeus Press, 1995.

Les Huguenots

References and Scores:

Dutronc, Jean-Louis (discography); Giuliani, Elisabeth (bibliography). *Meyerbeer: 'Les Huguenots' (L'Avant-Scène Opéra*, 134). Ed. Michel Pazdro. (Sept.–Oct. 1990). Paris: ABexpress, 1990; pp. 108–13, 120, 122.

Meyerbeer, Giacomo. *Les Huguenots: The Manuscript Facsimile.* Intro. and ed. by Robert Letellier. Newcastle: Cambridge Scholars Press, 2006; pp. xvi + 888.

Böhmel, Bernd and Zimmermann, Reiner (eds) (1973). *Les Huguenots (Die Hugenotten): Leipziger Bühnenfassung.* Leipzig: C.F. Peters, 1973.

Gossett, Philip and Rosen, Charles (eds). *Les Huguenots: Facsimile of the Schlesinger Full Score (1836).* (Early Romantic Opera, 20). 2 vols. New York and London: Garland Publishing, Inc., 1980.

Sullivan, Arthur and Pittman, J. (eds). *Gli Ugonotti: Facsimile of the Boosey & Co. Vocal Score.* New York: Edwin F. Kalmus, 1985.

Bibliography:

Becker, Heinz. ""...Der Marcel von Meyerbeer": Anmerkungen zur Entstehungsgeschichte der *Hugenotten'. Jahrbuch des Staatlichen Instituts für Musikforschung Preussischer Kulturbesitz 1979–80* (Berlin, 1981): 79–100.

Berlioz, Hector. '*Les Huguenots'. Revue et Gazette musicale* (Paris) 3 (6, 13, 20 March 1836): 73, 81, 89.

Frese, Christhard. *Meyerbeer 'Les Huguenots': Materiallen zum Werk.* Leipzig: Peters, 1974.

Friedrichs, Henning. 'Das Rezitativ in den *Hugenotten* Giacomo Meyerbeers'. In *Beiträge zur Geschichte der Oper* (Studien zur Musikgeschichte des 19. Jahrhunderts, 15). Ed. Heinz Becker. Regensburg: Gustav Bosse, 1969; pp. 55–76.

Greenfield, Howard S. *Caruso. An Illustrated Life.* London: Collins & Brown, 1991; pp. 27–28, 81, 139, 157.

Kaufman, Thomas G. '*Les Huguenots*: One of the Greatest Successes of All Time'. Programme notes for the concert performance by the Opera Orchestra of New York, Carnegie Hall, April 2001. Includes a table of revivals of the opera since 1900. [12 pp.]

Kelly, Thomas Forrest. *First Nights at the Opera.* New Haven: Yale University Press, 2004; pp. 132–226.

Miller, Norbert. 'Grosse Oper als Historiengemälde: Überlegungen zur Zusammenarbeit von Eugène Scribe und Giacomo Meyerbeer (am Beispiel des 1. Aktes von *Les Huguenots*)' [exemplified by Act 1 of *Les Huguenots*]. In *Oper und Opertexte* (Reihe Siegen, Beiträge zur Literatur- und Sprachwissenschaft, 60). Ed. Jens Malte Fischer. Heidelberg, 1985; pp. 45–79.

Mongrédien, Jean. 'Aux sources du livret des *Huguenots*: La collaboration entre Scribe et Meyerbeer'. In Sieghart Döhring and Jürgen Schläder (eds). *Giacomo Meyerbeer: Musik als Welterfahrung: Heinz Becker zum 70. Geburtstag.* Munich: Ricordi, 1995; pp. 155–72.

Pendle, Karin. 'The Technique of Grand Opera and the Transformation of Literary Models: Meyerbeer's *Les Huguenots*'. In *Eugène Scribe and French Opera of the*

Nineteenth Century; (Studies in Musicology, 6). Ann Arbor: UMI Research Press, 1979; pp. 465–93.

Robinson, Francis. *Caruso. His Life in Pictures*. New York and London: The Studio Publications, Inc., 1957; see p. 62, also pp. 71, 92–3.

Sand, Georges. 'À Giacomo Meyerbeer'. Letter 11 in *Lettres d'un Voyageur*. Paris: Bonnaire, 1837. First published in the *Revue des deux Mondes* (15 November 1836).

Wagner, Richard. 'Über Meyerbeers *Hugenotten*'. In *Sämtliche Schriften und Dichtungen* (Leipzig, 1911–16); XII: 22–9.

Walter, Michael. *'Hugenotten'-Studien* (Europäische Hochschulschriften 36: Musicology 24). Bern, New York, Paris: Peter Lang, 1987.

Le Prophète

Scores:

Meyerbeer, Giacomo. *Le Prophète: The Manuscript Facsimile*. Introduced and edited by Robert Letellier. Newcastle: Cambridge Scholars Press, 2006; pp. xv, 963.

Gossett, Philip and Rosen, Charles (eds). *Le Prophète: Facsimile of the Brandus Full Score (1851)* (Early Romantic Opera, 21). 2 vols. NewYork and London: Garland Publishing, Inc., 1978.

Le Prophète, An Opera in 5 Acts, with French Text: Facsimile of the Brandus Vocal Score (1851). New York: Edwin F. Kalmus, 1988.

Bibliography:

Armstrong, Alan. 'Meyerbeer's *Le Prophète*: A history of its Composition and Early Performances'. Unpublished doctoral dissertation, Ohio State University, 1990.

——'Gilbert-Louis Duprez and Gustav Roger in the Composition of Meyerbeer's *Le Prophète*'. *Cambridge Opera Journal* 8:2 (1998): 147–65.

Berlioz, Hector. '*Le Prophète*'. *Journal des Débats* (Paris, 20 April 1849).

Dahlhaus, Carl. *Musikalischer Realismus*. Munich: Piper, 1980. [Discusses *Le Prophète*, pp. 105–10.]

Guest, Ivor. *The Ballet of the Second Empire*. London: Pitman Publishing, 1955, 1958. Reprinted in one vol., 1974; pp. 45–6.

Pendle, Karin. 'Historical Opera: Meyerbeer's *Le Prophète*'. In *Eugène Scribe and the French Opera of the Nineteenth Century* (Studies in Musicology, 6). Ann Arbor: UMI Research Press, 1979; pp. 495–534.

——and Wilkins, Stephen. '*Le Prophète*: The Triumph of the Grandiose', part of 'Paradise Found: The Salle le Peletier and French Grand Opera'. In *Opera in Context: Essays on Historical Staging from the Late Renaissance to the Time of Puccini*. Ed. Mark A. Radice. Portland, OR: Amadeus Press, 1998: 171–208.

L'Africaine (Vasco da Gama)

Score:

Meyerbeer, Giacomo. *L'Africaine: The Manuscript Facsimile*. Intro. and ed. Robert Letellier. Newcastle: Cambridge Scholars Press, 2005; pp. xvi + 888.

Gossett, Philip and Rosen, Charles (eds). *L'Africaine: Facsimile of the Brandus et Dufour Full Score, ed. F-J. Fétis (1865)* (Early Romantic Opera, 24). 2 vols. New York and London: Garland Publishing, Inc., 1980.

Haedler, Manfred and Kleffel, Arno (eds). *Die Afrikanerin (L'Africaine)*. Berlin and Wiesbaden: Bote & Bock, 1990.

Bibliography:

Camoens, Luis Vaz de. *The Lusiads*. Trans. William C. Atkinson. Harmondsworth: Penguin Books, 1952.

Cruz, Gabriela. 'Laughing at History: The Third Act of Meyerbeer's *L'Africaine*'. *Cambridge Opera Journal* 11:1 (March 1999): 31–76.

Higgins, John. 'How Placido Domingo sees Vasco da Gama'. In *The Times* (London, 9 November 1978).

Letellier, Robert Ignatius. 'History, Myth and Music in a Theme of Exploration: Some Reflections on the Musico-Dramatic Language of *L'Africaine*'. See *Meyerbeer Studies. A Series of Lectures, Essays, and Articles on the Life and Work of Giacomo Meyerbeer*. Madison, Teaneck: Fairleigh Dickinson University Press and Associated University Presses, 2005; pp. 20–40.

Roberts, John Howell. 'The Genesis of Meyerbeer's *L'Africaine*'. Unpubublished doctoral dissertation, University of California (Berkeley), 1977.

Schläder, Jürgen. 'Sélikas Sterbeszene in *L'Africaine*'. See Thurnau Symposium 1991. Also in Sieghart Döhring and Arnold Jacobshagen (eds). *Meyerbeer und das europäische Musiktheater*, 'Die Sterbeszene der Sélika: zur Dramaturgie des Finales in Meyerbeers *L'Africaine*' (Thurnauer Schriften zum Musiktheater, 16). Laaber: Laaber, 1998; pp. 169–82.

Subrahmanyam, Sanjay. *The Career and Legend of Vasco da Gama*. Cambridge: Cambridge University Press, 1997; 2nd ed. 1998.

4) French Operas: *Opéra Comique*

L'Étoile du Nord

Score:

Gossett, Philip and Rosen, Charles (eds). *L'Etoile du Nord: Facsimile of the Brandus Full Score (1854)* (Early Romantic Opera, 22). 2 vols. Garland Publishing, Inc., 1980.

Bibliography:

Becker, Heinz and Becker, Gudrun. 'Giacomo Meyerbeers Opéra comique *L'Etoile du Nord*: Anmerkungen zur Entstehungsgeschichtedes Librettos'. In *Festschrift Hubert Unverricht zum 65. Geburtstag*. Tutzing: Hans Schneider, 1992; pp. 17–34.

Crichton, Ronald. 'Meyerbeer and *L'Etoile du Nord*'. Introductory essay to the Marco Polo Recording of the Wexford Festival revival (1997); pp. 6–11.

Everist, Mark. 'Der Lieblingswunsch meines Lebens: Contexts and Continuity in Meyerbeer's *Opéras Comiques*'. See *Giacomo Meyerbeer and Music Drama in Nineteenth-Century Paris* (Variorum Collected Studies Series). Aldershot: Ashgate, 2005.

Letellier, Robert Ignatius. '*Che sarà, sarà*: The "Star" of Which Dreams are Made, Meyerbeer's *L'Étoile du Nord*'. *The Opera Quarterly* 18:1 (Winter 2002): 40–57. Also in Arnold Jacobshagen and Milan Pospísil (eds). *Meyerbeer und die Opéra comique um die Mitte des 19. Jahrhunderts* (Thurnauer Schriften zum Musiktheater, 19). Laaber: Laaber, 2000.

Loppert, Max. 'An Introduction to *L'Etoile du Nord*'. *The Musical Times* 116:1584 (1975): 130–33.

Le Pardon de Ploërmel [Dinorah]

Score:

Gossett, Philip and Rosen, Charles (eds). *Le Pardon de Ploërmel: Facsimile of the Brandus et Dufour Full Score (1859)* (Early Romantic Opera, 23). New York and London: Garland Publishing, Inc., 1981.

Bibliography:

Basevi, Abramo. 'Illustrazione della sinfonia all'opera *Le Pardon de Ploërmel*, Gran Sinfonia descrittiva con coro, dal maestro G. Meyerbeer' (Biblioteca del Sinfonista: Raccolta delle più celebri Sinfonie [overture] in partitura a piena orchestra). Florence: G.G. Guidi, 1863; pp. i–vii. [Introduction to the miniature full-score.]

Coudroy-Saghai, Marie-Hélène (ed.). '*Le Pardon de Ploërmel*': dossier de presse parisienne (1859) édité par Marie-Hélène Coudroy-Saghai* (Critique de l'opéra parisien du xixe siècle, 2). Saarbrücken: Musik-Edition Lucie Galland, 1992.

Law, Joe K. 'Meyerbeer's Variations on a Theme by Laurence Sterne: or "Why a Goat?"'. *The Opera Journal* 22:4 (1989): 3–8.

Letellier, Robert Ignatius. 'Meyerbeer and the Comic Spirit: Miniature Variations on Grand Themes' (Bristol Symposium 1998.) [Reprinted in *Meyerbeer Studies. A Series of Lectures, Essays, and Articles on the Life and Work of Giacomo Meyerbeer*. Madison, Teaneck: Fairleigh Dickinson University Press and Associated University Presses, 2005; pp. 96–105].

5. PLAYS (MASQUE/INCIDENTAL MUSIC)

Das Hoffest zu Ferrara

Anon. '*Die Hoffest zu Ferrara*, ein verschollenes Werk Meyerbeers'. *Blätter der Staatsoper* 2:6 (n.d.).

Raupach, Ernst von. *Das Hoffest zu Ferrara*. Libretto. Berlin, 1843. Copy in the New York Public Library [15 pp.].

Struensee

Score:

Meyerbeer, Giacomo. *Struensee. Trauerspiel von Michael Beer. Musik von Giacomo Meyerbeer*. Berlin: Schlesinger, 1847.

———*Struensée. Tragédie de Michael Beer. Musique de G. Meyerbeer. Partition de Piano & Chant avec un Arrangement pour son éxécution dans les concerts par M.J. Fétis*. Paris: G. Brangus & S. Dufour, 1867.

Bibliography:

Beer, Michael. *Sämmtliche Werke von Michael Beer. Herausgegeben von Eduard von Schenk. Mit dem Bildnisse des Dichters.* Leipzig: F.A. Brockhaus, 1835. [*Struensee*, pp. 285–520.]

Basevi, Abramo. 'Illustrazione della sinfonia alla tragedia *Struensée* del maestro G. Meyerbeer' (Biblioteca del Sinfonista: Raccolta delle più celebri Sinfonia [overture] in partitura a piena orchestra). Florence: G.G. Guidi, 1862; pp. i–vii. [Introduction to the miniature full-score.]

Chapman, Hester W. *Caroline Matilda, Queen of Denmark 1751–1775*. London: Jonathan Cape, 1971.

Gautier, Théophile. *Prologue de Struensée*. In *Théatre, mystère, comédies et ballets*. Paris. G.Charpentier 1882: 229–31. [Reprint in *Oeuvres complètes*, VIII. Genève: Slatkine Reprints 1978.]

Kahn, Lothar. 'Michael Beer'. *Year Book XII of the Leo Baeck Institute*. London, 1967; pp. 149–60.

Schwab, Christian Theodor. 'Ein Bruder Meyerbeers'. *Sonntagsblätter* 52 (Vienna, 27 Dec. 1846).

Index